ERNESTO LACLAU is Professor of Political Theory at the University of Essex. He is the author of *Politics and Ideology in Marxist Theory*, *New Reflections on the Revolution of our Time*, *Emancipation(s)*, *The Making of Political Identities* and, with Judith Butler and Slavoj Žižek *Contingency, Hegemony, Universality*.

CHANTAL MOUFFE is Professor of Political Theory at the Centre for the Study of Democracy at the University of Westminster. She is the author of, among other works, *The Return of the Political*, *The Dimensions of Radical Democracy*, *The Challenge of Carl Schmitt* and *The Democratic Paradox*.

Hegemony and Socialist Strategy

Towards a Radical Democratic Politics

Second Edition

◆

ERNESTO LACLAU
and
CHANTAL MOUFFE

VERSO

London • New York

First published by Verso 1985
© Ernesto Laclau and Chantal Mouffe 1985
This second edition first published by Verso 2001
© Ernesto Laclau and Chantal Mouffe 2001

3 5 7 9 10 8 6 4

Verso
UK: 6 Meard Street, London W1F 0EG
US: 180 Varick Street, New York, NY 10014–4606

Verso is the imprint of New Left Books
www.versobooks.com

ISBN 1–85984–621–1
ISBN 1–85984–330–1 (pbk)

British Library Cataloguing in Publication Data
A catalogue record for this book is available from the British Library

Library of Congress Cataloging-in-Publication Data
A catalog record for this book is available from the Library of Congress

Printed and bound in Great Britain by
Biddles Ltd, King's Lynn, Norfolk

Contents

Preface to the Second Edition

Hegemony and Socialist Strategy was originally published in 1985, and since then it has been at the centre of many important theoretico-political discussions, both in the Anglo-Saxon world and elsewhere. Many things have changed in the contemporary scene since that time. To refer just to the most important developments, it is enough to mention the end of the Cold War and the disintegration of the Soviet system. To this we should add drastic transformations of the social structure, which are at the root of new paradigms in the constitution of social and political identities. To perceive the epochal distance between the early 1980s, when this book was originally written, and the present, we have only to remember that, at that time, Eurocommunism was still seen as a viable political project, going beyond both Leninism and social democracy; and that, since then, the major debates which have absorbed the intellectual reflection of the Left have been those around the new social movements, multiculturalism, the globalization and deterritorialization of the economy and the ensemble of issues linked to the question of postmodernity. We could say — paraphrasing Hobsbawm — that the 'short twentieth century' ended at some point in the early 1990s, and that today we have to face problems of a substantially new order.

Given the magnitude of these epochal changes, we were surprised, in going through the pages of this not-so-recent book again, at how little we have to put into question the intellectual and political perspective developed therein. Most of what has happened since then has closely followed the pattern suggested in our book, and those issues which were central to our concerns at that moment have become ever more prominent in contemporary discussions. We could even say that we see the theoretical perspective developed then — rooted as it was in the Gramscian matrix and in the centrality of the category of hegemony — as a far more adequate approach to contemporary issues than the intellectual apparatus which has often accompanied recent discussions on political subjectivity, on democracy, and on the trends and political consequences of a globalized economy. This is why we want to recapitulate, as a way of introducing this second edition, some central points of our theoretical intervention, and to counterpose some of its political conclusions to recent trends in the discussion about democracy.

Let us start by saying something about the intellectual project of *Hegemony* and the theoretical perspective from which it was written. In the mid-1970s, Marxist theorization had clearly reached an impasse. After an exceptionally rich and creative period in the 1960s, the limits of that expansion — which had its epicentre in Althusserianism, but also in a renewed interest in Gramsci and in the theoreticians of the Frankfurt School — were only too visible. There was an increasing gap between the realities of contemporary capitalism and what Marxism could legitimately subsume under its own categories. It is enough to remember the increasingly desperate contortions which took place around notions such as 'determination in the last instance' and 'relative autonomy'. This situation, on the whole, provoked two types of attitude: either to negate the changes, and to retreat unconvincingly to an orthodox bunker; or to add, in an *ad hoc* way, descriptive analyses of the new trends which were simply juxtaposed — without integration — to a theoretical body which remained largely unchanged.

Our way of dealing with the Marxist tradition was entirely different and could, perhaps, be expressed in terms of the Husserlian distinction between 'sedimentation' and 'reactivation'. Sedimented theoretical categories are those which conceal the acts of their original institution, while the reactivating moment makes those acts visible again. For us — as opposed to Husserl — that reactivation had to show the original contingency of the synthesis that the Marxian categories attempted to establish. Instead of dealing with notions such as 'class', the triad of levels (the economic, the political and the ideological) or the contradiction between forces and relations of production as sedimented fetishes, we tried to revive the preconditions which make their discursive operation possible, and asked ourselves questions concerning their continuity or discontinuity in contemporary capitalism. The result of this exercise was the realization that the field of Marxist theorization had been far more ambivalent and diversified than the monolithic transvestite that Marxism–Leninism presented as the history of Marxism. It has to be clearly stated: the lasting *theoretical* effect of Leninism has been an appalling impoverishment of the field of Marxian diversity. While, at the end of the period of the Second International, the fields in which Marxist discursivity was operating were becoming increasingly diversified — ranging, especially in Austro-Marxism, from the problem of the intellectuals to the national question, and from the internal inconsistencies of the labour theory of value to the relationship between socialism and ethics — the division of the international workers' movement, and the reorganization of its revolutionary wing around the Soviet experience, led to a discontinuity of this creative process. The pathetic case of a Lukács, who contributed his undeniable intellectual skills to the consolidation of a theoretico-political horizon which did not transcend the whole gamut of shibboleths of the Third International, is an extreme but far from isolated example. It is worth pointing out that many of the problems confronted by a socialist strategy in the conditions of late capitalism are already contained *in nuce* in the theorization of Austro-Marxism, but had little continuity in the inter-war period. Only the isolated example of Gramsci, writing from the Mussolinian jails, can be quoted as a new departure producing a new arsenal of concepts — war of position, historical bloc, collective will, hegemony, intellectual and moral leadership — which are the starting point of our reflections in *Hegemony and Socialist Strategy.*

Revisiting (reactivating) the Marxist categories in the light of these series of new problems and development had to lead, necessarily, to deconstructing the former — that is, to displacing some of their conditions of possibility and developing new possibilities which transcend anything which could be characterized as the *application* of a category. We know from Wittgenstein that there is no such thing as the 'application of a rule' — the instance of application becomes part of the rule itself. To reread Marxist theory in the light of contemporary problems necessarily involves deconstructing the central categories of that theory. This is what has been called our 'post-Marxism'. We did not invent this label — it only marginally appears (not as a label) in the Introduction to our book. But since it has become generalized in characterizing our work, we can say that we do not oppose it insofar as it is properly understood: as the process of reappropriation of an intellectual tradition, as well as the process of going beyond it. And in developing this task, it is important to point out that it cannot be conceived just as an *internal* history of Marxism. Many social antagonisms, many issues which are crucial to the understanding of contemporary societies, belong to fields of discursivity which are *external* to Marxism, and cannot be reconceptualized in terms of Marxist categories — given, especially, that their very presence is what puts Marxism as a closed theoretical system into question, and leads to the postulation of new starting points for social analysis.

There is one aspect in particular that we want to underline at this point. Any substantial change in the *ontic* content of a field of research leads also to a new *ontological* paradigm. Althusser used to say that behind Plato's philosophy, there was Greek mathematics; behind seventeenth-century rationalism, Galilean physics; and behind Kant's philosophy, Newtonian theory. To put the argument in a transcendental fashion: the strictly ontological question asks how entities have to be, so that the objectivity of a particular field is possible. There is a process of mutual feedback between the incorporation of new fields of objects and the general ontological categories governing, at a certain time, what is thinkable within the general field of objectivity. The ontology implicit in Freudianism, for instance, is different and incompatible with a biologist paradigm. From this point of view, it is our conviction that in the transition from Marxism to post-Marxism, the change is not only ontic but also ontological. The problems of a globalized and information-ruled society are unthinkable within the two ontological paradigms governing the field of Marxist discursivity: first the Hegelian, and later the naturalistic.

Our approach is grounded in privileging the moment of *political* articulation, and the central category of political analysis is, in our view, *hegemony*. In that case, how — to repeat our transcendental question — does a relation between entities have to be, for a hegemonic relation to become possible? Its very condition is that a *particular* social force assumes the representation of a *totality* that is radically incommensurable with it. Such a form of 'hegemonic universality' is the only one that a political community can reach. From this point of view, our analysis should be differentiated from analyses in which universality finds in the social field a direct, non-hegemonically mediated expression, and those in which particularities are merely added up without any mediation between them being thinkable — as in some forms of post-modernism. But if a relation of hegemonic representation is to be possible, its ontological status has to be defined. This is the point at which, for our analysis, a notion of the social conceived as a *discursive* space — that is, making possible relations of representation strictly unthinkable within a physicalist or naturalistic paradigm — becomes of paramount importance. In other works, we have shown that the category of 'discourse' has a pedigree in contemporary thought going back to the three main intellectual currents of the twentieth century: analytical philosophy, phenomenology, and structuralism. In these three the century started with an illusion of immediacy, of a non-discursively mediated access to the things themselves — the referent, the phenomenon and the sign, respectively. In all three, however, this illusion of immediacy dissolved at some point, and had to be replaced by one form or another of discursive mediation. This is what happened in analytical philosophy with the work of the later Wittgenstein, in phenomenology with the existential analytic of Heidegger, and in structuralism with the post-structuralist critique of the sign. It is also, in our view, what happened in epistemology with the transition verificationism — Popper — Kuhn — Feyerabend, and in Marxism with the work of Gramsci, where the fullness of class identities of classical Marxism has to be replaced by hegemonic identities constituted through non-dialectical mediations.

All these currents have fed our thought to some extent, but post-structuralism is the terrain where we have found the main source of our theoretical reflection and, within the post-structuralist field, deconstruction and Lacanian theory have had a decisive importance in the formulation of our approach to hegemony. From deconstruction, the notion of undecidability has been crucial. If, as shown in the work of Derrida, undecidables permeate the field which had previously been seen as governed by structural determination, one can see hegemony as a theory of the decision taken in an undecidable terrain. Deeper levels of contingency require hegemonic — that is, contingent — articulations, which is another way of saying that the moment of reactivation means nothing other than retrieving an act of political institution that finds its source and motivation nowhere but in itself. For not unrelated reasons, Lacanian theory contributes decisive tools to the formulation of a theory of hegemony. Thus, the category of *point de capiton* (nodal point, in our terminology) or master-signifier involves the notion of a particular element assuming a 'universal' structuring function within a certain discursive field — actually, whatever organization that field has is only the result of that function — without the particularity of the element *per se* predetermining such a function. In a similar way, the notion of the subject before subjectivation establishes the centrality of the category of 'identification' and makes it possible, in that sense, to think of hegemonic transitions which are fully dependent on political articulations and not on entities constituted outside the political field — such as 'class interests'. Indeed, politico-hegemonic articulations retroactively create the interests they claim to represent.

'Hegemony' has very precise conditions of possibility, both from the point of view of what a relation requires to be conceived as hegemonic, and from the perspective of the construction of a hegemonic subject. As for the first aspect, the already mentioned dimension of structural undecidability is the very condition of hegemony. If social objectivity, through its internal laws, determined whatever structural arrangement exists (as in a purely sociologistic conception of society), there would be no room for contingent hegemonic rearticulations — nor, indeed, for politics as an autonomous activity. In order to have hegemony, the requirement is that elements whose own nature does not predetermine them to enter into one type of arrangement rather than another, nevertheless coalesce, as a result of an external or articulating practice. The visibility of the acts of originary institution — in their specific contingency — is, in this respect, the requirement of any hegemonic formation. But to say *contingent articulation* is to enounce a central dimension of 'politics'. This privileging of the political moment in the structuration of society is an essential aspect of our approach. Our book shows how, historically, the category of hegemony was originally elaborated in Russian social democracy as an attempt at addressing the autonomous political intervention which was made possible by the structural dislocation between actors and democratic tasks that resulted from the late development of capitalism in Russia; how, later, the notion of 'combined and uneven development' extended it to the general conditions of politics in the imperialist age; and how, with Gramsci, this hegemonic dimension was made constitutive of the subjectivity of historical actors (who thus cease to be merely *class* actors). We could add that this dimension of contingency, and the concomitant autonomization of the political, are even more visible in the contemporary world, in the conditions of advanced capitalism, where hegemonic rearticulations are far more generalized than they were in Gramsci's time.

As for hegemonic subjectivity, our argument dovetails with the whole debate about the relation between universalism and particularism which has become quite central in recent years. A hegemonic relation has, no doubt, a universalistic dimension, but it is a very particular type of universalism whose main features it is important to point out. It is not the result of a contractual decision, as in the case of Hobbes's *Leviathan*, for the hegemonic link transforms the identity of the hegemonic subjects. It is not necessarily linked to a public space, as with Hegel's notion of a 'universal class', for hegemonic rearticulations start at the level of civil society. It is not, finally, like the Marxian notion of the proletariat as a universal class, for it does not result from an ultimate human reconciliation leading to the withering away of the State and the end of politics; the hegemonic link is, on the contrary, constitutively political.

What, in that case, is the specific universality inherent in hegemony? It results, we argue in the text, from the specific dialectic between what we call logics of difference and logics of equivalence. Social actors occupy differential positions within the discourses that constitute the social fabric. In that sense they are all, strictly speaking, particularities. On the other hand, there are social antagonisms creating internal frontiers within society. Vis-à-vis oppressive forces, for instance, a set of particularities establish relations of equivalence between themselves. It becomes necessary, however, to represent the totality of the chain, beyond the mere differential particularisms of the equivalential links. What are the means of representation? As we argue, only one particularity whose body is split, for without ceasing to be its own particularity, it transforms its body in the representation of a universality transcending it (that of the equivalential chain). This relation, by which a certain particularity assumes the representation of a universality entirely incommensurable with it, is what we call a *hegemonic relation.* As a result, its universality is a *contaminated* universality: (1) it lives in this unresolvable tension between universality and particularity; (2) its function of hegemonic universality is not acquired for good but is, on the contrary, always reversible. Although we are no doubt radicalizing the Gramscian intuition in several respects, we think that something of the sort is implicit in Gramsci's distinction between corporative and hegemonic class. Our notion of a contaminated universality parts company with a conception such as that of Habermas, for whom universality has a content of its own, independent of any hegemonic articulation. But it also avoids the other extreme — represented, perhaps, at its purest in the particularism of Lyotard, whose conception of society as consisting in a plurality of incommensurable language games, whose interactions can be conceived only as *tort,* makes any *political* rearticulation impossible.

As a result, our approach conceives of universality as a *political* universality and, in that sense, as depending on internal frontiers within society. This leads us to what is, perhaps, the most central argument of our book, which is linked to the notion of *antagonism.* We have explained why, in our view, neither real oppositions (Kant's *Realrepugnanz*) nor dialectical contradiction can account for the specific relation that we call 'social antagonism'. Our thesis is that antagonisms are not *objective* relations, but relations which reveal the limits of all objectivity. Society is constituted around these limits, and they are antagonistic limits. And the notion of antagonistic limit has to be conceived literally — that is to say, there is no 'cunning of reason' which would realize itself through antagonistic relations. Nor is there any kind of supergame that would submit antagonisms to its system of rules. This is why we conceive of the political not as a superstructure but as having the status of an *ontology of the social*.

From this argument it follows that, for us, social division is inherent in the possibility of politics, and — as we argue in the last part of the book — in the very possibility of a democratic politics.

We would like to emphasize this point. Antagonism is indeed at the centre of the current relevance of our approach, on both the theoretical and the political level. This might seem paradoxical, considering that one of the principal consequences of the profound transformations which have taken place in the fifteen years since the publication of this book has precisely been that the notion of antagonism has been erased from the political discourse of the Left. But unlike those who see that as progress, we believe this is where the main problem lies. Let us examine how and why it happened. One could have hoped that the collapse of the Soviet model would have given a renewed impetus to democratic socialist parties, finally freed of the negative image of the socialist project that their old antagonist presented. However, with the failure of its communist variant, it is the very idea of socialism that became discredited. Far from being given new life, social democracy was thrown into disarray. Instead of a recasting of the socialist project, what we have witnessed in the last decade has been the triumph of neo-liberalism, whose hegemony has become so pervasive that it has had a profound effect on the very identity of the Left. It can even be argued that the left-wing project is in an even deeper crisis today than at the time in which we were writing, at the beginning of the 1980s. Under the pretence of 'modernization', an increasing number of social-democratic parties have been discarding their left identity, redefining themselves euphemistically as 'centre-left'. They claim that the notions of Left and Right have become obsolete, and that what is needed is a politics of the 'radical Centre'. The basic tenet of what is presented as the 'third way' is that with the demise of communism and the socio-economic transformations linked to the advent of the information society and the process of globalization, antagonisms have disappeared. A politics without frontiers would now be possible — a 'win–win politics' where solutions could be found that favoured everybody in society. This implies that politics is no longer structured around social division, and that political problems have become merely technical. According to Ulrich Beck and Anthony Giddens — the theorists of this new politics — we are now living under conditions of 'reflexive modernization' where the adversarial model of politics, of us versus them, does not apply any more. They affirm that we have entered a new era in which politics needs to be envisaged in a completely different way. Radical politics should concern 'life' issues and be 'generative', allowing people and groups to make things happen; and democracy should be envisaged inthe form of a 'dialogue', controversial issues being resolved through listening to each other.

There is much talk nowadays of a 'democratization of democracy'. There is nothing wrong, in principle, with such a perspective, and at first sight it seems to chime with our idea of a 'radical and plural democracy'. There is, however, a crucial difference because we never envisaged the process of a radicalization of democracy that we were advocating as taking place within a neutral terrain, whose topology would not be affected, but as a profound transformation of the existing relations of power. For us, the objective was the establishment of a new hegemony, which requires the creation of new political frontiers, not their disappearance. No doubt it is a good thing that the Left has finally come to terms with the importance of pluralism and of liberal-democratic institutions, but the problem is that this has been accompanied by the mistaken belief that it meant abandoning any attempt at transforming the present hegemonic order. Hence the sacralization of consensus, the blurring of the frontiers between Left and Right, and the move towards the Centre.

But this is to draw the wrong conclusion from the fall of communism. Certainly it is important to understand that liberal democracy is not the enemy to be destroyed in order to create, through revolution, a completely new society. This is indeed what we were already arguing in this book when we insisted on the necessity of redefining the project of the Left in terms of a 'radicalization' of democracy. In our view, the problem with 'actually existing' liberal democracies is not with their constitutive values crystallized in the principles of liberty and equality for all, but with the system of power which redefines and limits the operation of those values. This is why our project of 'radical and plural democracy' was conceived as a new stage in the deepening of the 'democratic revolution', as the extension of the democratic struggles for equality and liberty to a wider range of social relations.

We never thought, though, that discarding the Jacobin friend/enemy model of politics as an adequate paradigm for democratic politics should lead to the adoption of the liberal one, which envisages democracy as simple competition among interests taking place in a neutral terrain — even if the accent is put on the 'dialogic' dimension. This, however, is precisely the way in which many left-wing parties are now visualizing the democratic process. This is why they are unable to grasp the structure of power relations, and even begin to imagine the possibility of establishing a new hegemony. As a consequence, the anti-capitalist element which had always been present in social democracy — in both its right-wing and its left-wing variants — has now been eradicated from its supposedly modernized version. Hence the lack in their discourse of any reference to a possible alternative to the present economic order, which is taken as the only feasible one — as if acknowledging the illusory character of a total break with a market economy necessarily precluded the possibility of different modes of regulation of market forces, and meant that there was no alternative to a total acceptance of their logics.

The usual justification for the 'no alternative dogma' is globalization, and the argument generally rehearsed against redistributive social-democratic policies is that the tight fiscal constraints faced by governments are the only realistic possibility in a world where global markets would not permit any deviation from neo-liberal orthodoxy. This argument takes for granted the ideological terrain which has been created as a result of years of neo-liberal hegemony, and transforms what is a conjunctural state of affairs into a historical necessity. Presented as driven exclusively by the information revolution, the forces of globalization are detached from their political dimensions and appear as a fate to which we all have to submit. So we are told that there are no more left-wing or right-wing economic policies, only good and bad ones!

To think in terms of hegemonic relations is to break with such fallacies. Indeed, scrutinizing the so-called 'globalized world' through the category of hegemony elaborated in this book can help us to understand that the present conjuncture, far from being the only natural or possible societal order, is the expression of a certain configuration of power relations. It is the result of hegemonic moves on the part of specific social forces which have been able to implement a profound transformation in the relations between capitalist corporations and the nation-states. This hegemony can be challenged. The Left should start elaborating a credible alternative to the neo-liberal order, instead of simply trying to manage it in a more humane way. This, of course, requires drawing new political frontiers and acknowledging that there cannot be a radical politics without the definition of an adversary. That is to say, it requires the acceptance of the ineradicability of antagonism.

There is another way in which the theoretical perspective developed in this book can contribute to restoring the centrality of the political — by bringing to the fore the shortcomings of what is currently presented as the most promising and sophisticated vision of a progressive politics: the model of 'deliberative democracy' which has been put forward by Habermas and his followers. It is useful to contrast our approach with theirs, because some similarities do actually exist between the conception of radical democracy we advocate and the one they defend. Like them, we criticize the aggregative model of democracy, which reduces the democratic process to the expression of those interests and preferences which are registered in a vote aiming at selecting leaders who will carry out the chosen policies. Like them, we object that this is an impoverished conception of democratic politics, which does not acknowledge the way in which political identities are not pre-given but constituted and reconstituted through debate in the public sphere. Politics, we argue, does not consist in simply registering already existing interests, but plays a crucial role in shaping political subjects. On these topics, we are at one with the Habermasians. Moreover, we agree with them on the need to take account of the many different voices that a democratic society encompasses and to widen the field of democratic struggles.

There are, however, important points of divergence between our view and theirs which hinge on the theoretical framework that informs our respective conceptions. The central role that the notion of antagonism plays in our work forecloses any possibility of a final reconciliation, of any kind of rational consensus, of a fully inclusive 'we'. For us, a non-exclusive public sphere of rational argument is a conceptual impossibility. Conflict and division, in our view, are neither disturbances that unfortunately cannot be eliminated nor empirical impediments that render impossible the full realization of a harmony that we cannot attain because we will never be able to leave our particularities completely aside in order to act in accordance with our rational self — a harmony which should nonetheless constitute the ideal towards which we strive. Indeed, we maintain that without conflict and division, a pluralist democratic politics would be impossible. To believe that a final resolution of conflicts is eventually possible — even if it is seen as an asymptotic approach to the regulative idea of a rational consensus — far from providing the necessary horizon for the democratic project, is to put it at risk. Conceived in such a way, pluralist democracy becomes a 'self-refuting ideal', because the very moment of its realization would coincide with its disintegration. This is why we stress that it is vital for democratic politics to acknowledge that any form of consensus is the result of a hegemonic articulation, and that it always has an 'outside' that impedes its full realization. Unlike the Habermasians, we do not see this as something that undermines the democratic project, but as its very condition of possibility.

A final word about the way we envisage the most urgent tasks for the Left. Several voices have been heard recently calling: 'Back to the class struggle'. They claim that the Left has become too closely identified with 'cultural' issues, and that it has abandoned the struggle against economic inequalities. It is time, they say, to leave aside the obsession with 'identity politics', and to listen again to the demands of the working class. What should we make of such critiques? Are we, today, in an opposite conjuncture to that which provided the background of our reflection, based as it was in criticizing the Left for not taking the struggles of the 'new movements' into consideration? It is true that the evolution of the parties of the Left has been such that they have become concerned mainly with the middle classes, to the detriment of the workers. But this is due to their incapacity to envisage an alternative to neo-liberalism and their uncritical acceptance of the imperatives of 'flexibility', not to a supposed infatuation with issues of 'identity'. The solution is not to abandon the 'cultural' struggle to go back to 'real' politics. One of the central tenets of *Hegemony and Socialist Strategy* is the need to create a chain of equivalence among the various democratic struggles against different forms of subordination. We argued that struggles against sexism, racism, sexual discrimination, and in the defence of the environment needed to be articulated with those of the workers in a new left-wing hegemonic project. To put it in terminology which has recently become fashionable, we insisted that the Left needed to tackle issues of both 'redistribution' and 'recognition'. This is what we meant by 'radical and plural democracy'.

Today, such a project remains as pertinent as ever — which is not to say that it has become easier to realize. Indeed, it appears sometimes as if, rather than thinking of 'radicalizing' democracy, the first priority is to defend it against the forces which insidiously threaten it from within. Instead of reinforcing its institutions, it seems that the triumph of democracy over its communist adversary has contributed to their weakening. Disaffection with the democratic process is reaching worrying proportions, and cynicism about the political class is so widespread that it is undermining citizens' basic trust in the parliamentary system. There is certainly no ground for rejoicing about the current state of politics in liberal-democratic societies. In some countries this situation is being cleverly exploited by right-wing populist demagogues, and the success of people like Haider and Berlusconi is there to testify that such rhetorics can attract a very significant following. As long as the Left relinquishes the hegemonic struggle, and insists on occupying the centre ground, there is very little hope that such a situation could be reversed. To be sure, we have begun to see the emergence of a series of resistances to the transnational corporations' attempt to impose their power over the entire planet. But without a vision about what could be a different way of organizing social relations, one which restores the centrality of politics over the tyranny of market forces, those movements will remain of a defensive nature. If one is to build a chain of equivalences among democratic struggles, one needs to establish a frontier and define an adversary, but this is not enough. One also needs to know for what one is fighting, what kind of society one wants to establish. This requires from the Left an adequate grasp of the nature of power relations, and the dynamics of politics. What is at stake is the building of a new hegemony. So our motto is: 'Back to the hegemonic struggle'.

Ernesto Laclau and Chantal Mouffe
November 2000

Introduction

Left-wing thought today stands at a crossroads. The 'evident truths' of the past — the classical forms of analysis and political calculation, the nature of the forces in conflict, the very meaning of the Left's struggles and objectives — have been seriously challenged by an avalanche of historical mutations which have riven the ground on which those truths were constituted. Some of these mutations doubtless correspond to failures and disappointments: from Budapest to Prague and the Polish coup d'etat, from Kabul to the sequels of Communist victory in Vietnam and Cambodia, a question-mark has fallen more and more heavily over a whole way of conceiving both socialism and the roads that should lead to it. This has recharged critical thinking, at once corrosive and necessary, on the theoretical and political bases on which the intellectual horizon of the Left was traditionally constituted. But there is more to it than this. A whole series of positive new phenomena underlie those mutations which have made so urgent the task of theoretical reconsideration: the rise of the new feminism, the protest movements of ethnic, national and sexual minorities, the anti-institutional ecology struggles waged by marginalized layers of the population, the anti-nuclear movement, the atypical forms of social struggle in countries on the capitalist periphery — all these imply an extension of social conflictuality to a wide range of areas, which creates the potential, but no more than the potential, for an advance towards more free, democratic and egalitarian societies.

This proliferation of struggles presents itself, first of all, as a 'surplus' of the social vis-à-vis the rational and organized structures of society — that is, of the social 'order'. Numerous voices, deriving especially from the liberal-conservative camp, have insistently argued that Western societies face a crisis of governability and a threat of dissolution at the hands of the egalitarian danger. However, the new forms of social conflict have also thrown into crisis theoretical and political frameworks closer to the ones that we shall seek to engage in dialogue in the major part of this book. These correspond to the classical discourses of the Left, and the characteristic modes in which it has conceived the agents of social change, the structuring of political spaces, and the privileged points for the unleashing of historical transformations. What is now in crisis is a whole conception of socialism which rests upon the ontological centrality of the working class, upon the role of Revolution, with a capital 'r', as the founding moment in the transition from one type of society to another, and upon the illusory prospect of a perfectly unitary and homogeneous collective will that will render pointless the moment of politics. The plural and multifarious character of contemporary social struggles has finally dissolved the last foundation for that political imaginary. Peopled with 'universal' subjects and conceptually built around History in the singular, it has postulated 'society' as an intelligible structure that could be intellectually mastered on the basis of certain class positions and reconstituted, as a rational, transparent order, through a founding act of a political character. Today, the Left is witnessing the final act of the dissolution of that Jacobin imaginary.

Thus, the very wealth and plurality of contemporary social struggles has given rise to a theoretical crisis. It is at the middle point of this two-way movement between the theoretical and the political that our own discourse will be located. At every moment, we have tried to prevent an impressionist and sociologistic descriptivism, which lives on ignorance of the conditions of its own discursivity, from filling the theoretical voids generated by the crisis. Our aim has been the exact opposite: to focus on certain discursive categories which, at first sight, appeared to be privileged condensation-points for many aspects of the crisis; and to unravel the possible meaning of a history in the various facets of this multiple refraction. All discursive eclecticism or wavering was excluded from the very start. As is said in an inaugural 'manifesto' of the classical period, when one enters new territory, one must follow the example of 'travellers who, finding themselves lost in a forest, know that they ought not to wander first to one side and then to the other, nor, still less, to stop in one place, but understand that they should continue to walk as straight as they can in one direction, not diverging for any slight reason, even though it was possibly chance alone that first determined them in their choice. By this means if they do not go exactly where they wish, they will at least arrive somewhere at the end, where probably they will be better off than in the middle of a forest.'[1]

The guiding thread of our analysis has been the transformations in the concept of hegemony, considered as a discursive surface and fundamental nodal point of Marxist political theorization. Our principal conclusion is that behind the concept of 'hegemony' lies hidden something more than a type of political relation *complementary* to the basic categories of Marxist theory. In fact, it introduces a *logic of the social* which is incompatible with those categories. Faced with the rationalism of classical Marxism, which presented history and society as intelligible totalities constituted around conceptually explicable laws, the logic of hegemony presented itself from the outset as a *complementary* and *contingent* operation, required for conjunctural imbalances within an evolutionary paradigm whose essential or 'morphological' validity was not for a moment placed in question. (One of the central tasks of this book will be to determine this specific logic of contingency.) As the areas of the concept's application grew broader, from Lenin to Gramsci, the field of contingent articulations also expanded, and the category of 'historical necessity' — which had been the cornerstone of classical Marxism — withdrew to the horizon of theory. As we shall argue in the last two chapters, the expansion and determination of the social logic implicit in the concept of 'hegemony' — in a direction that goes far beyond Gramsci — will provide us with an *anchorage* from which contemporary social struggles are *thinkable* in their specificity, as well as permitting us to outline a new politics for the Left based upon the project of a radical democracy.

One question remains to be answered: why should we broach this task through a critique and a deconstruction of the various discursive surfaces of classical Marxism? Let us first say that there is not *one* discourse and *one* system of categories through which the 'real' might speak without mediations. In operating deconstructively within Marxist categories, we do not claim to be writing 'universal history', to be inscribing our discourse as a moment of a single, linear process of knowledge. Just as the era of normative epistemologies has come to an end, so too has the era of universal discourses. Political conclusions similar to those set forth in this book could have been approximated from very different discursive formations — for example, from certain forms of Christianity, or from libertarian discourses alien to the socialist tradition — none of which could aspire to be *the* truth of society (or 'the insurpassable philosophy of our time', as Sartre put it). For this very reason, however, Marxism is *one* of the traditions through which it becomes possible to formulate this new conception of politics. For us, the validity of this point of departure is simply based on the fact that it constitutes our own past.

Is it not the case that, in scaling down the pretensions and the area of validity of Marxist theory, we are breaking with something deeply inherent in that theory: namely, its monist aspiration to capture with its categories the essence or underlying meaning of History? The answer can only be in the affirmative. Only if we renounce any epistemological prerogative based upon the ontologically privileged position of a 'universal class', will it be possible seriously to discuss the present degree of validity of the Marxist categories. At this point we should state quite plainly that we are now situated in a post-Marxist terrain. It is no longer possible to maintain the conception of subjectivity and classes elaborated by Marxism, nor its vision of the historical course of capitalist development, nor, of course, the conception of communism as a transparent society from which antagonisms have disappeared. But if our intellectual project in this book is *post*-Marxist, it is evidently also post-*Marxist*. It has been through the development of certain intuitions and discursive forms constituted within Marxism, and the inhibition or elimination of certain others, that we have constructed a concept of hegemony which, in our view, may be a useful instrument in the struggle for a radical, libertarian and plural democracy. Here the reference to Gramsci, though partially critical, is of capital importance. In the text we have tried to recover some of the variety and richness of Marxist discursivity in the era of the Second International, which tended to be obliterated by that impoverished monolithic image of 'Marxism–Leninism' current in the Stalin and post-Stalin eras and now reproduced, almost intact though with opposite sign, by certain forms of contemporary 'anti-Marxism'. Neither the defenders of a glorious, homogeneous and invulnerable 'historical materialism', nor the professionals of an anti-Marxism à la nouveaux philosophes, realize the extent to which their apologias or diatribes are equally rooted in an ingenuous and primitive conception of a doctrine's role and degree of unity which, in all its essential determinations, is still tributary to the Stalinist imaginary. Our own approach to the Marxist texts has, on the contrary, sought to recover their plurality, to grasp the numerous discursive sequences — to a considerable extent heterogeneous and contradictory — which constitute their inner structure and wealth, and guarantee their survival as a reference point for political analysis. The surpassing of a great intellectual tradition never takes place in the sudden form of a collapse, but in the way that river waters, having originated at a common source, spread in various directions and mingle with currents flowing down from other sources. This is how the discourses that constituted the field of classical Marxism may help to form the thinking of a new left: by bequeathing some of their concepts, transforming or abandoning others, and diluting themselves in that infinite intertextuality of emancipatory discourses in which the plurality of the social takes shape.

Note to Introduction

1. Descartes, 'Discourse on Method', in *Philosophical Works* Vol. 1, Cambridge 1968, p. 96.

Hegemony: the Genealogy of a Concept

We will start by tracing the *genealogy* of the concept of 'hegemony'. It should be stressed that this will not be the genealogy of a concept endowed from the beginning with full positivity. In fact, using somewhat freely an expression of Foucault, we could say that our aim is to establish the 'archaeology of a silence'. The concept of hegemony did not emerge to define a new type of relation in its specific identity, but to fill a hiatus that had opened in the chain of historical necessity. 'Hegemony' will allude to an absent totality, and to the diverse attempts at recomposition and rearticulation which, in overcoming this original absence, made it possible for struggles to be given a meaning and for historical forces to be endowed with full positivity. The contexts in which the concept appear will be those of a *fault* (in the geological sense), of a fissure that had to be filled up, of a contingency that had to be overcome. 'Hegemony' will be not the majestic unfolding of an identity but the response to a crisis.

Even in its humble origins in Russian Social Democracy, where it is called upon to cover a limited area of political effects, the concept of 'hegemony' already alludes to a kind of *contingent* intervention required by the crisis or collapse of what would have been a 'normal' historical development. Later, with Leninism, it is a keystone in the new form of political calculation required by the contingent 'concrete situations' in which the class struggle occurs in the age of imperialism. Finally, with Gramsci, the term acquires a new type of centrality that transcends its tactical or strategic uses: 'hegemony' becomes the key concept in understanding the very unity existing in a concrete social formation. Each of these extensions of the term, however, was accompanied by an expansion of what we could provisionally call a 'logic of the contingent'. In its turn, this expression stemmed from the fracture, and withdrawal to the explanatory horizon of the social, of the category of 'historical necessity' which had been the cornerstone of Second International Marxism. The alternatives within this advancing crisis — and the different responses to it, of which the theory of hegemony is but one — form the object of our study.

The Dilemmas of Rosa Luxemburg

Let us avoid any temptation to go back to the 'origins'. Let us simply pierce a moment in time and try to detect the presence of that void which the logic of hegemony will attempt to fill. This arbitrary beginning, projected in a variety of directions, will offer us, if not the sense of a trajectory, at least the dimensions of a crisis. It is in the multiple, meandering reflections in the broken mirror of 'historical necessity' that a new logic of the social begins to insinuate itself, one that will only manage to think itself by questioning the very literality of the terms it articulates.

In 1906 Rosa Luxemburg published *The Mass Strike, the Political Party and the Trade Unions*. A brief analysis of this text — which already presents all the ambiguities and critical areas important to our theme — will provide us with an initial point of reference. Rosa Luxemburg deals with a specific theme: the efficacy and significance of the mass strike as a political tool. But for her this implies consideration of two vital problems for the socialist cause: the unity of the working class and the path to revolution in Europe. Mass strike, the dominant form of struggle in the first Russian revolution, is dealt with in its specific mechanisms as well as in its possible projections for the workers' struggle in Germany. The theses of Rosa Luxemburg are well known: while debate concerning the efficacy of the mass strike in Germany had centred almost exclusively on the political strike, the Russian experience had demonstrated an interaction and a mutual and constant enrichment between the political and economic dimensions of the mass strike. In the repressive context of the Tsarist state, no movement for partial demands could remain confined within itself: it was inevitably transformed into an example and symbol of resistance, thus fuelling and giving birth to other movements. These emerged at unpreconceived points and tended to expand and generalize in unforeseeable forms, so that they were beyond the capacity of regulation and organization of any political or trade union leadership. This is the meaning of Luxemburg's 'spontaneism'. The unity between the economic and the political struggle — that is to say, the very unity of the working class — is a consequence of this movement of feedback and interaction. But this movement in turn is nothing other than the process of revolution.

If we move from Russia to Germany, Rosa Luxemburg argues, the situation becomes very different. The dominant trend is the fragmentation among diverse categories of workers, between the different demands of various movements, between economic struggle and political struggle. 'Only in the sultry air of the period of revolution can any partial little conflict between labour and capital grow into a general explosion. In Germany the most violent, most brutal collisions between the workers and the employers take place every day without the struggle over-leaping the bound of the individual factories . . . None of these cases . . . changes suddenly into a common class action. And when they grow into isolated mass strikes which have without question a political colouring, they do not bring about a general storm.'[1] This isolation and fragmentation is not a contingent event: it is a structural effect of the capitalist state, which is only overcome in a revolutionary atmosphere. 'As a matter of fact the separation of the political and the economic struggle and the independence of each is nothing but an artificial product of the parliamentarian period, even if historically determined. On the one hand, in the peaceful, "normal" course of bourgeois society the economic struggle is split into a multitude of individual struggles in every undertaking and dissolved in every branch of production. On the other hand, the political struggle is not directed by the masses themselves in a direct action, but in correspondence with the form of the bourgeois State, in a representative fashion, by the presence of legislative representation.'[2]

In these conditions and given that the revolutionary outbreaks in Russia could be explained by factors such as the comparative backwardness of the country, the absence of political liberties, or the poverty of the Russian proletariat — were not the perspectives for revolution in the West postponed *sine die*? Here Rosa Luxemburg's response becomes hesitant and less convincing as it assumes a characteristic course: namely, an attempt to minimize the differences between the Russian and the German proletariat, showing the areas of poverty and the absence of organization in various sectors of the German working class, as well as the presence of inverse phenomena in the most advanced sectors of the Russian proletariat. But what of those pockets of backwardness in Germany? Were they not residual sectors which would be swept away by capitalist expansion? And in that case, what guaranteed the emergence of a revolutionary situation? The answer to *our* question — Rosa Luxemburg does not at any point formulate it in this text — comes to us abruptly and unequivocably a few pages later: '(The social democrats) must now and always hasten the development of things and endeavour to accelerate events. This they cannot do, however, by suddenly issuing the "slogan" for a mass strike at random at any moment, but first and foremost, by making clear to the widest layers of the proletariat the *inevitable advent* of this revolutionary period, the inner *social* factors making for it and the *political* consequences of it.'[3] Thus, the 'necessary laws of capitalist development' establish themselves as a guarantee for the future revolutionary situation in Germany. Everything is now clear: as there were no more bourgeois-democratic changes to be achieved in Germany (*sic*), the coming of a revolutionary situation could only be resolved in a socialist direction; the Russian proletariat — struggling against absolutism, but in a historical context dominated by the maturity of world capitalism which prevented it from stabilizing its own struggles in a bourgeois stage — was the vanguard of the European proletariat and pointed out to the German working class its own future. The problem of the differences between East and West, so important in the strategic debates of European socialism from Bernstein to Gramsci, was here resolved by being discarded.[4]

Let us analyse the various moments of this remarkable sequence. Concerning the constitutive mechanism of class unity, Rosa Luxemburg's position is clear: in capitalist society, the working class is necessarily fragmented and the recomposition of its unity only occurs through the very process of revolution. Yet the *form* of this revolutionary recomposition consists of a specific mechanism which has little to do with any mechanistic explanation. It is here that spontaneism comes into play. One could think that the 'spontaneist' theory simply affirms the impossibility of *foreseeing* the direction of a revolutionary process, given the complexity and variety of forms which it adopts. Nevertheless, this explanation is insufficient. For what is at stake is not merely the complexity and diversity inherent in a dispersion of struggles — when these are seen from the point of view of an analyst or a political leader — but also the constitution of the *unity* of the revolutionary subject on the basis of this complexity and diversity. This alone shows us that in attempting to determine the meaning of Luxemburgist 'spontaneism', we must concentrate not only on the plurality of forms of struggle but also on the relations which they establish among themselves and on the unifying effects which follow from them. And here, the mechanism of unification is clear: in a revolutionary situation, it is impossible *to fix the literal sense* of each isolated struggle, because each struggle overflows its own literality and comes to represent, in the consciousness of the masses, a simple moment of a more global struggle against the system. And so it is that while in a period of stability the class consciousness of the worker — as a global consciousness constituted around his 'historical interests' — is 'latent' and 'theoretical', in a revolutionary situation it becomes 'active' and 'practical'. Thus, in a revolutionary situation the *meaning* of every mobilization appears, so to speak, as split: aside from its specific literal demands, each mobilization represents the revolutionary process as a whole; and these totalizing effects are visible in the overdetermination of some struggles by others. This is, however, nothing other than the defining characteristic of the symbol: the overflowing of the signifier by the signified.[5] *The unity of the class is therefore a symbolic unity.* Undoubtedly this is the highest point in Luxemburg's analysis, one which establishes the maximum distance from the orthodox theoreticians of the Second International (for whom class unity is simply laid down by the laws of the economic base). Although in many other analyses of the period a role is given to the contingent — exceeding the moment of 'structural' theorization — few texts advance as much as Rosa Luxemburg's in determining the specific mechanisms of this contingency and in recognizing the extent of its practical effects.[6]

Now, on the one hand, the analysis of Rosa Luxemburg has multiplied the points of antagonism and the forms of struggle — which we will from now on call the *subject positions* — up to the point of exploding all capacity for control or planning of these struggles by a trade-union or political leadership; on the other hand, it has proposed symbolic overdetermination as a concrete mechanism for the unification of these struggles. Here, however, the problems begin, since for Rosa Luxemburg this process of overdetermination constitutes a very precise unity: a *class unity*. Yet there is nothing in the theory of spontaneism which logically supports her conclusion. On the contrary, the very logic of spontaneism seems to imply that the resulting type of unitary subject should remain largely indeterminate. In the case of the Tsarist state, if the condition of overdetermination of the points of antagonism and the diverse struggles is a repressive political context, why cannot the class limits be surpassed and lead to the construction of, for example, partially unified subjects whose fundamental determination is popular or democratic? Even in Rosa Luxemburg's text — notwithstanding the dogmatic rigidity of the author, for whom every subject has to be a class subject — the surpassing of classist categories appears at a number of points. 'Throughout the whole of the spring of 1905 and into the middle of summer there fermented throughout the whole empire an uninterrupted economic strike of almost the entire proletariat against capital — a struggle which on the one hand caught all the petty-bourgeois and liberal professions, and on the other hand penetrated to the domestic servants, the minor police officials and even to the stratum of the lumpen proletariat, and simultaneously surged from the towns to the country districts and even knocked at the iron gates of the military barracks.'[7]

Let us be clear about the meaning of our question: if the unity of the working class were an infrastructural datum constituted *outside* the process of revolutionary overdetermination, the question concerning the class character of the revolutionary subject would not arise. Indeed, both political and economic struggle would be symmetrical expressions of a class subject constituted prior to the struggles themselves. But if the unity *is* this process of overdetermination, an independent explanation has to be offered as to why there should be a necessary overlap between political subjectivity and class positions. Although Rosa Luxemburg does not offer such an explanation — in fact, she does not even perceive the problem — the background of her thought makes clear what this would have been: namely, an affirmation of the necessary character of the objective laws of capitalist development, which lead to an increasing proletarianization of the middle sectors and the peasantry and, thus, to a straightforward confrontation between bourgeoisie and proletariat. Consequently the innovatory effects of the logic of spontaneism appear to be strictly limited from the beginning.[8]

The effects are so limited, no doubt, because the area in which they operate is extremely circumscribed. But also because, in a second and more important sense, the logic of spontaneism and the logic of necessity do not converge as two distinct and positive principles to explain certain historical situations, but function instead as antithetical logics which only interact with each other through the reciprocal limitation of their effects. Let us carefully examine the point where they diverge. The logic of spontaneism is a logic of the symbol inasmuch as it operates precisely through the disruption of every literal meaning. The logic of necessity is a logic of the literal: it operates through fixations which, precisely because they are necessary, establish a meaning that eliminates any contingent variation. In this case, however, the relation between the two logics is a relation of frontiers, which can expand in one or another direction but never overcome the irreducible dualism introduced into the analysis.

In reality, we here witness the emergence of a *double void*. Seen from the category of necessity, the duality of logics merges with the determinable/indeterminable opposition: that is to say, it only points to the operational limits of that category. But the same thing occurs from the point of view of spontaneism: the field of 'historical necessity' presents itself as a limit to the working of the symbolic. The *limits* are, in actual fact, *limitations*. If the specificity of this limitation of effects is not immediately evident, this is because it is thought of as a confluence of two positive and different explanatory principles, each valid in its own area, and not as what each of them is: the purely negative reverse of the other. The double void created by dualism hereby becomes invisible. However, to make a void invisible is not the same as to fill it up.

Before we examine the changing forms of this double void, we may for a moment place ourselves within it and practise the only game it allows us: that is, to move the frontiers separating the two opposed logics. If we broaden the area corresponding to historical necessity, the result is a well-known alternative: either capitalism leads through its necessary laws to proletarianization and crisis; or else these necessary laws do not function as expected, in which case, following the very logic of Luxemburgist discourse, the fragmentation between different subject positions ceases to be an 'artificial product' of the capitalist state and becomes a permanent reality. It is the zero-sum game intrinsic to all economistic and reductionist conceptions. If, on the contrary, we move the boundary in the opposite direction, to the point where the class nature of political subjects loses its necessary character, the spectacle that appears before our eyes is not at all imaginary: it is the original forms of overdetermination assumed by social struggles in the Third World, with the construction of political identities having little to do with strict class boundaries; it is the rise of fascism, which would brutally dispel the illusion of the necessary character of certain class articulations; it is the new forms of struggle in the advanced capitalist countries, where during the last few decades we have witnessed the constant emergence of new forms of political subjectivity cutting across the categories of the social and economic structure. The concept of 'hegemony' will emerge precisely in a context dominated by the experience of fragmentation and by the indeterminacy of the articulations between different struggles and subject positions. It will offer a socialist answer in a politico–discursive universe that has witnessed a withdrawal of the category of 'necessity' to the horizon of the social. Faced with attempts to tackle the crisis of an essentialist monism through a proliferation of dualisms — free-will/determinism; science/ethics; individual/collectivity; causality/teleology — the theory of hegemony will ground its response on a displacement of the terrain which made possible the monist/dualist alternative.

One final point before leaving Rosa Luxemburg. The limitation of effects which the 'necessary laws' produce in her discourse also functions in another important direction: as a limitation of the political conclusions capable of being derived from the 'observable tendencies' in advanced capitalism. The role of theory is not to elaborate intellectually the observable tendencies of fragmentation and dispersion, but to ensure that such tendencies have a transitory character. There is a split between 'theory' and 'practice' which is a clear symptom of a crisis. This crisis — to which the emergence of Marxist 'orthodoxy' represents only one answer — is the starting-point of our analysis. Yet it requires that we place ourselves at a point prior to this beginning, in order to identify the paradigm that entered into crisis. For this we can refer to a document of exceptional clarity and systematicity: Kautsky's 1892 commentary to the Erfurt Programme, the seminal manifesto of German Social Democracy.[9]

Crisis, Degree Zero

The Class Struggle is a typical Kautskian text which puts forward an indissociable unity of theory, history and strategy.[10] From our present-day perspective, of course, it appears extremely naïve and simplistic. Yet we must inquire into the various dimensions of this simplicity, for they will permit us to understand both the structural characteristics of the paradigm and the reasons that led to its crisis at the turn of the century.

The paradigm is simple, in a primary and literal sense that Kautsky quite explicitly presents a theory of the increasing *simplification* of the social structure and the antagonisms within it. Capitalist society advances towards an increasing concentration of property and wealth in the hands of a few enterprises; and a rapid proletarianization of the most diverse social strata and occupational categories is combined with a growing impoverishment of the working class. This impoverishment, and the necessary laws of capitalist development that are at its origin, hinder a real autonomization of spheres and functions within the working class: the economic struggle can have only modest and precarious successes, and this leads to a *de facto* subordination of trade-union to party organization, which alone can substantially modify the position of the proletariat through the conquest of political power. The structural moments or instances of capitalist society also lack any form of relative autonomy. The state, for example, is presented in terms of the most crass instrumentalism. Thus, the simplicity of the Kautskian paradigm consists, first of all, in a simplification of the system of structural differences constitutive of capitalist society.

Yet the Kautskian paradigm is also simple in a second and less frequently mentioned sense, which is of crucial importance for our analysis. Here, the point is not so much that the paradigm reduces the number of pertinent structural differences, but that it fixes them through the attribution to each of a *single meaning,* understood as a precise location within a totality. In the first sense, Kautsky's analysis was simply economistic and reductionist; but if this were the only problem, the corrective would merely have to introduce the 'relative autonomies' of the political and the ideological, and render the analysis more complex through the multiplication of instances within a topography of the social. *Yet each one of these multiplied instances or structural moments would have an identity as fixed and singular as the instances of the Kautskian paradigm.*

In order to illustrate this *unicity of meaning,* let us examine how Kautsky explains the relationship between economic and political struggle: 'Occasionally someone has attempted to oppose the political struggle to the economic, and declared that the proletariat should give its exclusive attention to one or the other. The fact is that the two cannot be separated. The economic struggle demands political rights and these will not fall from heaven. To secure and maintain them the most vigorous political struggle is necessary. The political struggle is, in the last analysis, an economic struggle'.[11] Rosa Luxemburg also affirmed the unity of the two types of struggle, but she began from an *initial diversity*, and unity was a *unification*, the result of an overdetermination of discrete elements without any forms of fixed, a priori articulation. For Kautsky, however, unity is the starting-point: the working class struggles in the field of politics by virtue of an economic calculation. It is possible to pass from one struggle to the other through a purely logical transition. In the case of Rosa Luxemburg, each struggle had more than one meaning — as we have seen, it was reduplicated in a second symbolic dimension. Nor was its meaning fixed: for it depended upon variable articulations which, from her spontaneist perspective repelled any a priori determination (within the limits we have signalled). Kautsky, on the other hand, simplified the meaning of every social antagonism or element by reducing it to a specific structural location, already fixed by the logic of the capitalist mode of production. The history of capitalism set out in *The Class Struggle* consists of *pure relations of interiority*. We can pass from working class to capitalists, from the economic sphere to the political sphere, from manufacture to monopoly capitalism, without having to depart for one instant from the internal rationality and intelligibility of a closed paradigm. Capitalism is, no doubt, presented to us as acting upon an external social reality, yet the latter simply dissolves upon entering into contact with the former. Capitalism changes, yet this change is nothing more than the unfolding of its endogenous tendencies and contradictions. Here the logic of necessity is not limited by anything: this is what makes *The Class Struggle* a pre-crisis text.

Finally, simplicity is present in a third dimension — that which refers to the role of theory itself. If this early Kautskian text is compared with others belonging to an earlier or later Marxist tradition, we find that it contains a rather surprising feature: it presents itself not as an intervention to unravel the underlying sense of history, but as the systematization and generalization of a transparent experience which is there for all to see. As there is no social hieroglyph to decode, there is a perfect correspondence between theory and the practices of the workers movement. With regard to the constitution of class unity, Adam Przeworski has pointed out the peculiarity of Kautsky's text: whereas Marx, from the time of the *Poverty of Philosophy,* presented the unity of the economic insertion and political organization of the working class as an unfinished process — this was the hiatus which the distinction between 'class in itself' and 'class for itself' tried to fill — Kautsky argues as if the working class has already completed the formation of its unity. 'It seems that Kautsky believed that by 1890 the formation of the proletariat into a class was a *fait accompli*; it was already formed as a class and would remain so in the future. The organized proletariat had nothing left to do but to pursue its historical mission, and the party could only participate in its realization.'[12] Similarly, when Kautsky refers to growing proletarianization and impoverishment, to the inevitable crises of capitalism, or to the necessary advent of socialism, he seems to be speaking not of potential tendencies revealed by analysis, but of empirically observable realities in the first two cases, and of a short-term transition in the third. Despite the fact that necessity is the dominant category in his discourse, its function is not to guarantee a meaning beyond experience, but to systematize experience itself.

Now, although the combination of elements underlying this optimism and simplicity is presented as part of a universal process of class constitution, it merely represented the crowning of the very specific historical formation of the *German* working class. Firstly, the political autonomy of the German working class was the result of two failures: that of the German bourgeoisie, after 1849, to set itself up as the hegemonic force of a liberal-democratic movement; and that of the Lassalleans' corporatist attempt to integrate the working class into the Bismarckian state. Secondly, the great depression of 1873–96, and the accompanying economic insecurity which affected all social strata, nurtured a general optimism about the imminent collapse of capitalism and the advent of proletarian revolution. Thirdly, the working class had a low degree of structural complexity: the trade unions were incipient and subordinated to the party both politically and financially; and in the context of the twenty-year depression, the prospects for an improvement in the workers' condition through trade-union activity seemed extremely limited. Only with difficulty was the General Commission of the German trade unions, established in 1890, able to impose its hegemony over the workers movement, amid the resistance of local trade union powers and the overall scepticism of Social Democracy.[13]

Under these conditions, the unity and autonomy of the working class, and the collapse of the capitalist system, virtually appeared as facts of experience. These were the reading parameters which gave the Kautskian discourse its acceptability. In reality, however, the situation was strictly German — or, at most, typical of certain European countries where the liberal bourgeoisie was weak — and certainly did not correspond to those processes of working-class formation in countries with a strong liberal (England) or democratic-Jacobin tradition (France), or where ethnic and religious identities predominated over those of class (the United States). But since, in the Marxist Vulgate, history advanced towards an ever greater simplification of social antagonisms, the extreme isolation and confrontation course of the German workers movement would acquire the prestige of a paradigm towards which other national situations had to converge and in relation to which they were merely inadequate approximations.[14]

The end of the depression brought the beginning of the crisis of this paradigm. The transition to 'organized capitalism', and the ensuing boom that lasted until 1914, made uncertain the prospect of a 'general crisis of capitalism'. Under the new conditions, a wave of successful trade union economic struggles enabled the workers to consolidate their organizational power and influence within Social Democracy. But at this point, a steady tension began to assert itself between the trade unions and the political leadership within the party, so that the unity and socialist determination of the working class became increasingly problematic. In all areas of society, an *autonomization of spheres* was taking place — which implied that any type of unity could only be attained through unstable and complex forms of rearticulation. From this new perspective, a serious question-mark appeared over the seemingly logical and simple sequence of the various structural moments of the 1892 Kautskian paradigm. And as the relationship between theory and programme was one of total implication, the political crisis was reduplicated in a theoretical one. In 1898 Thomas Masaryk coined an expression that soon became popular: the 'crisis of Marxism'.

This crisis, which served as the background to all Marxist debates from the turn of the century until the war, seems to have been dominated by two basic moments: the new awareness of the opacity of the social, of the complexities and resistances of an increasingly organized capitalism; and the fragmentation of the different positions of social agents which, according to the classical paradigm, should have been united.[15] In a famous passage of a letter to Lagardelle, Antonio Labriola stated at the beginning of the revisionism debate: 'Truly, behind all this rumour of controversy, there is a serious and essential problem: the ardent, lively and precocious hopes of some years ago — those expectations of over-precise details and contours — are now running up against the most complex resistance of economic relations and the most intricate meshing of the political world.'[16]

It would be wrong to see this as a merely transitory crisis; on the contrary, Marxism finally lost its innocence at that time. In so far as the paradigmatic sequence of its categories was subjected to the 'structural pressure' of increasingly atypical situations, it became ever more difficult to reduce social relations to structural moments internal to those categories. A proliferation of caesurae and discontinuities start to break down the unity of a discourse that considered itself profoundly monist. From then on, the problem of Marxism has been *to think those discontinuities* and, at the same time, to find *forms reconstituting* the unity of scattered and heterogeneous elements. The transitions between different structural moments have lost their originary logical transparency and reveal an opacity pertaining to contingent and laboriously constructed relations. The specificity of the different responses to the crisis of this paradigm resides in the way of conceiving this relational moment — whose importance increases to the extent that its nature becomes less evident. This is what we must now analyse.

The First Response to the Crisis: the Formation of Marxist Orthodoxy

Marxist orthodoxy, as it is constituted in Kautsky and Plekhanov, is not a simple continuation of classical Marxism. It involves a very particular inflection, characterized by the new role assigned to theory. Instead of serving to systematize observable historical tendencies — as it did in Kautsky's text of 1892 — theory sets itself up as a guarantee that these tendencies will eventually coincide with the type of social articulation proposed by the Marxist paradigm. In other words, orthodoxy is constituted on the ground of a growing disjuncture between Marxist theory and the political practice of Social Democracy. It is the laws of motion of the infrastructure, guaranteed by Marxist 'science', which provide the terrain for the overcoming of this disjuncture and assure both the transitory character of the existing tendencies and the future revolutionary reconstitution of the working class.

Let us examine, in this regard, Kautsky's position on the relationship between party and unions, as expressed in his polemic with the theoreticians of the trade union movement.[17] Kautsky is perfectly aware of the strong tendencies toward fragmentation within the German working class: the rise of a labour aristocracy; the opposition between unionized and non-unionized workers; the counterposed interests of different wage categories; the conscious policy of the bourgeoisie to divide the working class; the presence of masses of Catholic workers subjected to a church populism which distances them from the Social Democrats, and so forth. He is equally conscious of the fact that the more *immediate material interests* predominate, the more tendencies toward fragmentation assert themselves; and that hence pure trade-union action cannot guarantee either the unity or the socialist determination of the working class.[18] These can be consolidated only if the immediate material interests of the working class are subordinated to the *Endziel,* the final socialist objective, and this presupposes the subordination of economic struggle to political struggle, and thus of the trade unions to the party.[19] But the party can represent this totalizing instance only insofar as it is the depository of science — that is, of Marxist theory. The obvious fact that the working class was not following a socialist direction — English trade unionism was a resounding example of this, and by the turn of the century could no longer be ignored — led Kautsky to affirm a new privileged role for intellectuals which was to have such an important influence on Lenin's *What is to be Done*. Such intellectual mediation is limited in its effects, for, according to the Spinozist formula, its sole freedom consists in being the consciousness of necessity. However, it does entail the emergence of an articulating nexus that cannot simply be referred to the chain of a monistically conceived necessity.

The fissure that opened up in the identity of the class, the growing dissociation between the different subject positions of the workers, could only be surpassed by a future movement of the economic base whose advent was guaranteed by Marxist science. Consequently, everything depends on the predictive capacity of this science and on the necessary character of such predictions. It is no accident that the category of 'necessity' has to be affirmed with ever increasing virulence. It is well known how 'necessity' was understood by the Second International: as a natural necessity, founded on a combination of Marxism and Darwinism. The Darwinist influence has frequently been presented as a vulgar Marxist substitute for Hegelian dialectics; but the truth is that in the orthodox conception, Hegelianism and Darwinism combined to form a hybrid capable of satisfying strategic requirements. Darwinism alone does not offer 'guarantees for the future', since natural selection does not operate in a direction predetermined from the beginning.[20] Only if a Hegelian type of teleology is added to Darwinism — which is totally incompatible with it — can an evolutionary process be presented as a guarantee of future transitions.

This conception of class unity as a future unity assured by the action of ineluctable laws, had effects at a number of levels: on the type of articulation attributed to diverse subject positions; on the way of treating differences which could not be assimilated to the paradigm; and on the strategy for analysis of historical events. Concerning the first point, it is evident that if the revolutionary subject establishes its class identity at the level of the relations of production,[21] its presence at other levels can only be one of *exteriority* and it must adopt the form of *'representation of interests'*. The terrain of politics can only be a superstructure, insofar as it is a terrain of struggle between agents whose identity, conceived under the form of 'interests', has set itself up at another level. This essential identity was thus *fixed,* once and for all, as an unalterable fact relating to the various forms of political and ideological representation into which the working class entered.[22]

Secondly, this reductionist problematic used two types of reasoning — which we may call the *argument from appearance* and the *argument from contingency* — to deal with differences that could not be assimilated to its own categories. The argument from appearance: everything presenting itself as different can be reduced to identity. This may take two forms: either appearance is a mere artifice of concealment, or it is a necessary form of the manifestation of essence. (An example of the first form: 'nationalism is a screen which hides the interests of the bourgeoisie'; an example of the second: 'the Liberal State is a necessary political form of capitalism'.) The argument from contingency: a social category or sector may not be reducible to the central identities of a certain form of society, but in that case its very marginality vis-à-vis the fundamental line of historical development allows us to discard it as irrelevant. (For example: 'because capitalism leads to the proletarianization of the middle classes and the peasantry, we can ignore these and concentrate our strategy on the conflict between the bourgeoisie and the proletariat'.) Thus, in the argument from contingency, identity is rediscovered in a diachronic totality: an inexorable succession of stages allows existing social reality to be divided into phenomena that are necessary or contingent, according to the stage of that society's approaching maturity. History is therefore a continuous concretization of the abstract, an approximation to a paradigmatic purity which appears as both sense and direction of the process.

Finally the orthodox paradigm, qua analytic of the present, postulates a strategy of *recognition.* In as much as Marxism claims to know the unavoidable course of history in its essential determinations, the understanding of an actual event can only mean to identify it as a moment in a temporal succession that is fixed a priori. Hence discussions such as: is the revolution of year *x* in country *y the* bourgeois–democratic revolution? Or, what forms should the transition to socialism assume in this or that country?

The three areas of effects analysed above present a common characteristic: the concrete is reduced to the abstract. Diverse subject positions are reduced to manifestations of a single position; the plurality of differences is either reduced or rejected as contingent; the sense of the present is revealed through its location in an a priori succession of stages. It is precisely because the concrete is in this way reduced to the abstract, that history, society and social agents have, for orthodoxy, *an essence which operates as their principle of unification*. And as this essence is not immediately visible, it is necessary to distinguish between a *surface* or appearance of society and an *underlying reality* to which the ultimate sense of every concrete presence must necessarily be referred, whatever the level of complexity in the system of mediations.

It is clear which strategic conception could be derived from this vision of the course of capitalism. The subject of this strategy was, of course, the workers' party. Kautsky vigorously rejected the revisionist notion of a 'popular party' because, in his view, it involved a transference of the interests of other classes to the interior of the party and, consequently, a loss of the revolutionary character of the movement. However, his supposedly radical position, based on the rejection of any compromise or alliance, was the centrepiece of a fundamentally conservative strategy.[23] Since his radicalism relied on a process which did not require political initiatives, it could only lead to quietism and waiting. Propaganda and organization were the two basic — in fact the only — tasks of the party. Propaganda was geared not to the creation of a broader 'popular will', through the winning of new sectors to the socialist cause, but above all to the reinforcing of working-class identity. As to organization, its expansion did not involve greater political participation in a number of fronts, but the construction of a ghetto where the working class led a self-focused and segregated existence. This progressive institutionalization of the movement was well suited to a perspective in which the final crisis of the capitalist system would come from the bourgeoisie's own labours, while the working class merely prepared for its intervention at the appropriate moment. Since 1881 Kautsky had stated: 'Our task is not to organize the revolution but to organize ourselves for the revolution; not *to make* the revolution but to take advantage of it.'[24]

Obviously, alliances did not represent for Kautsky a fundamental strategic principle. In concrete circumstances, a variety of alliances were possible at the level of empirical tactics; but in the long term, just as the revolution would have a purely proletarian character, so did the working class occupy an isolated position in the anti-capitalist struggle. Kautsky's analysis of internal contradictions in other sectors precisely demonstrates the impossibility of establishing long-term democratic and anti-capitalist alliances with them. In the case of the peasantry, he attempts to prove that it is a disintegrating sector, so that working-class defence of its interests is a reactionary policy opposed to the general line of economic progress. Similarly, in the Kautskian analysis of imperialism, the middle classes are increasingly united under the ideological domination of finance capital and militarism. Characteristically, Kautsky is never for one moment aware that this political and ideological hold dangerously accentuates the workers' isolation, and that, faced with the offensive of capital, the working class should respond with a counter-offensive to win over these middle sectors to the anti-capitalist cause. This line of thought is closed because, in his analysis, the increasingly reactionary character of the middle sectors corresponds to objective and unalterable processes. For the same reason, the isolation of the workers is not a threat to socialism, because this is guaranteed by historically given laws which in the long term will prove the powerlessness of all bourgeois machinations.

A good example of how Kautsky conceived the proletarian struggle may be found in his concept of 'war of attrition'. This refers not to a special tactic but to the totality of political actions undertaken by the working class since the 1860s. Three aspects are involved in war of attrition: (1) the preconstituted identity of the working class, which increasingly undermines the opponent's power but is not significantly modified in the course of the struggle; (2) an equally preconstituted identity of the bourgeoisie, which increases or reduces its capacity for domination but under no circumstances alters its own nature; (3) a prefixed line of development — once again the 'inexorable laws' — which gives a directional tendency to the war of attrition. This strategy has been compared to Gramsci's 'war of position',[25] but in reality the two are profoundly different. War of position presupposes the concept of hegemony which, as we shall see, is incompatible with the idea of a linear, predetermined development and, above all, with the preconstituted character of Kautskian subjects.

The role assigned by orthodox Marxism to theory confronts us with a paradox. On the one hand, its role increases as the widening gap between 'present consciousness' and 'historical mission' of the class can only be externally bridged through political intervention. On the other hand, since the theory underpinning political intervention is presented as consciousness of a necessary and mechanical determination, the analysis becomes ever more determinist and economist to the very extent that *the composition of historical forces depends more on theoretical mediation*. This is even more evident in Plekhanov than in Kautsky. The incipient development of capitalism in Russia failed to create a bourgeois civilization, with the result that the meaning of Russian reality could only be unravelled through a comparison with Western capitalist development. For Russian Marxists, therefore, the social phenomena of their country were symbols of a text which transcended them and was available for a full and explicit reading only in the capitalist West. This meant that theory was incomparably more important in Russia than in the West: if the 'necessary laws of history' were not universally valid, the fleeting reality of a strike, of a demonstration, of a process of accumulation, threatened to melt away. A reformist like Guglielmo Ferrero[26] could wax ironic about the orthodox claim that Marxism constituted a coherent and homogeneous theoretical field. In the end, if the doctrine was eclectic and heteroclite, this scarcely affected the materiality of a social practice sanctioned by the ensemble of proletarian institutions — a practice which, in the revisionism controversy, began to establish its own relations of exteriority with theory. This, however, could not be Plekhanov's position, for he confronted phenomena which did not spontaneously point in a precise direction, but whose meaning relied on their insertion within an interpretative system. The more the meaning of the social depended upon theoretical formulation, the more the defence of orthodoxy turned into a political problem.

With these points in mind, it is not surprising that the principles of Marxist orthodoxy were given a much more rigid formulation in Plekhanov than in Kautsky. It is well known, for example, that he coined the term 'dialectical materialism'. But he was also responsible for the radical naturalism which led to such a strict separation between base and superstructure that the latter was considered to be no more than a combination of necessary expressions of the former. Moreover, Plekhanov's concept of economic base allows for no intervention by social forces: the economic process is completely determined by the productive forces, conceived as technology.[27] This rigid determination enables him to present society as a strict hierarchy of instances, with decreasing degrees of efficacy: '1) *the state of the productive forces*; 2) the economic relations these forces condition; 3) the socio-*political system* that has developed on the given economic "basis"; 4) the mentality of social man, which is determined in part by the economic conditions obtaining, and in part by the entire socio-political system that has arisen on that foundation; 5) the various ideologies that reflect the properties of that mentality.'[28] In *Socialism and Political Struggle* and *Our Differences*, Plekhanov formulated an equally rigid succession of stages through which the Russian revolutionary process had to pass, so that any 'uneven and combined development' was eliminated from the field of strategy.

All the early analysis of Russian Marxism — from Peter Struve's 'legal Marxism', through Plekhanov as the central moment, to Lenin's *Development of Capitalism in Russia* — tended to obliterate the study of specificities, representing these as nothing other than outwardly apparent or contingent forms of an essential reality: the abstract development of capitalism through which every society must pass.

Let us now make a final observation on orthodoxy. As we have seen, theory maintained that the growing disjuncture between final objective and current political practices would be resolved at some future moment, which operated as a *coincidentia oppositorum*. As this practice of recomposition, however, could not be left *entirely* to the future, a struggle had somehow to be waged in the present against the tendencies towards fragmentation. But since this struggle entailed forms of articulation which did not at that time *spontaneously* result from the laws of capitalism, it was necessary to introduce a social logic different from mechanical determinism — that is to say, a space that would restore *the autonomy of political initiative*. Although minimal, this space is present in Kautsky: it comprises the relations of exteriority, between the working class and socialism, which require the political mediation of intellectuals. There is a link here which cannot simply be explained by 'objective' historical determination. This space was necessarily broader for those tendencies which, in order to overcome the split between day-to-day practices and final objective, strove hardest to break with quietism and to achieve current political effects.[29] Rosa Luxemburg's spontaneism, and, more generally, the political strategies of the *Neue Linke* confirm this. The most creative tendencies within orthodoxy attempted to limit the effects of the 'logic of necessity', but the inevitable outcome was that they placed their discourse in a permanent dualism between a 'logic of necessity', producing ever fewer effects in terms of political practice, and a 'logic of contingency' which, by not determining its specificity, was incapable of theorizing itself.

Let us give two examples of the dualism created by these partial attempts to 'open the game'. The first is the concept of *morphological prediction* in Labriola. He stated: 'Historical foresight . . . (in *The Communist Manifesto*) does not imply, and this is still the case, either a chronological date or an advance picture of a social configuration, as was and is typical of old and new apocalypses and prophecies . . . In the theory of critical communism, it is the whole of society which, at a moment in the process, discovers the reason for its inevitable course, and which, at a salient point in its curve, sheds light on itself and reveals its laws of motion. The prediction to which the *Manifesto* alludes for the first time was not chronological, of an anticipatory or promise-like nature; it was morphological, a word which, in my opinion, succinctly expresses everything.'[30] Labriola was here waging a twofold battle. The first was directed against tendencies critical of Marxism — Croce, Gentile[31] — who, basing the unpredictability of history on the non-systematic character of events, found a unitary order only in the consciousness of the historian. For his part, Labriola stressed the objective character of historical laws. However, these were *morphological* — that is, their area of validity was restricted to certain fundamental tendencies. Labriola's second battle, then, was against the forms of dogmatism which converted general tendencies into immediately legible facts on the surface of historical life. It is now clear that the way in which this twofold battle was waged could not but introduce a dualism which, in Labriola, found expression in the counterposition of historical development as narration and as morphology; and, more generally, in the decreasing capacity of Engels's dialectical paradigm to explain history.[32] Moreover, this dichotomy presents the same double void that we found in Rosa Luxemburg. For, the 'narrative' elements are counterposed to the 'morphological' ones not as something positive, with its own internal necessity, but as the contingent reverse of morphological necessity. According to Badaloni, the 'real unfolding of events can (for Labriola) give rise to intricate and unforeseeable vicissitudes. Nonetheless, what counts is that the understanding of these vicissitudes should occur within the genetical hypothesis (class contradiction and its progressive simplification). Thus, the proletariat is located not in an indeterminate historical time, but in that peculiar historical time which is dominated by the crisis of the bourgeois social formation.'[33] In other words, 'morphological necessity' constitutes a theoretico-discursive terrain which comprises not only its own distinctive territory but also what it excludes from itself — contingency. If an ensemble of 'events' are conceptualized as 'contingent', they are not conceptualized at all, except in their lack of certain attributes existent in the morphological tendencies opposed to them. However, since the life of society is ever more complex than the morphological categories of Marxist discourse — and this complexity was Labriola's starting point — the only possible consequence is that theory becomes an increasingly irrelevant tool for the understanding of concrete social processes.

Thus, to avoid falling into complete agnosticism, it is necessary at some point to introduce other explanatory categories. Labriola does this, for example, in his concrete analyses, where diverse social categories are not simply conceptualized in their 'contingency', but are each endowed with a certain necessity or lawfulness of their own. What is the relationship between these 'factual' structural complexes and the structures which are the object of morphological prediction? A first possible solution would be 'dialectical': to maintain a monist perspective which conceives complexity as a system of mediations.[34] Labriola could not adopt this solution, however, because it would have forced him to extend the effects of necessity to the surface of historical life — the very area from which he wanted to displace them. But if the dialectical solution is rejected, it is not possible to pass logically from morphological analysis to the distinctive lawfulness of partial totalities. The transition therefore assumes an *external character* — which is to say that the conceptualization of these legalities is *external to Marxist theory*. Marxist theory cannot, then, be the 'complete and harmonious world-system' presented by Plekhanov and thinkable only within a closed model. The necessity/contingency dualism opens the way to a pluralism of structural legalities whose internal logics and mutual relations have to be determined.

This can be seen even more clearly if we examine Austro-Marxism, our second example of an 'open orthodoxy'. Here we find a more radical and systematic effort than Labriola's to diversify the starting points, to multiply the theoretical categories, and to autonomize areas of society in their specific determinations. Otto Bauer, in his obituary on Max Adler, referred to the beginning of the school in the following terms: 'Whereas Marx and Engels began from Hegel, and the later Marxists from materialism, the more recent "Austro-Marxists" had at their point of departure Kant and Mach.'[35] The Austro-Marxists were conscious of the obstacles to working-class unity in the dual monarchy, and of the fact that such unity depended upon constant political initiative. They therefore understood well what, from the different perspective of the Leninist tradition, was termed 'uneven and combined development'. 'In the Austro-Hungarian monarchy there are examples of all the economic forms to be found in Europe, including Turkey . . . The light of socialist propaganda shines everywhere in the midst of these divergent economic and political conditions. This creates a picture of extreme diversity . . . What exists in the International as a chronological development — the socialism of artisans, journeymen, workers in manufacture, factory workers, and agricultural workers, which undergoes alterations, with the political, the social, or the intellectual aspect of the movement predominating at any given moment — takes places contemporaneously in Austria.'[36]

In this mosaic of social and national situations, it was impossible to think of national identities as 'superstructural' or of class unity as a necessary consequence of the infrastructure. Indeed, such a unity depended on a complex political construction. In the words of Otto Bauer: 'It is an intellectual force which maintains unity . . . "Austro-Marxism" today, as a product of unity and a force for the maintenance of unity, is nothing but the ideology of unity of the workers movement.'[37]

The moment of class unity is, thus, a political moment. The constitutive centre of what we might call a society's *relational configuration* or *articulatory form* is displaced towards the field of the superstructures, so that the very distinction between economic base and superstructure becomes blurred and problematic. Three main types of Austro-Marxist theoretical intervention are closely linked to this new strategic perspective: the attempt to limit the area of validity of 'historical necessity'; the suggestion of new fronts of struggle based upon the complexity of the social that was characteristic of mature capitalism; and the effort to think in a non-reductive manner the specificity of subject positions other than those of class. The first type of intervention is mainly connected with Max Adler's philosophical reformulation and his peculiar form of neo-Kantianism. The Kantian rethinking of Marxism produced a number of liberating effects: it broadened the audience for socialism, insofar as the justness of its postulates could be posed in terms of a universality transcending class bounds; it broke with the naturalist conception of social relations and, by elaborating concepts such as the 'social a priori', introduced a strictly discursive element into the constitution of social objectivity; and finally, it allowed Marxists to conceive the infrastructure as a terrain whose conformation depended upon forms of consciousness, and not upon the naturalistic movement of the forces of production. The second type of intervention also placed the base/superstructure distinction into question. In the discussion regarding Kautsky's *Road to Power*, Bauer, for example,[38] tried to show how wrong it was to conceive the economy as a homogeneous field dominated by an endogenous logic, given that in the monopoly and imperialist phase political, technico-organizational and scientific transformations were increasingly part of the industrial apparatus. In his view, if the laws of competition previously functioned as natural powers, they now had to pass through the minds of men and women. Hence the emphasis on the growing interlock between state and economy, which in the

1920s led to the debate about 'organized capitalism'. Views also changed about the points of rupture and antagonism created by the new configuration of capitalism: these were now located not solely in the relations of production, but in a number of areas of the social and political structure. Hence too, the new importance attributed to the very dispersion of the day-to-day struggle (*revolutionäre Kleinarbeit*), conceived in neither an evolutionary nor a reformist sense,[39] and the fresh significance acquired by the moment of political articulation. (This is reflected, among other things, in the new way of posing the relationship between party and intellectuals.[40]) Finally, with regard to the new subject positions and the ensuing break with class reductionism, it is sufficient to mention Bauer's work on the national question and Renner's on legal institutions.

The general pattern of the theoretico-strategic intervention of Austro-Marxism should now be clear: insofar as the practical efficacy of autonomous political intervention is broadened, the discourse of 'historical necessity' loses its relevance and withdraws to the horizon of the social (in exactly the same way that, in deist discourse, the effects of God's presence in the world are drastically reduced). This, in turn, requires a proliferation of new discursive forms to occupy the terrain left vacant. The Austro-Marxists, however, failed to reach the point of breaking with dualism and eliminating the moment of 'morphological' necessity. In the theoretico-political universe of *fin-de-siècle* Marxism, this decisive step was taken only by Sorel, through his contrast between '*mélange*' and '*bloc*'. We shall return to this below.

The Second Response to the Crisis: Revisionism

The orthodox response to the 'crisis of Marxism' sought to overcome the disjuncture between 'theory' and 'observable tendencies of capitalism' by intransigently affirming the validity of the former and the artificial or transitory character of the latter. Thus it would seem very simple to conclude that the revisionist response was symmetrically opposed, especially since Bernstein himself insisted on many occasions that he had no major disagreements with the programme and practices of the SPD as they had materialized since the Erfurt Congress, and that the only purpose of his intervention was to realize an *aggiornamento* adapting the theory to the concrete practices of the movement. Nevertheless, such a conclusion would obscure important dimensions of Bernstein's intervention. In particular, it would lead us into the error of identifying *reformism* with *revision-*

ism.[41] The trade union leaders, who were the true spokesmen for a reformist policy within the SPD, expressed little interest in Bernstein's theoretical propositions and remained strictly neutral in the ensuing controversy — when they did not openly support orthodoxy.[42] Moreover, in crucial political debates on the mass strike[43] and the attitude to war, Bernstein's position was not only different from but strictly opposed to that of the reformist leaders in the trade unions and the party. Thus, in attempting to identify the precise difference between reformism and revisionism, we must stress that *what is essential in a reformist practice is political quietism and the corporatist confinement of the working class*. The reformist leader attempts to defend the gains and immediate interests of the class, and he consequently tends to consider it as a segregated sector, endowed with a perfectly defined identity and limits. But a 'revisionist' theory is not necessary for this; indeed, a 'revolutionary' theory can — in many cases — better fulfil the same role by isolating the working class and leaving to an indeterminate future any questioning of the existing power structure. We have already referred to the conservative character of Kautskian revolutionism. Reformism does not identify with either term of the revisionism/orthodoxy alternative but cuts across the two.

The basic issue confronting revisionist and orthodox theoreticians was not, therefore, the question of reformism. Neither was it the problem of peaceful or violent transition from capitalism to socialism — in relation to which the 'orthodox' did not have a clear and unanimous position. *The main point of divergence was that, whereas orthodoxy considered that the fragmentation and division characteristic of the new stage of capitalism would be overcome through changes in the infrastructure, revisionism held that this was to be achieved through autonomous political intervention*. The autonomy of the political from the economic base is the true novelty of Bernstein's argument. In fact, it has been pointed out[44] that behind each of Bernstein's critiques of classical Marxist theory, there was an attempt to recover the political initiative in particular spheres. Revisionism, at its best moments, represented a real effort to break with the corporative isolation of the working class. It is, also true, however, that just as the political was emerging as an autonomous instance, it was used to validate a 'reformist' practice which was to a large extent its opposite. This is the paradox that we must try to explain. It refers us to certain limitations in Bernstein's rupture with economism which would only be rigorously overcome in Gramsci. Autonomy of the political and its limits: we must examine how these two moments are structured.

It is important to recognize that Bernstein, more clearly than any representative of orthodoxy, understood the changes affecting capitalism as it entered the monopoly era. His analyses were, in this sense, closer to the problematic of a Hilferding or a Lenin than to the orthodox theorizations of the time.[45] Bernstein also grasped the political consequences of capitalist reorganization. The three main changes — a-symmetry between the concentration of enterprises and the concentration of patrimonies; the subsistence and growth of the middle strata; the role of economic planning in the prevention of crises — could only involve a total change in the assumptions upon which Social Democracy had hitherto been based. It was not the case that the evolution of the economy was proletarianizing the middle classes and the peasantry and heightening the polarization of society, nor that the transition to socialism could be expected to follow from a revolutionary outbreak consequent upon a serious economic crisis. Under such conditions, socialism had to change its terrain and strategy, and the key theoretical moment was the break with the rigid base/superstructure distinction that had prevented any conception of the autonomy of the political. It was this latter instance to which the moment of recomposition and overcoming of fragmentation was now transferred in the revisionist analysis. 'Sciences, arts, a whole series of social relations are today much less dependent on economics than formerly, or, in order to give no room for misconception, the point of economic development attained today leaves the ideological, and especially the ethical, factors greater space for independent activity than was formerly the case. In consequence of this the interdependency of cause and effect between technical, economic evolution of other social tendencies is becoming always more indirect, and from that the necessities of the first are losing much of their power of dictating the form of the latter.'[46]

It is only this autonomization of the political, as opposed to the dictates of the economic base, that permits it to play this role of recomposition and reunification against infrastructural tendencies which, if abandoned to themselves, can only lead to fragmentation. This can clearly be seen in Bernstein's conception of the dialectic of working-class unity and division. Economically, the working class always appears more and more divided. The modern proletariat is not that dispossessed mass of which Marx and Engels wrote in the *Manifesto*: 'it is just in the most advanced of manufacturing industries that a whole hierarchy of differentiated workmen are to be found, between those groups only a moderate feeling of identity exists.'[47] This diversification of interests — which was most apparent in the English case — was not simply the residue of a guildist past, as Cunow had argued, but was the result of the establishment of a democratic State. Although, under conditions of political repression, unity in struggle placed sectoral interests on a secondary level, these tended to blossom once again in a context of freedom.

Now, if the tendency towards division is inscribed in the very structure of modern capitalism, what is the source of the opposite moment, the tendency towards unification? According to Bernstein, it is the party. Thus, he speaks of the 'necessity of an organ of the class struggle which holds the entire class together in spite of its fragmentation through different employment, and that is the Social Democracy as a political party. In it, the special interest of the economic group is submerged in favour of the general interest of those who depend on income for their labour, of all the under-privileged.'[48] As we saw earlier, in Kautsky the party also represented the universal moment of the class; but while in his case political unity was the scientific prefiguration of a real unity to be achieved by the movements of the infrastructure, in Bernstein the moment of political articulation could not be reduced to such movements. The specificity of the political link escapes the chain of necessity; the irreducible space of the political, which in Kautsky was limited to the mediating role of the intelligentsia, appears here considerably enlarged.

However, in Bernstein's analysis of political mediation as consti-tutive of class unity, a barely perceptible ambiguity has slipped through to vitiate his entire theoretical construction. The ambiguity is this: if the working class appears increasingly divided in the economic sphere, and if its unity is autonomously constructed at the political level, in what sense is this political unity a *class* unity? The problem was not posed for orthodoxy, as the non–correspondence between economic and political identity was ultimately to be resolved by the evolution of the economy itself. In Bernstein's case, the logical conclusion would seem to be that political unity can be constituted only through an overcoming of the *class limitations* of the different fractions of workers, and that there should thus be a perma-nent structural hiatus between economic and political subjectivity. This is, however, a conclusion which Bernstein never reaches in his analysis. On the one hand, he insists that Social Democracy must be a party of all the oppressed and not only of the workers, but on the other he conceives this unity as that of an ensemble of sectors which 'accept the point of view of the workers and recognize them as the leading class'. As his biographer Peter Gay indicates,[49] Bernstein never went beyond this point. Consequently, a link is missing in his reasoning. The *class* character of the unification between the political and the economic is not produced in either of the two spheres, and the argument remains suspended in a void.

This conclusion may perhaps be excessive, because it assumes that Bernstein's reasoning moves on the same level as that of Kautsky or Rosa Luxemburg — that he is referring to *necessary* subjects of an ineluctable historical process. The truth is, however, that by denying that history is dominated by an abstract determinist logic, Bernstein precisely shifted the debate from this plane. In his conception, the centrality of the workers seems instead to refer to a historically contingent line of argument — for example, that the working class is better prepared than other sectors to fulfil the leading role, given its degree of concentration and organization. Yet the problem remains of why Bernstein presented these advantages — which were at most conjunctural — as *irreversible achievements*. The same ambiguity can be found in Bernstein's *dictum* that 'the path is everything and the goal is nothing'. Traditionally, this has been considered a typical 'gradualist' slogan.[50] However, in some of its meanings, *which produce both theoretical and political effects within the revisionist discourse,* gradualism is not *logically* entailed. The only necessary implication of this statement is that the working class *can* obtain concrete gains within the capitalist system, and that revolution cannot therefore be considered as an absolute moment in the passage from total dispossession to radical liberation. This does not *necessarily* imply the gradualist conception of slow, unilinear and irreversible advances, although it is true that Bernstein's line of argument concerning democratic advances links them to a gradualist perspective. Once again, we must therefore pose the problem of the terrain where these logically distinct structural moments unite.

This brings our investigation to the concrete forms of Bernstein's rupture with orthodox determinism, and to the type of concepts he deploys in order to fill the space opened by its collapse. When Bernstein questions whether any general mechanism can validly explain the course of history, his argument assumes a characteristic form: he does not criticise the type of historical causality proposed by orthodoxy, but attempts to create a space where the free play of subjectivity will be possible in history. Accepting the orthodox identification of objectivity and mechanical causality, he merely tries to limit its effects.[51] He does not deny the scientific character of a part of Marxism, but he refuses to extend it to the point of creating a closed system that will cover the entire field of political prediction. The critique of the dogmatic rationalism of orthodoxy takes the form of a Kantian dualism. For Bernstein, there were three particular objections to the consideration of Marxism as a closed scientific system. First, Marxism had failed to show that socialism necessarily followed from capitalism's collapse. Secondly, this could not be demonstrated because history was not a simple objective process: *will* also played a role in it. Hence, history could only be explained as the result of an interaction between objective and subjective factors. Thirdly, as socialism was a *party programme* and therefore founded upon ethical decision, it could not be entirely scientific — could not be based upon objective statements whose truth or falsehood had to be accepted by all. Thus, the autonomy of the ethical subject was the basis of Bernstein's break with determinism.

Now — and this point is crucial — the introduction of the ethical subject cannot dispel the ambiguities we found earlier in Bernstein's reasoning. The ethical subject's free decision can at most create an area of indeterminacy in history, but it cannot be the foundation for a gradualist thesis. It is here that a new postulate — the progressive and ascending character of human history — intervenes to provide the terrain on which the political and the economic combine, imparting a sense of direction to every concrete achievement. The concept of evolution, *Entwicklung*,[52] plays a decisive role in the Bernsteinian discourse: in fact, his entire schema obtains its coherence from it. The unification of the political and economic spheres takes place not on the basis of theoretically defined articulations, but through a tendential movement underlying them both and dictated by the laws of evolution. For Bernstein, these laws are not at all the same as in the orthodox system: they include not only antagonistic but also harmonious processes. Yet in both cases they are conceived as *totalizing contexts* which fix a priori the meaning of every event. Thus, although 'the facts' are freed from the essentialist connections which linked them together in the orthodox conception, they are later reunited in a general theory of progress unconnected to any determinable mechanism. The rupture with mechanist objectivism, which considered classes as transcendent subjects, is achieved through the postulation of a new transcendent subject — the ethical subject — which imposes ascendancy in a humanity increasingly freed from economic necessity.[53] From here, it is impossible to move towards a theory of articulation and hegemony.

This clarifies why, in Bernstein, the autonomization of the political can be linked to acceptance of a reformist practice and a gradualist strategy. For if every advance is irreversible — given the *Entwicklung* postulate — its consolidation no longer depends upon an unstable articulation of forces and *ceases to be a political problem*. If, on the other hand, the ensemble of democratic advances depended upon a contingent correlation of forces, then abstract consideration of the justness of each demand would not be sufficient reason to assert its progressiveness. For example, a negative realignment of forces might be brought about by an ultra-left demand or its opposite, an absence of radical political initiatives in a critical conjuncture. But if the ensemble of democratic advances depends solely upon a law of progress, then the progressive character of any struggle or conjunctural demand is defined independently of its correlation with other forces operating at a given moment. The fact that the demands of the workers movement are considered just and progressive, and judged separately from their correlation with other forces, erases the only basis for criticism of the corporative confinement of the working class. Here lie the premises for a coincidence between theoretical revisionism and practical reformism: the broadening of political initiative to a number of democratic fronts never enters into contradiction with the quietism and corporatism of the working class.

This can be clearly seen if we consider the revisionist theory of the State. For orthodoxy, the problem was straightforward: the State was an instrument of class domination, and Social Democracy could only participate in its institutions with the purpose of spreading its own ideology, and defending and organizing the working class. Such participation was therefore marked by exteriority. Bernstein sees this problem from the opposite perspective: the growing economic power of the working class, the advance in social legislation, the 'humanization' of capitalism, all lead to the 'nationalization' of the working class; the worker is not merely a proletarian, he has also become a citizen. Consequently, according to Bernstein, the functions of social organization have a greater influence within the State than do those of class domination; its democratization transforms it into a State 'of all the people'. Once again, Bernstein has understood better than orthodoxy the basic truth that the working class is *already* on the terrain of the State, and that it is sterile dogmatism to seek to maintain with it pure relations of exteriority. In his discourse, however, this is immediately transformed into a totally illegitimate prediction: namely, that the State will become increasingly democratic as a necessary consequence of 'historical evolution'.

Having reached this point, we may now apply the test we used for Rosa Luxemburg: to follow the logical lines of Bernstein's argument, while eliminating the essentialist presuppositions (in this case, the postulate of progress as a unifying tendency) which limit its effects. Two conclusions immediately arise from this test. First, democratic advances within the State cease to be cumulative and begin to depend upon a relationship of forces that cannot be determined a priori. The object of struggle is not simply punctual gains, but forms of articulating forces that will allow these gains to be consolidated. *And these forms are always reversible*. In that fight, the working class must struggle from where it really is: both *within* and *outside* the State. But — and this is the second conclusion — Bernstein's very clearsightedness opens up a much more disquieting possibility. If the worker is no longer just proletarian but also citizen, consumer, and participant in a plurality of positions within the country's cultural and institutional apparatus; if, moreover, this ensemble of positions is no longer united by any 'law of progress' (nor, of course, by the 'necessary laws' of orthodoxy), then the relations between them become an open articulation which offers no a priori guarantee that it will adopt a given form. There is also a possibility that contradictory and mutually neutralizing subject positions will arise. In that case, more than ever, democratic advance will necessitate a proliferation of political initiatives in different social areas — as required by revisionism, but with the difference that the meaning of each initiative comes to depend upon its relation with the others. To think this dispersion of elements and points of antagonism, and to conceive their articulation outside any a priori schema of unification, is something that goes far beyond the field of revisionism. Although it was the revisionists who first posed the problem in its most general terms, the beginnings of an adequate response would only be found in the Gramscian conception of 'war of position'.

The Third Response to the Crisis: Revolutionary Syndicalism

Our inquiry into revisionism has brought us to the point where Bernstein, paradoxically, faces the same dilemma as all orthodox currents (including his arch-enemy Rosa Luxemburg): the economic base is incapable of assuring class unity *in the present*; while politics, the sole terrain where that present unity can be constructed, is unable convincingly to guarantee the *class* character of the unitary subjects. This antinomy can be perceived more clearly in revolutionary syndicalism, which constituted a third type of response to the 'crisis of Marxism'. In Sorel the antinomy is drawn with particularly sharp lines, because he was more conscious than Bernstein, or any orthodox theoretician, of the true dimensions of the crisis and of the price theory had to pay in order to overcome it in a satisfactory manner. We find in Sorel not only the postulation of an area of 'contingency' and 'freedom', replacing the broken links in the chain of necessity, but also an effort to think the specificity of that 'logic of contingency', of that new terrain on which a field of totalizing effects is reconstituted. In this sense, it is instructive to refer to the key moments of his evolution.[54]

Even in the relatively orthodox beginnings of Sorel's Marxist career, both the sources of his political interest and the theoretical assumptions behind his analysis showed a marked originality and were considerably more sophisticated than those of a Kautsky or a Plekhanov. He was far from keeping to the established idea of an underlying historical mechanism that both unified a given form of society and governed the transitions between diverse forms. Indeed, Sorel's chief focus of interest — and hence his frequent reference to Vico — was the type of moral qualities which allowed a society to remain united and in a process of ascension. Having no guarantee of positivity, social transformations were penetrated by negativity as one of their possible destinies. It was not simply the case that a given form of society was opposed by a different, positive form destined to replace it; it also faced the possibility of its own decay and disintegration, as was the case of the ancient world. What Sorel found attractive in Marxism was not in fact a theory of the necessary laws of historical evolution, but rather the theory of the formation of a new agent — the proletariat — capable of operating as an agglutinative force that would reconstitute around itself a higher form of civilization and supplant declining bourgeois society.

This dimension of Sorel's thought is present from the beginning. In his writings prior to the revisionism controversy, however, it is combined with an acceptance of the tendencies of capitalist development postulated by orthodoxy. In these writings, Sorel sees Marxism as a 'new real metaphysics'. All real science, he argues, is constituted on the basis of an 'expressive support', which introduces an artificial element into analysis. This can be the origin of utopian or mythical errors, but in the case of industrial society there is a growing unification of the social terrain around the image of the mechanism. The expressive support of Marxism — the social character of labour and the category of 'commodity', which increasingly eliminates qualitative disctinctions — is not an arbitrary base, because it is the moulding and constitutive paradigm of social relations. Socialism, qua collective appropriation of the means of production, represents the necessary culmination of the growing socialization and homogenization of labour. The increasing sway of this productivist paradigm relies on the laws of motion of capitalism, which are not questioned by Sorel at this point of his career. But even so, the agent conscious of its own interests — the one that will shift society to a higher form — is not constituted by a simple objective movement. Here another element of Sorel's analysis intervenes: Marxism is not for him merely a scientific analysis of society; it is also the ideology uniting the proletariat and giving a sense of direction to its struggles. The 'expressive supports', therefore, operate as elements aggregating and condensing the historical forces that Sorel will call blocs. It should be clear that, vis-à-vis orthodox Marxism, this analysis already shifts the terrain on a crucial point: the field of so-called 'objective laws' has lost its character as the rational substratum of the social, becoming instead the ensemble of forms through which a class constitutes itself as a dominant force and imposes its will on the rest of society. However, as the validity of these laws is not questioned, the distance from orthodoxy is ultimately not that considerable.

The separation begins when Sorel, starting from the revisionism debate, accepts *en bloc* Bernstein's and Croce's critiques of Marxism, but in order to extract very different conclusions. What is striking in Sorel is the *radicalism* with which he accepts the consequences of the 'crisis of Marxism'. Unlike Bernstein, he does not make the slightest attempt to replace orthodoxy's historical rationalism with an alternative evolutionist view, and the possibility that a form of civilization may disintegrate always remains open in his analysis. The *totality* as a founding rational substratum has been dissolved, and what now exists is *mélange*. Under these circumstances, how can one think the possibility of a process of recomposition? Sorel's answer centres on social classes, which no longer play the role of structural locations in an objective system, but are rather poles of reaggregation that he calls *'blocs'*. The possibility of unity in society is thus referred to the will of certain groups to impose their conception of economic organization. Sorel's philosophy, in fact — influenced by Nietzsche and in particular by Bergson — is one of action and will, in which the future is unforeseeable, and hinges on will. Furthermore, the level at which the forces in struggle find their unity is that of an ensemble of images or 'language figures' — foreshadowing the theory of myth. However, the consolidation of classes as historical forces cemented by a 'political idea' is reliant upon their confrontation with opposing forces. Once its identity ceased to be based on a process of infrastructural unity (at this level there is only *mélange*), the working class came to depend upon a *split* from the capitalist class which could only be completed in struggle against it. For Sorel, 'war' thus becomes the condition for working-class identity, and the search for common areas with the bourgeoisie can only lead to its own weakening. This consciousness of a *split* is a juridical consciousness — Sorel sees the construction of revolutionary subjectivity as a process in which the proletariat becomes aware of a set of rights opposing it to the class adversary and establishes a set of new institutions that will consolidate these rights.[55] Sorel, however, an ardent Dreyfusard, does not see a necessary contradiction between the plurality of working-class positions within the political and economic system: he is a partisan of democracy and of the political struggle of the proletariat, and even considers the possibility that the working class, while in no way *economically* linked to the middle sectors, could become a pole for their political regroupment.

We see a clear pattern in Sorel's evolution: like all the tendencies struggling against the quietism of orthodoxy, he is compelled to displace the constitutive moment of class unity to the political level; but as his break with the category of 'historical necessity' is more radical than in other tendencies, he also feels obliged to specify the founding bond of political unity. This can be seen even more clearly when we move to the third stage of his thought, which corresponds to the great disillusion following the triumph of the Dreyfusard coalition. Millerand's brand of socialism is integrated into the system; corruption spreads; there is a continuous loss of proletarian identity; and energy saps away from the only class which, in Sorel's eyes, has the possibility of a heroic future that will remodel declining bourgeois civilization. Sorel then becomes a decided enemy of democracy, seeing it as the main culprit for that dispersion and fragmentation of subject positions with which Marxism had to grapple at the turn of the century. It was therefore necessary, at whatever cost, to restore the split and to reconstitute the working class as a unitary subject. As is well known, this led Sorel to reject political struggle and to affirm the syndicalist myth of the general strike. '(We) know that the general strike is indeed what I have said: the *myth* in which Socialism is wholly comprised, *i.e.* a body of images capable of evoking instinctively all the sentiments which correspond to the different manifestations of the war undertaken by Socialism against modern society. Strikes have engendered in the proletariat the noblest, deepest and most moving sentiments that they possess; the general strike groups them all in a co-ordinated picture, and, by bringing them together, gives to each one of them its maximum of intensity; appealing to their painful memories of particular conflicts, it colours with an intense life all the details of the composition presented to consciousness. We thus obtain that intuition of Socialism which language cannot give us with perfect clearness — and we obtain it as a whole, perceive it instantaneously.'[56]

The syndicalist 'general strike', or the 'revolution' in Marx, is a myth in that it functions as an ideological point of condensation for proletarian identity, constituted on the basis of the dispersion of subject positions. It is the one type of recomposing link that remains once political struggle has been discarded, and once it is thought that the economy of monopolies and imperialism — seen by Sorel as involving a process of refeudalization — is heightening the tendencies toward disintegration. More generally, one recognizes the old theme of *anti-physis* in Sorel's affirmation that societies have a 'natural' tendency to decay, and that the tendency to greatness is 'artificial'. Thus, violence is the only force which can keep alive the antagonism described by Marx. 'If a capitalist class is energetic, it is constantly affirming its determination to defend itself; its frank and consistently reactionary attitude contributes at least as greatly as proletarian violence towards keeping distinct that cleavage between classes which is the basis of all Socialism.'[57] From this perspective, it matters little whether or not the general strike can be realized: its role is that of a regulating principle, which allows the proletariat to think the *mélange* of social relations as organized around a clear line of demarcation; the category of totality, eliminated as an objective description of reality, is reintroduced as a mythical element establishing the unity of the workers' consciousness. As de Paola has pointed out,[58] the notion of 'cognitive instrument' — or expressive support — whose artificiality was recognized from the beginning, has been broadened to include fictions.`

For Sorel, then, the possibility of a dichotomous division of society is given not as a datum of the social structure, but as a construction at the level of the 'moral factors' governing group conflict. Here we come face to face with the problem that we have found whenever a Marxist tendency has attempted to break with economism and to establish class unity at some other level. Why does this politically or mythically reconstituted subject have to be a *class* subject? But whereas the inadequacy of Rosa Luxemburg's or Labriola's rupture with economism created the conditions for the invisibility of the double void that appeared in their discourses, in Sorel's case the very radicality of his anti-economism made this void clearly visible. So much so that some of his followers, having abandoned hope of a revolutionary recovery of the working class, gave themselves to a search for some other substitute myth capable of assuring the struggle against bourgeois decadence. It is known that they found it in nationalism. This was the avenue through which a *part* of Sorel's intellectual legacy contributed to the rise of fascism. Thus, in 1912 his disciple Edouard Berth was able to affirm: 'In fact, it is necessary that the two-sided nationalist and syndicalist movement, both parallel and synchronic, should lead to the complete expulsion of the kingdom of gold and to the triumph of heroic values over the ignoble bourgeois materialism in which present-day Europe is suffocating. In other words, it is necessary that this awakening of Force and Blood against Gold — whose first symptoms have been revealed by Pareto and whose signal has been given by Sorel in his *Réflexions sur la violence* and by Maurras in *Si le coup de force est possible* — should conclude with the absolute defeat of plutocracy.'[59]

Of course, this is merely *one* of the possible derivations from Sorel's analysis, and it would be historically false and analytically unfounded to conclude that it is a necessary outcome.[60] Historically false, because Sorel's influence made itself felt in a number of directions — it was, for example, crucial in the formation of Gramsci's thought. Analytically unfounded, because such a teleological interpretation assumes that the transition from *class* to *nation* was necessarily determined by the very structure of Sorel's thought, whereas the latter's most specific and original moment was precisely the indeterminate, non-apriori character of the mythically constituted subjects. Furthermore, this indeterminacy is not a weakness of the theory, for it affirms that social reality itself is indeterminate (*mélange*) and that any unification turns on the recomposing practices of a *bloc*. In this sense, there is no *theoretical* reason why the mythical reconstitution should not move in the direction of fascism, but equally none to exclude its advance in another direction — such as Bolshevism, for example, which Sorel enthusiastically welcomed. The decisive point — and this is what makes Sorel the most profound and original thinker of the Second International — is that the very identity of social agents becomes indeterminate and that every 'mythical' fixation of it depends upon a struggle. The concept of 'hegemony' as it emerged in Russian Social Democracy — which, as we shall see, also supposed a logic of contingency — was from this point of view much less radical. Neither Lenin nor Trotsky was capable of questioning the *necessity* for social agents to have a class character. Only with Gramsci did the two traditions converge in his concept of 'historical bloc', where the concept of 'hegemony' derived from Leninism meets in a new synthesis with the concept of 'bloc' derived from Sorel.

Notes to Chapter One

1. R. Luxemburg, *The Mass Strike, the Political Party and the Trade Unions,* London (n.d.), p. 48.

2. Ibid., pp. 73–74.

3. Ibid., pp. 64–65. Emphasis in the original.

4. It is important to note that Bernstein's intervention in the German debate on the mass strike (*Der Politische Massenstreik und die Politische Lage der Sozialdemokratie in Deutschland*) refers to two basic differences between East and West — the complexity and resistance of civil society in the West, and the weakness of the State in Russia — which will later be central to Gramsci's argument. For an overview of the debate, see M. Salvadori, 'La socialdemocrazia tedesca e la rivoluzione russa del 1905. Il dibattito sullo sciopero di massa e sulle differenze fra Oriente e Occidente', in E.J. Hobsbawm et al., eds., *Storia del marxismo,* Milan 1979, vol. 2, pp. 547–594.

5. Cf. T. Todorov, *Théories du symbole,* Paris 1977, p. 291. 'One could say that there is a condensation every time a single signifier leads us to comprehend more than one signified; or more plainly: *every time that the signified is more abundant than the signifier.* The great German mythologist Creuzer already defined the symbol in that way: by "the inadequacy of being and form, and by the overflowing of the content compared to its expression".'

6. Although Rosa Luxemburg's work is the highest point in the *theoretical* elaboration of the mechanism of mass strike, the latter was posed as the fundamental form of struggle by the entire *Neue Linke.* See for example, A. Pannekoek, 'Marxist Theory and Revolutionary Tactics', in A. Smart, ed., *Pannekoek and Gorter's Marxism,* London 1978, pp. 50–73.

7. R. Luxemburg, p. 30.

8. Recently, a number of studies have discussed the fatalist or non-fatalist character of Luxemburgist spontaneism. In our opinion, however, these have given excessive emphasis to a relatively secondary problem, such as the alternative between mechanical collapse and conscious intervention of the class. The assertion that capitalism will mechanically collapse is so absurd that, as far as we know, nobody has upheld it. The decisive problem is, instead, that of knowing whether the subject of the anti-capitalist struggle does or does not constitute its entire identity within the capitalist relations of production; and, in this respect, Rosa Luxemburg's position is unequivocally affirmative. For that reason, statements concerning the inevitability of socialism are not simply concessions to the rhetoric of the time or the result of a psychological need, as Norman Geras maintains (Cf. N. Geras, *The Legacy of Rosa Luxemburg,* London 1976, p. 36), but rather the nodal point giving meaning to her entire theoretical and strategic

structure. As, according to Rosa Luxemburg, the advent of socialism has to be entirely explained *on the basis of the logic of capitalist development,* the revolutionary subject can only be the working class. (On Luxemburg's dogmatic adherence to Marx's theory of pauperization as the basis for the revolutionary determination of the working class, see G. Badia, 'L'analisi dello sviluppo capitalistico in Rosa Luxemburg', Feltrinelli Institute, *Annali,* Milan, p. 252.)

9. K. Kautsky, *The Class Struggle,* New York 1971.

10. 'The object of his (Kautsky's) entire struggle against revisionism was to be that of preserving a notion of the programme not as a complex of determinate political demands — destined to establish the initiative of the party in specific phases of struggle, and as such modifiable from time to time — but as an indissoluble bloc of theory and politics, within which the two terms lost their respective fields of autonomy and Marxism became the finalist ideology of the proletariat.' (L. Paggi, 'Intellettuali, teoria e partito nel marxismo della Seconda Internazionale'. Introduction to M. Adler, *Il socialismo e gli intellettuali,* Bari 1974.)

11. K. Kautsky, pp. 185-6.

12. A. Przeworski, 'Proletariat into a Class. The Process of Class Formation from Karl Kautsky's *The Class Struggle* to Recent Controversies', *Politics and Society,* 7, 1977.

13. For example, at the 1893 Cologne Congress of the SPD, Legien protested against statements by *Vorwärts* according to which 'the struggle for political power remains the most important at every moment, while the economic struggle always finds the workers deeply divided, and the more hopeless the situation is, the more acute and damaging the division becomes. Small-scale struggle would also certainly have its advantages, but these would be of secondary importance for the final objective of the party.' Legien asked: 'Are these arguments from a party organ adequate to attract indifferent workers to the movement? I seriously doubt it.' Quoted from N. Benvenuti's anthology of documents on the relationship between party and trade unions, *Partito e Sindicati in Germania: 1880–1914),* Milan 1981, pp. 70-1.

14. This way of approaching the problem of class unity, according to which deviations from a paradigm are conceptualized in terms of contingent 'obstacles' and 'impediments' to its full validity, continues to dominate certain historiographical traditions. Mike Davis, for example, in a stimulating and highly interesting article ('Why the US Working Class is Different', *New Left Review* 123, Sept.-Oct. 1980), while showing the specificities of the formation of the American working class, conceptualizes these as deviations from a normal pattern which, at some moment of history, will eventually impose itself.

15. We must make clear that when we speak of 'fragmentation' or 'dispersion', it is always with reference to a discourse which postulates the unity of the dispersed and fragmented elements. If these 'elements' are considered without reference to any discourse, the application to them of terms such as 'dispersion' or 'fragmentation' lacks any meaning whatsoever.

16. A. Labriola, *Saggi sul materialismo storico,* Rome 1968, p. 302.

17. Kautsky's main writings on this matter are contained in the anthology by Benvenuti, *Partito e Sindicati.*

18. 'The nature of the trade unions is not therefore defined from the beginning. They may become an instrument of class struggle, but they may also become a fetter on it.' Kautsky in Benvenuti, p. 186.

19. 'The party seeks . . . to reach a final objective which once and for all does away with capitalist exploitation. With regard to this final objective, trade union activity, despite its importance and indispensability, can well be defined as a labour of Sisyphus, not in the sense of useless work, but of work which is never concluded and

44

has always to be begun again. It follows from all this that where a strong social-democratic party exists and has to be reckoned with, it has a greater possibility than the trade unions to establish the necessary line for the class struggle, and hence to indicate the direction which individual proletarian organizations not directly belonging to the party should take. In this way the indispensable unity of the class struggle can be safeguarded.' Kautsky in Benvenuti, p. 195.

20. Cf. Lucio Colletti's remarks in *Tramonto dell'ideologia*, Rome 1980, pp. 173-76. Jacques Monod argues in *Le hasard et la nécessité* (Paris 1970, pp. 46-7): 'In trying to base upon the laws of nature the edifice of their social doctrines, Marx and Engels also had to make a more clear and deliberate use of the "animist projection" than Spencer had done . . . Hegel's postulate that the more general laws which govern the universe in its evolution are of a dialectical order, finds its place within a system which does not recognize any permanent reality other than mind . . . But to preserve these subjective "laws" as such, so as to make them rule a purely material universe, is to carry out the animist projection in all its clarity, with all its consequences, starting with the abandonment of the postulate of objectivity.'

21. This does not contradict our earlier assertion that for Kautsky immediate material interests cannot constitute the unity and identity of the class. The point here is that the 'scientific' instance, as a separate moment, determines the totality of implications of the workers' insertion into the productive process. Science, therefore, *recognizes* the interests of which the different class fragments, in their partiality, do not have full consciousness.

22. This obviously simplified the problem of calculation, in a situation in which the clarity and transparency of interests reduced the problem of strategies to the ideal conditions of a 'rational choice'. Michel de Certeau has recently stated: 'I call "strategy" the calculation of those relations of force that are possible from the moment in which a subject of will (a proprietor, an enterprise, a city, a scientific institution) is isolated from an "environment" . . . Political, economic and scientific rationality is constructed upon this strategic model. Contrary to this, I call "tactics", a calculation that cannot count upon something of its own, nor therefore upon a frontier distinguishing the other as a visible totality.' *L'invention du quotidien*, Paris 1980, vol. 1, pp. 20-1. In the light of this distinction, it is clear that, inasmuch as the 'interests' of the Kautskian subjects are transparent, every calculation is of a strategic nature.

23. Cf. E. Matthias, *Kautsky e il kautskismo*, Rome 1971, *passim*.

24. Symmachos (K. Kautsky), 'Verschwörung oder Revolution?', *Der Sozialdemokrat*, 20/2/1881, quoted in H.J. Steinberg, 'Il partito e la formazione dell' ortodossia marxista', in E.J. Hobsbawm et al., vol. 2, p. 190.

25. See Perry Anderson, 'The Antinomies of Antonio Gramsci', *New Left Review* 100, Nov. 1976/Jan. 1977.

26. Guglielmo Ferrero, *L'Europa giovane. Studi e viaggi nei paesi del Nord,* Milan 1897, p. 95.

27. Cf. Andrew Arato, L'antinomia del marxismo classico: marxismo e filosofia', in E.J. Hobsbawm et al., vol. 2, pp. 702-7.

28. G. Plekhanov, *Fundamental Problems of Marxism*, New York 1969, p. 80.

29. This relation between the logic of necessity and quietism was clearly perceived by the critics of orthodoxy. Sorel affirmed: 'Reading the works of the democratic socialists, one is surprised by the certainty with which they have their future at their disposal; they know the world is moving towards an inevitable revolution, of which they know the general consequences. Some of them have such a faith in their own theory that they end up in quietism.' Georges Sorel, *Saggi di critica del marxismo,*

Palermo 1903, p. 59.

30. Antonio Labriola, 'In memoria del Manifesto dei Comunisti', in *Saggi del materialismo storico*, pp. 34-5.

31. With regard to Labriola's intervention in the debate on the revision of Marxism, see Roberto Racinaro, *La crisi del marxismo nella revisione de fine secolo*, Bari 1978, *passim*.

32. Cf. Nicola Badaloni, *Il marxismo de Gramsci*, Turin 1975, pp. 27-8.

33. Ibid., p. 13.

34. According to Badaloni, this is the solution which Labriola should have followed: 'Perhaps the alternative proposed by him was erroneous and the true alternative lay in a deepening and development of historical morphology, which was excessively simplified in Engels's exposition.' Badaloni, p. 27. With this, of course, the dualism would have been suppressed, but at the price of eliminating the area of morphological indeterminacy whose existence was essential for Labriola's theoretical project.

35. Otto Bauer, 'Was ist Austro-Marxismus', *Arbeiter-Zeitung*, 3/11/ 1927. Translated in the anthology of Austro-Marxist texts: Tom Bottomore and Patrick Goode, *Austro-Marxism*, Oxford 1978, pp. 45-8.

36. Editorial in the first number of *Der Kampf*, 1907-8, reproduced in Bottomore and Goode, pp. 52-6.

37. Ibid., p. 55.

38. On this discussion, and the general politico-intellectual trajectory of Austro-Marxism, see the excellent introduction by Giacomo Marramao to his anthology of Austro-Marxist texts, *Austro-marxismo e socialismo di sinistra fra le due guerre*, Milan 1977.

39. 'To see the process of transformation of capitalist society into socialist society no longer as following the tempo of a unified and homogeneous logico-historical mechanism, but as the result of a multiplication and proliferation of endogenous factors of mutation of the relations of production and power — this implies, at the theoretical level, a major effort of empirico-analytical disaggregation of Marx's morphological prediction, and, at the political level, a supersession of the mystifying alternative between "reform" and "revolution". However, it does not in any way involve an evolutionist type of option, as if socialism were realizable through homeopathic doses.' Giacomo Marramao, 'Tra bolscevismo e socialdemocrazia: Otto Bauer e la cultura politica dell' austro-marxismo', in E.J. Hobsbawm et al., vol. 3, p. 259.

40. See Max Adler, *Il socialismo e gli intellettuali*.

41. 'The peculiarity of revisionism is misunderstood when it is a-critically placed on the same plane as reformism or when it is simply viewed as the expression, since 1890, of the social-reformist practice of the party. The problem of revisionism must, therefore, substantially limit itself to the person of Bernstein and cannot be extended to either Vollmar or Höchberg.' Hans-Josef Steinberg, *Il socialismo tedesco da Bebel a Kautsky*, Rome 1979, p. 118.

42. On the relationship between revisionism and trade unions, see Peter Gay, *The Dilemma of Democratic Socialism*, London 1962, pp. 137-140.

43. Bernstein's defence of the mass strike as a defensive weapon provoked the following commentary by the trade union leader Bömelburg: 'At one time, Eduard Bernstein does not know how far he ought to move to the right, another time he talks about political mass strike. These *litterati* . . . are doing a disservice to the labour movement.' Quoted in Peter Gay, p. 138.

44. Leonardo Paggi, p. 29.

45. Cf. Lucio Colletti, *From Rousseau to Lenin*, NLB, London 1972, p. 62.

46. E. Bernstein, *Evolutionary Socialism*, New York 1978, pp. 15-6.

47. Ibid., p. 103.

48. E. Bernstein, *Die heutige Sozialdemokratie in Theorie und Praxis*, p. 133. Quoted by P. Gay, p. 207.

49. P. Gay, p. 120.

50. Earlier we distinguished between *reformism* and *revisionism*. We must now establish a second distinction between *reformism* and *gradualism*. The basic point of differentiation is that reformism is a political and trade-union *practice*, whereas gradualism is a *theory* about the transition to socialism. Revisionism is distinguished from both insofar as it is a critique of classical Marxism based on the autonomization of the political. These distinctions are important if, as we argue in the text, each of these terms does not necessarily imply the others and has an area of theoretical and political effects which may lead it in very different directions.

51. Hence his acceptance of a naive and technologistic notion of the economy, which is in the last instance identical to that found in Plekhanov. Cf. Colletti, pp. 63ff.

52. On Bernstein's concept of *Entwicklung* see Vernon L. Lidtke, 'Le premesse teoriche del socialismo in Bernstein', Feltrinelli Institute, *Annali*, 15th year, 1973, pp. 155-8.

53. The sense of our critique should not be misunderstood. We do not question the need for ethical judgements in the founding of a socialist politics — Kautsky's absurd denial of this, and his attempt to reduce the adherence to socialism to a mere awareness of its historical necessity, has been subjected to a devastating critique. Our argument is that from the presence of ethical judgements it does not follow that these should be attributed to a transcendental subject, constituted outside every discursive condition of emergence.

54. Among modern works on Sorel, we found the following particularly useful: Michele Maggi, *La formazione dell' egemonia in Francia*, Bari 1977; Michel Charzat, *Georges Sorel et la révolution au XXe siècle*, Paris 1977; Jacques Julliard, *Fernand Pelloutier et les origines du syndicalisme d'action directe*, Paris 1971; Gregorio de Paola, 'Georges Sorel, dalla metafisica al mito', in E.J. Hobsbawm et al., vol. 2, pp. 662-692; and with serious reservations, Zeev Sternhell, *Ni droite ni gauche. L'idéologie fasciste en France*, Paris 1983.

55. See Shlomo Sand, 'Lutte de classes et conscience juridique dans la pensée de Sorel', *Esprit* 3, March 1983, pp. 20-35.

56. G. Sorel, *Reflections on Violence*, New York 1961, p. 127.

57. Ibid., p. 182.

58. G. de Paola, p. 688.

59. Quoted by Z. Sternhell, p. 105.

60. This is what weakens Sternhell's analysis (*Ni droite ni gauche*), despite his richness of information. The history presented by him seems organized around an extremely simple teleology, according to which every rupture with a materialist or positivist view can only be considered a forerunner of fascism.

2
Hegemony: The Difficult Emergence of a New Political Logic

It is necessary at this point to clarify the relationship between the double void that emerged in the essentialist discourse of the Second International, and the peculiar dislocation of stages to which the problematic of hegemony will constitute a political response. Let us begin by specifying those characteristics of the double void which make possible its comparison with the hegemonic suture.[1] Firstly, that void appears in the form of a dualism: its founding discourse does not seek to determine differential degrees of efficacity *within* a topography of the social, but to set limits on the embracing and determining capacity of *every* topographical structuration. Hence such formulations as: 'the infrastructure does not determine everything, because consciousness or will also intervenes in history'; or 'the general theory cannot account for concrete situations, because every prediction has a morphological character'. This dualism is constructed through a hypostasis of the indeterminate *qua* indeterminate: entities which escape structural determination are understood as the negative reverse of the latter. This is what makes dualism a relation of frontiers. If we observe closely, however, this response does not break at all with structural determinism: it merely comes down to a limitation of its effects. For example, it is perfectly possible to argue both that there are vast areas of social life which escape economic determinism, and that, in the limited area in which its effects are operative, the action of the economy must be understood according to a determinist paradigm. Nonetheless there is an obvious problem with this argument: in order to affirm that something is *absolutely* determined and to establish a clear line separating it from the indeterminate, it is not sufficient to establish the *specificity* of the determination; its *necessary character* must also be asserted. For this reason the supposed dualism is a spurious one: its two poles are not at the same level. The determinate, in establishing its specificity as necessary, sets the limits of variation of the indeterminate. The indeterminate is thus reduced to a mere *supplement*[2] of the determinate.

Secondly, as we have already seen, this apparent dualism responds to the fact that structural determination does not provide the foundation for a political logic in which a struggle can be waged here and now against tendencies towards fragmentation. It is immediately apparent, however, that the only terrain permitting the specificity of such a logic to be thought has been erased from the picture: as every theoretically determinable specificity is referred to the terrain of the infrastructure and the resulting class system, any other logic disappears into the general terrain of contingent variation, or is referred to entities escaping all theoretical determination, such as will or ethical decision.

Thirdly, and finally, in the Second International's discourse, the *class* unity of social agents rested upon the ever weaker base of mirror play: economic fragmentation was unable to constitute class unity and referred us on to political recomposition; yet political recomposition was unable to found the *necessary* class character of social agents.

Combined Development and the Logic of the Contingent

Let us now compare this ensemble of fissures, present in the theoretical discourse of the Second International, with the dislocations that the concept of hegemony will attempt to suture. Perry Anderson[3] has studied the emergence of the concept of hegemony in Russian Social Democracy — the theoreticians of the Comintern took it from there, and it reached Gramsci through them — and the results of his investigation are clear: the concept of hegemony fills a space left vacant by a crisis of what, according to Plekhanov's 'stagist' conception, should have been a normal historical development. For that reason, the hegemonization of a task or an ensemble of political forces belongs to the terrain of historical contingency. In European Social Democracy, the main problem had been the dispersion of working-class positions and the shattering of the unity postulated among these by Marxist theory. The very degree of maturity of bourgeois civilization reflected its structural order within the working class, subverting the latter's unity. By contrast, in the theory of hegemony as it was posed in the Russian context, the limits of an insufficiently developed bourgeois civilization forced the working class to come out of itself and to take on tasks that were not its own. The problem, then, was no longer to assure class unity, but to maximize the political efficacity of working-class struggle in a historical terrain where contingency arose from the structural weakness of the bourgeoisie to assume its own tasks.

Let us examine how the steps leading to the emergence of the concept of 'hegemony' were structured. In the writings of Plekhanov and Axelrod, the term 'hegemony' was introduced to describe the process whereby the impotence of the Russian bourgeoisie to carry through its 'normal' struggle for political liberty forced the working class to intervene decisively to achieve it. There was thus a split between the class nature of the task and the historical agent carrying it out. This created a space of indeterminacy whose dimensions would vary considerably — they were minimal in Plekhanov, and expanded to a maximum in Trotsky. But at any event, this space was to be the crucial point from which the various revolutionary orientations divided. The Russian revolution — the revolution 'against *Capital*', as Gramsci called it — had to justify its strategy by broadening to the maximum the space of indeterminacy characteristic of the struggle for hegemony. Consequently, an opposition arose between a *necessary interior* (corresponding to the tasks of the class in a 'normal' development) and a *contingent exterior* (the ensemble of tasks alien to the class nature of the social agents which they had to assume at a given moment).

There are significant differences between these historical dislocations of the orthodox paradigm and those we found in the case of Western Europe. In both the dislocation produced a *displacement*; but whereas in Western Europe this involved a displacement of levels from the economic to the political within the same class, the displacement was much greater in Russia because it occurred between different classes. In Western Europe — with the exception of Austro-Marxism, where a multiplicity of national situations was presented as a dislocation of *stages* — we were confronted with a dissociation of the structural moments of a synchronic paradigm. Hence the thinking of the dissociation could not, as in Russian Social Democracy, take the form of a narrative. Finally, whereas the dislocation and crisis of the paradigm was a negative phenomenon in the other cases, in Russia it became a positive phenomenon: the disharmony between bourgeois tasks and the bourgeoisie's capacity to carry them out was the stepping-stone for the seizure of political power by the proletariat. For the same reason, the European forms of dislocation could be conceptualized purely through reference to negative categories — transience and contingency — which had to be overcome; but in the Russian case, since the dislocations expressed themselves as positive conjunctures permitting the advance of the working class — a certain way of infiltrating itself into history — it became necessary to characterize the new type of relationship between the working class and the alien tasks it had to assume at a given moment. This anomalous relation was called 'hegemony'.

We must now examine the specificity of the hegemonic relation in the discourse of Russian Social Democracy. In fact, 'hegemony' here designates, more than a relation, a *space* dominated by the tension between two very different relations: a) that of the hegemonized task and its 'natural' class agent; and b) that of the hegemonized task and the class hegemonizing it. If the coexistence of these two relations under imprecise conceptual forms is sufficient to give the term 'hegemony' a referential space, the precise determination of their logical articulation is a *sine qua non* for the conversion of 'hegemony' into a theoretical category. In this case, however, one has only to examine the two relations with care, in order to observe that they are not logically articulated at any point.

First of all, in the struggle against absolutism, none of the Russian Social Democratic analyses suggests that bourgeois tasks cease to be bourgeois when they are assumed by the proletariat. Class identity is constituted on the basis of the relations of production: for orthodoxy, it is within that primary structure that the antagonism between working class and bourgeoisie arises. This primary structure organizes itself like a narrative — we may call it *first narrative* — given that its movement is contradictory and tends to its self-elimination. In the structuring of this narrative, the laws of capitalist development are the plot, while the characters, with perfectly assigned roles, are the proletarian and capitalist classes. Now, the clarity of this history is marred by the emergence of an anomaly: the bourgeois class cannot fulfil its role, and this has to be taken over by the other character. We may call this role substitution the *second narrative* — in Trotsky's terms, the permanent revolution. What is the structural relation between these two narratives? It is sufficient to read briefly through the strategic debate, to convince ourselves that their articulation occurs in a theoretical terrain marked by the dominance of the first. Three considerations are enough to prove the point. (1.) The order of appearance of the characters is not altered by the second narrative: if the bourgeoisie is incapable of fulfilling 'its' tasks, these necessarily pass to the proletariat — yet the necessity of this transfer is only evident if one takes for granted the totality of the evolutionary schema constituted at the level of the first narrative. (2.) The class nature of the tasks is not altered by the fact that they are assumed by one class or the other — the democratic tasks remain bourgeois even when their historical agent is the working class. (3.) The very identity of the social agents is determined by their structural positions in the first narrative. Thus there is an unequal relation between the two narratives: hegemonic relations *supplement* class relations. Using a distinction of Saussure's, we could say that hegemonic relations are always facts of *parole,* while class relations are facts of *langue.*

The sense and identity of the hegemonic task and the agents which put it into effect are totally contained within relation (a), as defined above. Hence the relation between the two components of relation (b) can only be one of *exteriority.* Now, a relation of exteriority can be considered under two aspects: as a relation of *exteriority* and as a *relation* of exteriority. The first aspect presents no difficulty: a relation is one of exteriority if the identity of its components is entirely constituted outside the relation. As to the relational moment, in order that the relation may be one of strict exteriority, it is necessary that no conceptual specificity should be attributable to it. (Otherwise, such specificity would become a structurally definable moment. And since this would require a special theory of its forms of articulation with other structural moments constituting the class as such, the identity of the class would inevitably be modified.) In other words, the relation of exteriority can only be thought of as *pure contingency.* This explains why the spurious dualism found in the discourse of the Second International is, for the same reasons, reproduced in the theory of hegemony. Relation (a) and relation (b) cannot be conceptually articulated, simply because the latter has no positive conceptual specificity whatsoever, and is reduced to a contingently variant terrain of relations between agents constituted outside itself. But, it could be argued, in Russian Social Democracy, from Plekhanov and Axelrod to Lenin and Trotsky, there was a positive and increasingly complex theory of hegemony! This is true, but it is not an objection to our argument. For such positivity and complexity refer to the *typology of situations* making possible hegemonic relations among classes, and to the *variety of relations* among social groups acting in a given conjuncture. Yet, the *specificity of the hegemonic link as such* is never discussed or, rather, there is a subtle sleight-of-hand making it invisible.

In order to see how this sleight-of-hand occurs, we should not focus on those approaches for which 'normal' forms of development dominate the course of history and the hegemonic moment occupies a clearly marginal place. (This is the case with Plekhanov, who saw intervention by the working class as a means of pressing the bourgeoisie to fulfil its own tasks.) More pertinent are those other approaches in which the hegemonic transference of tasks constitutes the very substance of revolution, so that it is comparatively more difficult for the specificity of the hegemonic link to be made invisible. In this sense Trotsky's texts are of exemplary clarity, since they place extreme emphasis on the peculiarities of Russian development as opposed to the course of Western European capitalism. As is well known, in a number of writings published before and after the 1905 Russian Revolution,[4] Trotsky raised the possibility of a working-class government that would undertake a direct transition to socialism, as against the Menshevik perspective for a bourgeois-democratic republic following the collapse of Tsarism, and the Bolshevik notion of a workers' and peasants' government that would restrict its reforms to a bourgeois-democratic mould. This possibility was inscribed in the very peculiarities of Russia's historical development: weakness of the bourgeoisie and urban civilization; disproportionate growth of the State as a military–bureaucratic apparatus becoming autonomous from classes; insertion of advanced forms of capitalism resulting from the 'privilege of backwardness'; freshness of the Russian proletariat, due to the absence of traditions tying it to a complex civil society; and so on. As the bourgeoisie had arrived too late to assume the historical tasks of the struggle against absolutism, the proletariat became the key agent for their realization. This dislocation in the stagist paradigm, and the supersession of the resulting hegemonic transference, were the very axis of Trotsky's theory of the revolution.

It would seem that no greater centrality could have been given to the hegemonic relation, as the very possibility of revolution revolved around it. However, we should look more closely at the forms which this centrality assumes in Trotsky's discourse. On two fundamental points his analysis is confronted with the specificity of social relations that seem to resist strict class reductionism — that is, the necessary character of relation (a) — and on both points he shrinks from a theoretical advance that would determine this specificity. The first point concerns the correlation between the structural weakness of the bourgeoisie and the exceptional role played by the State in the historical formation of Russian society. Faced with the theoretical challenge posed by the Bolshevik historian Pokrovsky — who, from a crudely economist viewpoint, insists that to grant such importance to the State would be to detach it from its class bases — Trotsky fails to reply with a theoretical analysis of relative State autonomy in different capitalist social formations, appealing instead to the greenness of life against the greyness of theory: 'Comrade Pokrovsky's thought is gripped in a vice of rigid social categories which he puts in place of living historical forces . . . Where there are no "special features", there is no history, but only a sort of pseudo-materialist geometry. Instead of studying the living and changing matter of economic development, it is enough to notice a few outward symptoms and adapt them to a few ready-made clichés.'[5] With this, the 'special feature' constituted by the autonomization of the State from social classes is hereby placed on a terrain which severely limits its effects from the beginning: we are now dealing with *circumstances,* which belong to an eminently factual order and are capable of being incorporated into a *story* — hence the predominantly narrative tone of Trotsky's analysis — but which cannot be grasped conceptually.

This would not necessarily be negative if *all* social determinations were subjected to the same treatment, because Trotsky would then have to narrate — at the same level of Russia's specificities — the processes through which the economy manages to determine, in the last instance, all other social relations. This, however, does not happen; although there is a narration of the 'specificities', the features considered common to every capitalist social formation are not subjected to a narrative treatment. That the economy determines in the last instance the processes of history is something which, for Trotsky, is established at a level as extra-historical as Pokrovsky's, and in as dogmatic a manner. An order of 'essences' inescapably confronts an order of 'circumstances', and both are reproduced within the same social agents. What is liable in them to historical variation is reduced to that ensemble of characteristics which makes them deviate from a normal paradigm — the weakness of the bourgeoisie in Russia, the freshness of its proletariat, etc. These 'special features', however, do not in any way undermine the validity of the paradigm: this continues to produce its effects insofar as the social agents define their basic identity in relation to it, and insofar as the 'special features' present themselves merely as empirical advantages or disadvantages for the attainment of class objectives pre-established at the level of 'essences'.

This is clearly revealed in the second fundamental point where Trotsky's analysis touches the limits of the reductionist conception of classes: in the analysis of hegemony. As we saw earlier — and this can also be applied to Trotsky's analysis — there is a split between the 'natural' class agent of a historical task and the concrete agent that puts it into effect. But we also saw that, for the agent which undertakes it, the class nature of a task is not altered by this split. The agent does not, therefore, *identify* with the task undertaken; its relation with that task remains at the level of a circumstantial calculation — even when this may involve 'circumstances' of epochal dimensions. The splitting of the task is an empirical phenomenon that does not affect its nature; the agent's connection to the task is also empirical, and a permanent schism develops between an 'inside' and an 'outside' of the agent's identity. Never for a moment do we find in Trotsky the idea that the democratic and anti-absolutist identity of the masses constitutes a specific subject position which different classes can articulate and that, in doing so, they modify their own nature. The unfulfilled democratic tasks are simply a stepping-stone for the working class to advance towards its strictly class objectives. In this way, the conditions are created not only for the specificity of the hegemonic link to be systematically conjured away (given that its factual or circumstantial character eschews any conceptual construction), but also for its disappearance to be made invisible. Indeed, the insertion of the hegemonic relation into a *narrative* of adjustments and recompositions, into a succession which cannot be subsumed under the principle of repetition, seems to give a *meaning* to that conceptually evanescent presence. Thus, the historico-narrative form in which Russian specificities are presented, plays an ambiguous role: if, on the one hand, it limits them to the terrain of the circumstantial, on the other, the fact that they can be thought, even under the weak form of a narrative, gives them a principle of organization, a certain *discursive presence*. Yet this is an extremely ephemeral presence, since the saga of hegemony concludes very quickly: there is no specificity, either for Trotsky or for Lenin, which can assure the survival of a Soviet State unless a socialist revolution breaks out in Europe, unless the victorious working classes of the advanced industrial countries come to the assistance of the Russian revolutionaries. Here the 'abnormality' of the dislocation of stages in Russia links up with the 'normal' development of the West; what we have called a 'second narrative' is reintegrated into the 'first narrative'; 'hegemony' rapidly finds its limits.

'Class Alliances': Between Democracy and Authoritarianism

This conception of the hegemonic link as external to the class identity of the agents is not, of course, exclusive to Trotskyism but characterizes the whole Leninist tradition. For Leninism, hegemony involves *political leadership* within a *class alliance*. The political character of the hegemonic link is fundamental, implying as it does that the terrain on which the link establishes itself is different from that on which the social agents are constituted. As the field of the relations of production is the specific terrain of class constitution, the presence of classes in the political field can only be understood as a *representation of interests*. Through their representative parties they unite under the leadership of one class, in an alliance against a common enemy. This circumstantial unity does not, however, affect the identity of the classes comprising the alliance, since their identity is constituted around 'interests' which are in the end strictly incompatible ('strike together but march separately'). The identity of the social agents, rationalistically conceived under the form of 'interests', and the transparency of the means of representation in relation to what is represented, are the two conditions which permit the exteriority of the hegemonic link to be established. This exteriority was at the root of those paradoxical situations in which the communist militant typically found himself. Often in the vanguard of a struggle for democratic liberties, he nevertheless could not identify with them since he would be the first to abolish them once the 'bourgeois–democratic' stage was completed.

At this point, it is important to note the ambiguity and the contradictory effects that stem from the centrality of hegemony in Leninist discourse. On the one hand, the concept is undoubtedly associated with the more authoritarian and negative tendencies of the Leninist tradition, for it postulates a clear separation within the masses between the leading sectors and those which are led. (This separation is evidently absent in the revolutionary strategy of Kautskian orthodoxy, in which a complete coincidence between political leadership and social base leaves no necessity for hegemonic recompositions.) But, on the other hand, the hegemonic relation entails a conception of politics which is *potentially* more democratic than anything found within the tradition of the Second International. Tasks and demands which, in classist economism, would have corresponded to different stages are now seen to coexist in the same historical conjuncture. This results in the acceptance of current political validity for a plurality of antagonisms and points of rupture, so that revolutionary legitimacy is no longer exclusively concentrated in the working class. A structural dislocation thus emerges between 'masses' and 'classes', given that the line separating the former from the dominant sectors is not juxtaposed with class exploitation. Combined and uneven development becomes the terrain which for the first time allows Marxism to render more complex its conception of the nature of social struggles.

How, then, are we to account for this paradox: that at the very moment when the democratic dimension of the mass struggle was being enlarged, an ever more vanguardist and anti-democratic conception asserted itself in socialist political practice? Quite simply, by the fact that the ontological privilege granted to the working class by Marxism was transferred from the social base to the political leadership of the mass movement. In the Leninist conception, the working class and its vanguard do not transform their class identity by fusing it with the multiple democratic demands that are politically recomposed by the hegemonic practices; instead, they regard these demands as stages, as necessary yet transitory steps in pursuit of their own class objectives. Under such conditions, the relations between 'vanguard' and 'masses' cannot but have a predominantly external and manipulative character. Hence, to the extent that democratic demands become more diverse and the terrain of mass struggle more complex, a vanguard that continues to identify with the 'objective interests of the working class' must increasingly broaden the hiatus between its own identity and that of the sectors it seeks to lead. The very expansion of the democratic potential of the mass movement gives rise, in a strictly classist conception, to an increasingly authoritarian practice of politics. While democratization of the mass struggle depends upon a proliferation of points of rupture which overflow class boundaries, political authoritarianism emerges at the moment when, in order to ground the necessity of *class* hegemony, a distinction is established between leaders and led within mass movements. If this distinction were based upon a greater practical capacity for self-organization in the struggle for objectives shared by the entire movement, the consequences would not necessarily be authoritarian. But, as we have seen, it is actually posed in very different terms: one sector *knows* the underlying movement of history, and knows therefore the temporary character of the demands uniting the masses as a whole. The centrality attributed to the working class is not a practical but an *ontological* centrality, which is, at the same time, the seat of an *epistemological* privilege: as the 'universal' class, the proletariat — or rather its party — is the depository of science. At this point, the schism between class identity and the identity of the masses becomes permanent. The *possibility* of this authoritarian turn was, in some way, present from the beginnings of Marxist orthodoxy; that is to say, from the moment in which a limited actor — the working class — was raised to the status of 'universal class'. If none of the theoreticians of the Second International advanced in this authoritarian direction, this was because for them the political centrality of the working class had to coincide with the proletarianization of the other social strata, and there was thus no room for a schism between *class* and *masses*. All that was necessary for the authoritarian turn to become inevitable, however, was that the seizure of power should be conceived as an act of masses broader than the working class, while the latter's political centrality was upheld as a principle *in classical terms*.

Let us now bring together several links in our argument. It has become clearer why the tension between the two relations embraced by the concept of hegemony — the relation between the hegemonized task and the class hegemonizing it, and the relation between the hegemonized task and the class that is its 'natural' agent — could never be resolved in an effective conceptual articulation. The condition for the maintenance of working-class unity and identity on the terrain of economist stagism — the only terrain capable of constituting it as a 'universal class' — was that the hegemonized tasks should not transform the identity of the hegemonic class, but enter into a merely external and factual relation with it. Moreover, the only way of affirming the external character of this relation was to tighten the bond between the hegemonized task and its 'natural' class agent. The terrain of hegemonic relations was, therefore, one of essentially pragmatic discourses. All the terminological innovations which Leninism and the Comintern introduce to Marxism belong to military vocabulary (tactical alliance, strategic line, so many steps forward and so many back); none refers to the very structuring of the social relations, which Gramsci would later address with his concepts of historical bloc, integral State, and so forth.

Now, this tension between the two relations embraced by the concept of hegemony is not distinct from the ambiguity we have located between a democratic and an authoritarian practice of hegemony. The relation between a hegemonic class and a democratic task or demand assumes an external, manipulative character only insofar as this task is bonded to a different class, and to a necessary stage within the evolutionist paradigm. Conversely, the democratic potential can be developed only if this bond is broken, only if the conditions disappear which permitted the emergence of a rigid separation between leaders and led within the masses. At this point, we must present the conditions which would allow the original ambiguity to be overcome in either a democratic or an authoritarian practice of hegemony.

Democratic practice. As we have indicated, the terrain of hegemonic recomposition carries a potential for the democratic expansion and deepening of socialist political practice. Without hegemony, socialist practice can focus only on the demands and interests of the working class. But insofar as the dislocation of stages compels the working class to act on a *mass* terrain, it must abandon its class ghetto and transform itself into the articulator of a multiplicity of antagonisms and demands stretching beyond itself. From everything we have said, it is evident that the deepening of a mass democratic practice — which shuns vanguardist manipulation and an external characterization of the relation between class hegemony and democratic tasks — can be achieved only if it is recognized that these tasks do not have a necessary class character and if stagism is renounced in a thoroughgoing manner. It is necessary to break with the view that democratic tasks are bonded to a bourgeois stage — only then will the obstacle preventing a permanent articulation between socialism and democracy be eliminated. Four fundamental consequences follow from this. First, the very identity of classes is transformed by the hegemonic tasks they take on themselves: the rigid line of demarcation between the internal and the external has fallen. Second, inasmuch as the democratic demands of the masses lose their necessary class character, the field of hegemony ceases to involve a maximization of effects based on a zero-sum game among classes; the notion of 'class alliance' is also clearly insufficient, since hegemony supposes the construction of the very identity of social agents, and not just a rationalist coincidence of 'interests' among preconstituted agents. Thirdly, the field of politics can no longer be considered a 'representation of interests', given that the so-called 'representation' modifies the nature of what is represented. (In fact, the very notion of representation as transparency becomes untenable. What is actually called into question here, is the base/superstructure model itself.) Finally, insofar as the identity of social agents ceases to be exclusively constituted through their insertion in the relations of production, and becomes a precarious articulation among a number of subject positions, what is being implicitly challenged is the identification between social agents and classes.

Authoritarian practice. Here the conditions are the opposite. The class nature of every demand or task has to be fixed a priori. There are bourgeois–democratic demands, petty-bourgeois demands, etc., and their relative progressiveness is established through a political calculation which analyses every conjuncture in terms of the traditional model of stages and the changes introduced by their uneven combination. There is, obviously, a complete separation between the hegemonic tasks of the working class and its class identity. The military conception of politics dominates the whole range of strategic calculations. But since the real working class is, of course, far from fully identifying with its 'historical interests', the dissociation becomes permanent between the materiality of the class and the political instance representing its 'true identity'. From Lenin's *What is to be Done* to the Bolshevization of the Communist parties under the Comintern, this line of demarcation becomes increasingly rigid and is reflected in the growing authoritarian turn of Communist politics. It is important to clarify what makes this turn inevitable. We do not seek to deny the need for political mediation in the socialist determination of the working class; even less, to oppose it with a workerism based upon the myth of a spontaneously socialist determination of the class. What is decisive, however, is *how* the nature of this political link is understood; and Leninism evidently makes no attempt to construct, through struggle, a mass identity not predetermined by any necessary law of history. On the contrary, it maintains that there is a 'for itself' of the class accessible only to the enlightened vanguard — whose attitude towards the working class is therefore purely pedagogical. The roots of authoritarian politics lie in this interweaving of science and politics. As a consequence, there is no longer any problem in considering the party as representative of the class — not of the class as flesh and blood, of course, but of that entelechy constituted by its 'historical interests'. Whereas the democratic practice of hegemony increasingly calls into question the transparency of the process of representation, the authoritarian practice has laid the ground for the relation of representation to become the basic political mechanism. Once every political relation is conceived as a relation of representation, a progressive substitutionism moves from class to party (representation of the objective interests of the proletariat) and from party to Soviet State (representation of the world interests of the Communist movement). A martial conception of class struggle thus concludes in an eschatological epic.

As we have seen, the roots of this transference of class unity to the political sphere go back to Second International orthodoxy. In Leninism as in Kautskyism, the constitutive character of the political moment does not entail that a major role is attributed to super-structures, because the privilege granted to the party is not 'topo-graphical' but 'epistemological': it is founded not on the efficacy of the political level in constructing social relations, but on the scientific monopoly enjoyed by a given class perspective. This monopoly guaranteed, at a theoretical level, the overcoming of the split between the visible tendencies of capitalism and its underlying evolution. The difference between Kautskyism and Leninism is that for the former the split is purely temporary and internal to the class, and the process of overcoming it inscribed in the endogenous ten-dencies of capitalist accumulation; while for Leninism, the split is the terrain of a structural dislocation between 'class' and 'masses' which permanently defines the conditions of political struggle in the imperialist era.

This last point is decisive: hegemonic tasks become increasingly central to communist strategy, as they are bound up with the very conditions of development of the world capitalist system. For Lenin, the world economy is not a mere economic fact, but a political reality: it is an imperialist chain. The breaking points appear not at those links which are most advanced from the point of view of the contradiction between forces and relations of production, but instead, at those where the greatest number of contradictions have accumulated, and where the greatest number of tendencies and antagonisms — belonging, in the orthodox view, to diverse phases — merge into a ruptural unity.[6] This implies, however, that the revolutionary process can be understood only as a political articulation of dissimilar elements: there is no revolution without a social complexity external to the simple antagonism among classes; in other words, there is no revolution without hegemony. This moment of political articulation becomes more and more funda-mental when one encounters, in the stage of monopoly capitalism, a growing dissolution of old solidarities and a general politicization of social relations. Lenin clearly perceives the transition to a new bour-geois mass politics — labelled by him Lloyd Georgism[7] — which is profoundly transforming the historical arena of class struggle. This possibility of unsuspected articulations, altering the social and poli-tical identities that are permissible and even thinkable, increasingly dissolves the obviousness of the logical categories of classical stagism. Trotsky will draw the conclusion that combined and uneven development is the historical condition of our time. This can only mean an unceasing expansion of hegemonic tasks — as opposed to purely class tasks, whose terrain shrinks like a wild ass's skin. But if there is no historical process which does not involve a 'non-orthodox' combination of elements, what then is a normal development?

Communist discourse itself became increasingly dominated by the hegemonic character which every political initiative acquired in the new historical terrain of the imperialist era. As a result, however, it tended to oscillate in a contradictory manner between what we have called a democratic and an authoritarian practice of hegemony. In the 1920s economist stagism was everywhere in command, and as the prospect of revolution receded the class lines grew still more rigid. Since the European revolution was conceived purely in terms of working-class centrality, and since the Communist parties represented the 'historical interests' of the working class, the sole function of these parties was to maintain the revolutionary consciousness of the proletariat in opposition to the integrationist tendencies of social democracy. In periods of 'relative stabilization', therefore, it was necessary to strengthen the class barrier with even greater intransigence. Hence, the slogan launched in 1924 for the Bolshevization of the Communist parties. Zinoviev explained it as follows: 'Bolshevization means a firm will to struggle for the hegemony of the proletariat, it means a passionate hatred for the bourgeoisie, for the counter-revolutionary leaders of social democracy, for centrism and the centrists, for the semi-centrists and the pacifists, for all the miscarriages of bourgeois ideology . . . Bolshevization is Marxism in action; it is dedication to the idea of the dictatorship of the proletariat, to the idea of Leninism.'[8] As a renewal of the revolutionary process would inevitably follow upon a worsening economic crisis, political periodization was a mere reflection of economics: the only task left to the Communist parties in periods of stabilization was to accumulate forces around a wholly classist and 'rupturist' identity which, when the crisis arrived, would open the way to a new revolutionary initiative. (Characteristically, the 'united front' policy was reinterpreted as a united front from below and as an opportunity to expose the social democratic leaders.) Under these conditions a manipulative approach to other social and political forces could not fail to gain ascendancy.

The break with this reductionist and manipulative conception — or the beginnings of a break, as it has never been overcome in the communist tradition — was linked to the experience of fascism in Europe and the cycle of anti-colonial revolutions. In the first case the crisis of the liberal-democratic State, and the emergence of radical-popular ideologies of the Right, challenged the conception of democratic rights and freedoms as 'bourgeois' by nature; and, at the same time, the anti-fascist struggle created a popular and democratic mass subjectivity which could potentially be fused with a socialist identity. In the terms of our earlier analysis, the link uniting the hegemonized task to its 'natural' class agent began to dissolve, and it became possible to fuse that task with the identity of the hegemonic class. In this new perspective, hegemony was understood as the democractic reconstruction of the nation around a new class core. This tendency would later be reinforced by the varied experiences of national resistance against the Nazi occupation. But the change in communist policy started with Dimitrov's report to the Seventh Congress of the Comintern, where the Third Period line of 'class against class' was formally abandoned and the policy of the popular fronts first introduced.[9] While implicitly retaining the notion of hegemony as a merely external alliance of classes, the new strategy conceived democracy as a common ground which was not open to exclusive absorption by any one social sector. Under these conditions, it became more and more difficult to maintain a strict separation between hegemonic tasks and class identity. A number of formulas — ranging from Mao's 'new democracy' to Togliatti's 'progressive democracy' and 'national tasks of the working class' — attempted to locate themselves on a terrain that was difficult to define theoretically within Marxist parameters, since the 'popular' and the 'democratic' were tangible realities at the level of the mass struggle but could not be ascribed to a strict class belonging. Revolutions in the peripheral world which took place under a communist leadership present us with a similar phenomenon: from China to Vietnam or Cuba, the popular mass identity was other and broader than class identity. The structural split between 'masses' and 'class', which we saw insinuating itself from the very beginning of the Leninist tradition, here produced the totality of its effects.

At this point, communist discourse was confronted by a pair of crucial problems. How should one characterize that plurality of antagonisms emerging on a mass terrain different from that of classes? And how could the hegemonic force retain a strictly proletarian character, once it had incorporated the democratic demands of the masses in its own identity? The main response to the first question was to implement a set of discursive strategies whereby the relationship established between classes went beyond their specifically class character, while *formally* remaining on a classist terrain. Consider, for example, the use of enumeration in communist discourses. To enumerate is never an innocent operation; it involves major displacements of meaning. Communist enumeration occurs within a dichotomic space that establishes the antagonism between dominant and popular sectors; and the identity of both is constructed on the basis of enumerating their constitutive class sectors. On the side of the popular sectors, for example, would be included: the working class, the peasantry, the petty bourgeoisie, progressive fractions of the national bourgeoisie, etc. This enumeration, however, does not merely affirm the separate and literal *presence* of certain classes or class fractions at the popular pole; it also asserts their *equivalence* in the common confrontation with the dominant pole. A relation of equivalence is not a relation of identity among objects. Equivalence is never tautological, as the substitutability it establishes among certain objects is only valid for determinate positions within a given structural context. In this sense, equivalence displaces the identity which makes it possible, from the objects themselves to the contexts of their appearance or presence. This, however, means that in the relation of equivalence the identity of the object is split: on the one hand, it maintains its own 'literal' sense; on the other, it symbolizes the contextual position for which it is a substitutable element. This is exactly what occurs in the communist enumeration: from a strictly classist point of view, there is no identity whatsoever among the sectors of the popular pole, given that each one has differentiated and even antagonistic interests; yet, the relation of equivalence established among them, in the context of their opposition to the dominant pole, constructs a 'popular' discursive position that is irreducible to class positions. In the Marxist discourse of the Second International, there were no equivalential enumerations. For Kautsky, each class sector occupied a specific differential position within the logic of capitalist development; one of the constitutive characteristics of Marxist discourse had been, precisely, the dissolution of the 'people' as an amorphous and imprecise category, and the reduction of every antagonism to a class confrontation which exhausted itself in its own literality, without any equivalential dimension. As to the discourse of 'combined and uneven development', we have seen that the dislocation of stages and the hegemonic recompositions were merely thought of as a more complex movement among classes, whose factual character made room for a narrative of exceptionalities but not for a conceptualization of specificities. In Rosa Luxemburg we come closer to a symbolic–equivalential split which subverts the literal sense of each concrete struggle; but as we saw, her attribution of a necessary class character to the resulting social agent places a rigid limit on the expansive logic of equivalences. Only in the enumerative practices of the popular fronts period does the 'people' — that agent central to the political and social struggles of the nineteenth century — re-emerge, timidly at first, in the field of Marxist discursivity.

From what we have said, it is clear that the condition for the emergence of the 'people' as a political agent in communist discourse has been the relation of equivalence which splits the identity of classes and thereby constitutes a new type of polarization. Now, this process takes place entirely within the field of the hegemonic practices. Communist enumeration is not the confirmation of a de facto situation, but has a performative character. The unity of an ensemble of sectors is not a datum: it is a project to be built politically. The hegemonization of such an ensemble does not, therefore, involve a simple conjunctural or momentary agreement; it has to build a structurally new relation, different from class relations. This shows that the concept of 'class alliance' is as inadequate to characterize a hegemonic relation as the mere listing of bricks would be to describe a building. Nevertheless, given its internal logic, the relation of equivalence cannot display its presence simply through the incidental substitutability of its terms; it must give rise to a *general equivalent* in which the relation as such crystallizes symbolically. It is at this point, in the political case we are examining, that national-popular or popular-democratic symbols emerge to constitute subject positions different from those of class; the hegemonic relation then definitively loses its factual and episodic character, becoming instead a stable part of every politico-discursive formation. In this sense Mao's analyses of contradiction — despite their near-to-zero philosophical value — do have the great merit of presenting the terrain of social struggles as a proliferation of contradictions, not all of them referring back to the class principle.

The other series of problems facing communist discourse concerned the question of how to maintain the class identity of the hegemonic sector. Formulated in its most general terms, the issue is the following: if in the new conception the hegemonic relation transforms the identity of the hegemonic sector, and if the condition of social struggles in the imperialist era entails that these occur in an increasingly complex terrain dominated by recomposing practices, does it not follow that the class identity of the hegemonic subjects is put into question? Up to what point can we continue to refer to a class core as the articulating principle of the various subject positions? Two answers — or rather, two ways of arriving at an answer — are possible here. And in the end they depend on the two conceptions of hegemony — democratic and authoritarian — that we described earlier. For one of them, characterizing most of the communist tradition, the solution is found in an *ad nauseam* extension of the model of representation. Each instance is the representation of another, until a final class core is reached which supposedly gives meaning to the whole series. This response evidently denies all opacity and density to political relations, which are a bare stage on which characters constituted beyond them — the classes — wage their struggle. Furthermore, the class represented in this way cannot but be the class 'for itself', the finalist perspective incarnated in the 'scientific' cosmovision of the party; that is, the *ontologically* privileged agent. In this way, all concrete problems concerning the practice of representation are simply eliminated. The other response accepts the structural diversity of the relations in which social agents are immersed, and replaces the principle of representation with that of *articulation*. Unity between these agents is then not the expression of a common underlying essence but the result of political construction and struggle. If the working class, as a hegemonic agent, manages to articulate around itself a number of democratic demands and struggles, this is due not to any a priori structural privilege, but to a political initiative on the part of the class. Thus, the hegemonic subject is a class subject only in the sense that, on the basis of class positions, a certain hegemonic formation is *practically* articulated; but, in that case we are dealing with concrete workers and not with the entelechy constituted by their 'historical interests'. In the world of the Third International, there was only one thinker in whom the notion of politics and hegemony as articulation found — with all its ambiguities and limitations — a theoretically mature expression. We are, of course, referring to Antonio Gramsci.

The Gramscian Watershed

The specificity of Gramscian thought is usually presented in two different and apparently contradictory ways. In one interpretation, Gramsci was an eminently Italian theoretician whose conceptual innovations were related to the particular conditions of Italy's backwardness: failure of the Risorgimento project to construct a unified national State; strong regional split between industrial North and agrarian Mezzogiorno; lack of integration of the Catholic masses into the political life of the country, as a result of the Vatican question; insufficient and contradictory development of capitalism;

etc. In short, Gramsci was an original theoretician and a political strategist of 'uneven development', but his concepts are scarcely relevant to the conditions of advanced capitalism. A second, divergent reading presents him as a theoretician of revolution in the West,[10] whose strategic conception was based upon the complexity of advanced industrial civilizations and the density of their social and political relations. One of his interpreters goes so far as to see him as the theoretician of the capitalist restructuring which followed the 1929 world crisis, and of the complexity acquired by mass struggle within the context of a growing intertwining of politics and economics.[11] In fact, Gramsci's theoretical innovation is located at a more general level, so that both of these readings are possible — and partially valid. More than any other theoretician of his time, Gramsci broadened the terrain of political recomposition and hegemony, while offering a theorization of the hegemonic link which clearly went beyond the Leninist category of 'class alliance'. As, in both the advanced industrial countries and the capitalist periphery, the conditions of political struggle moved further and further away from the ones imagined by orthodox stagism, the Gramscian categories applied equally to both cases. Their relevance should therefore be situated at the level of the general theory of Marxism, and cannot be referred to specific geographical contexts.

The starting point was, however, a strictly Leninist approach. In *Notes on the Southern Question* (1926), the first Gramscian text in which the concept of hegemony is used, he states: 'The proletariat can become the leading and the dominant class to the extent that it succeeds in creating a system of alliances which allows it to mobilize the majority of the working population against capitalism and the bourgeois State. In Italy, in the real class relations which exist there, this means to the extent that it succeeds in gaining the consent of the broad peasant masses.'[12] The precondition of this leading role is that the working class should not remain confined to the narrow defence of its corporative interests, but should take up those of other sectors. However, the logic is still only one of preconstituted sectoral interests, which is perfectly compatible with the notion of a class alliance. As in Lenin, leadership is merely political and not 'moral and intellectual'.

It is in this movement, from the 'political' to the 'intellectual and moral' plane, that the decisive transition takes place toward a concept of hegemony beyond 'class alliances'. For, whereas political leadership can be grounded upon a conjunctural coincidence of interests in which the participating sectors retain their separate identity, moral and intellectual leadership requires that an ensemble of 'ideas' and 'values' be shared by a number of sectors — or, to use our own terminology, that certain subject positions traverse a number of class sectors. Intellectual and moral leadership constitutes, according to Gramsci, a higher synthesis, a 'collective will', which, through ideology, becomes the organic cement unifying a 'historical bloc'. All these are new concepts having an effect of displacement with regard to the Leninist perspective: the relational specificity of the hegemonic link is no longer concealed, but on the contrary becomes entirely visible and theorized. The analysis conceptually defines a new series of relations among groups which baffles their structural location within the revolutionary and relational schema of economism. At the same time, ideology is signalled as the precise terrain on which these relations are constituted.

Thus, everything depends on how ideology is conceived.[13] Here Gramsci brings about two new and fundamental displacements with regard to the classical problematic. The first is his conception of the materiality of ideology. Ideology is not identified with a 'system of ideas' or with the 'false consciousness' of social agents; it is instead an organic and relational whole, embodied in institutions and apparatuses, which welds together a historical bloc around a number of basic articulatory principles. This precludes the possibility of a 'superstructuralist' reading of the ideological. In fact, through the concepts of historical bloc and of ideology as organic cement, a new totalizing category takes us beyond the old base/superstructure distinction. This is not sufficient, however, because moral and intellectual leadership could still be understood as the ideological inculcation by a hegemonic class of a whole range of subordinate sectors. In that case, there would be no subject positions traversing classes, for any that seemed to do so would in fact be appurtenances of the dominant class, and their presence in other sectors could be understood only as a phenomenon of false consciousness. It is at this crucial point that Gramsci introduces his third and most important displacement: the break with the reductionist problematic of ideology. For Gramsci, political subjects are not — strictly speaking — classes, but complex 'collective wills'; similarly, the ideological elements articulated by a hegemonic class do not have a necessary class belonging. Concerning the first point, Gramsci's position is clear: the collective will is a result of the politico-ideological articulation of dispersed and fragmented historical forces. 'From this one can deduce the importance of the "cultural aspect", even in practical (collective) activity. An historical act can only be performed by "collective man", and this presupposes the attainment of a "cultural-social" unity through which a multiplicity of dispersed wills with heterogenous aims, are welded together with a single aim, on the basis of an equal and common conception of the world.'[14] Nothing more distant from this 'collective man', 'welded together with a single aim', than the Leninist notion of class alliance. With regard to the second point, it is equally evident that for Gramsci the organic ideology does not represent a purely classist and closed view of the world; it is formed instead through the articulation of elements which, considered in themselves, do not have any necessary class belonging. Let us examine, in this connection, the following critical passages: 'What matters is the criticism to which such an ideological complex is subjected by the first representation of a new historical phase. This criticism makes possible a process of differentiation and change in the relative weight that the elements of the old ideologies used to possess. What was previously secondary and subordinate, or even incidental, is now taken to be primary — becomes the nucleus of a new ideological and theoretical complex. The old collective will dissolves into its contradictory elements since the subordinate ones develop socially.'[15] 'How, on the other hand, should this theoretical consciousness, proposed as autonomous consciousness, be formed? How should everyone choose and combine the elements for the constitution of such an autonomous consciousness? Will each element imposed have to be repudiated a priori? It will have to be repudiated inasmuch as it is imposed, but not in itself; that is to say that it will be necessary to give a new form which is specific to the given group.'[16]

We can thus see the central point which demarcates Grasmci from other anti-economistic positions formulated within the communist movement of that period. Both Lukács and Korsch, for instance, also reproportioned the terrain classically attributed to the superstructures; but they did this within the parameters of a class-reductionist perspective which identified the revolutionary subject with the working class, such that hegemony in the sense of articulation was strictly unthinkable. It was precisely Gramsci's introduction of this latter concept which radically subverted the original conditions for the emergence of Second International dualism, and its reproduction on an extended scale in the discourse of the Third. On the one hand, the field of historical contingency has penetrated social relations more thoroughly than in any of the previous discourses: the social segments have lost those essential connections which turned them into moments of the stagist paradigm; and their own *meaning* depended upon hegemonic articulations whose success was not guaranteed by any law of history. In terms of our earlier analysis, we might say that the diverse 'elements' or 'tasks' no longer had any identity apart from their relation with the force hegemonizing them. On the other hand, these forms of precarious articulation began to receive names, to be theoretically thought, and were incorporated into the very identity of the social agents. This explains the importance attributed by Gramsci to the 'national-popular' and to the formulation of a concept such as 'integral State', in which the dominant sector modifies its very nature and identity through the practice of hegemony. For Gramsci a class does not *take State power*, it *becomes* State.

All the conditions would seem to be present here for what we have called the democratic practice of hegemony. Nonetheless, the entire construction rests upon an ultimately incoherent conception, which is unable fully to overcome the dualism of classical Marxism. For Gramsci, even though the diverse social elements have a merely relational identity — achieved through articulatory practices — there must always be a *single* unifying principle in every hegemonic formation, and this can only be a fundamental class. Thus two principles of the social order — the unicity of the unifying principle, and its necessary class character — are not the contingent result of hegemonic struggle, but the necessary structural framework within which every struggle occurs. Class hegemony is not a wholly practical result of struggle, but has an ultimate ontological foundation. The economic base may not assure the ultimate victory of the working class, since this depends upon its capacity for hegemonic leadership. However, a failure in the hegemony of the working class can only be followed by a reconstitution of bourgeois hegemony, so that in the end, political struggle is still a zero-sum game among classes. This is the inner essentialist core which continues to be present in Gramsci's thought, setting a limit to the deconstructive logic of hegemony. To assert, however, that hegemony must always correspond to a fundamental economic class is not merely to reaffirm determination in the last instance by the economy; it is also to predicate that, insofar as the economy constitutes an insurmountable limit to society's potential for hegemonic recomposition, the constitutive logic of the economic space is not itself hegemonic. Here the naturalist prejudice, which sees the economy as a homogeneous space unified by necessary laws, appears once again with all its force.

This fundamental ambiguity can clearly be seen in the Gramscian concept of 'war of position'. We have already noted the function of military metaphors in classical Marxist discourse, and it would be no exaggeration to say that, from Kautsky to Lenin, the Marxist conception of politics rested upon an imaginary owing a great deal to

Clausewitz.[17] The chief consequence was what might be called a *segregation* effect — for, if one understands relations with other social forces as military relations, then one will always keep one's own separate identity. From Kautsky's 'war of attrition' to the extreme militarism of the Bolshevization drive and 'class against class', the establishment of a strict dividing line was considered the very condition of politics — 'politics' being conceived simply as one of the terrains of *class* struggle. For Gramsci, by contrast, 'war of position' involves the progressive disaggregation of a civilization and the construction of another around a new class core. Thus, the identity of the opponents, far from being fixed from the beginning, constantly changes in the process. It is clear that this has little to do with 'war of position' in the strict military sense, where enemy forces are not continually passing to one's own side. Indeed, the military metaphor is here metaphorized in the opposite direction: if in Leninism there was a militarization of politics, in Gramsci there is a demilitarization of war.[18] Nevertheless, this transition to a non-military conception of politics reaches a limit precisely at the point where it is argued that the *class* core of the new hegemony — and, of course, also of the old — remains constant throughout the entire process. In this sense, *there is* an element of continuity in the confrontation, and the metaphor of the two armies in struggle can retain part of its productivity.

Thus, Gramsci's thought appears suspended around a basic ambiguity concerning the status of the working class which finally leads it to a contradictory position. On the one hand, the political centrality of the working class has a historical, contingent character: it requires the class to come out of itself, to transform its own identity by articulating to it a plurality of struggles and democratic demands. On the other hand, it would seem that this articulatory role is assigned to it by the economic base — hence, that the centrality has a necessary character. One cannot avoid the feeling that the transition from a morphological and essentialist conception à la Labriola, to a radical historicist one,[19] has not been coherently accomplished.

At any event, if we compare Gramsci's thought with the various classical tendencies of Second International Marxism, the radical novelty of his concept of hegemony is quite evident. After the war, Kautsky[20] formulated a democratic conception of the transition to socialism which used the Bolshevik experience as a counter-model, responsible — in his view — for dictatorial practices that were inevitable if an attempt was made to bring about a transition to socialism in Russian-like conditions of backwardness. However, the alternative he proposed was to wait until the mythical laws of capitalist development simplified social antagonisms: the conditions would then exist for the dislocation between 'masses' and 'classes' to disappear, and with it any possible split between leaders and led. The Gramscian theory of hegemony, on the contrary, accepts social complexity as the very condition of political struggle and — through its threefold displacement of the Leninist theory of 'class alliances' — sets the basis for a democratic practice of politics, compatible with a plurality of historical subjects.[21]

As to Bernstein, Gramsci shares his affirmation of the primacy of politics, and his acceptance of a plurality of struggles and democratic demands irreducible to class belonging. But unlike Bernstein, for whom these separate struggles and demands are united only at an epochal level, through the intervention of a general law of progress, Gramsci has no room for a principle of *Entwicklung*. Struggles derive their meaning from their hegemonic articulation, and their progressive character — from a socialist point of view — is not assured in advance. History, therefore, is regarded not as an ascendant *continuum* of democratic reforms, but as a discontinuous series of hegemonic formations or historical blocs. In the terms of a distinction we drew earlier, Gramsci might share with Bernstein his 'revisionism', but certainly not his 'gradualism'.

With regard to Sorel, the situation is more complicated. Undoubtedly, in his concepts of 'bloc' and 'myth', Sorel breaks more radically than Gramsci with the essentialist vision of an underlying morphology of history. In this respect, and this alone, Gramsci's concept of historical bloc represents a step backwards. At the same time, however, Gramsci's perspective marks a clear advance on Sorel, for his theory of hegemony as articulation entails the idea of *democratic plurality*, while the Sorelian myth was simply destined to recreate the unity *of the class*. Successive versions of this myth sought to secure a radical line of partition within society, and never to construct, through a process of hegemonic reaggregation, a new integral State. The idea of a 'war of position' would have been radically alien to Sorel's perspective.

Social Democracy: From Stagnation to 'Planism'

The political and theoretical void which the turn to a hegemonic politics tried to fill, can also be found in the practice of the social-democratic parties after the First World War. In their case, the dislocation between strictly class tasks and the new political tasks of the movement took a characteristic form: that of a contradiction between the limited list of demands and proposals coming forth from the labour movement, and the diversity and complexity of the political problems confronted by a social democracy *thrown* into power as a result of the post-war crisis. This new and peculiar form of 'uneven and combined' development could not but set up paralysing political effects in social forces which had placed all their bets on the progressive development of the productive forces, with the proviso that this would lead to power only when the 'objective conditions' matured. The narrowly classist mentality of the social-democratic parties would here produce all its negative consequences. This was evident in the limited capacity of the social-democratic parties to hegemonize the broad range of democratic demands and antagonisms resulting from the post-war crisis. 'From the turn of the century until the end of the First World War, the European Socialist movement, under its cloak of a revolutionary party, was thus a mere parliamentary instrument of trade unionism. Its real activity was restricted to trade union problems, its constructive action to questions of wages and hours, social insurance, tariff problems and, at the most, suffrage reform. The struggle against militarism, and the prevention of the war, important as it was, was "incidental" to the main work of the party.'[22] This mentality was to dominate social-democratic activity as a whole between the end of the war and the Great Depression. In Germany, for example, from November 1918 onwards, most of the decrees passed by the Socialist Council of People's Commissars referred almost exclusively to trade union demands and reforms in the suffrage system; no attempt whatsoever was made to face up to key political and economic problems. This narrow classist mentality was also reflected in the total absence of a policy of radical democratization in those societies where the social democrats came to government. The classist mentality — reformist or revolutionary, it matters little — closed the road to the construction of a collective will articulating a variety of democratic demands and antagonisms within a new popular hegemonic bloc. Neither the Army nor the bureaucracy was subjected to any reform whatsoever. And as for foreign policy, the social-democratic governments — and, above all, socialist ministers participating in cabinets dominated by other political forces — restricted themselves to following the dominant tendencies without formulating any political alternative.

In the strictly economic field, the dominant policy of the post-war social democracies was one of nationalizations (called 'socializations'). In *Der Weg zum Sozialismus*,[23] Otto Bauer proposed a graduated series of nationalizations together with democratic management of the enterprises. Projects for nationalization appeared in a number of other countries, and in some of them like Germany, Britain and Sweden, commissions were set up to study socialization plans. Yet nothing came of this activity. 'Although social democrats formed or entered government in several countries, the global result of the first attempts at socialization was nil: with the exception of the French armament industry in 1936, not a single company was nationalized in Western Europe by a social-democratic government during the entire inter-war period.'[24] After the socialization fiasco, social democracy did not have the least alternative economic project until the Great Depression.

There are various reasons for this failure, but they all come down to two main factors. First, there was a lack of a hegemonic project: having renounced any attempt to articulate a broad front of democratic struggles, and aspiring instead merely to represent workers' interests, social democracy found itself powerless to alter the social and political logic of the State apparatuses. At this point, an option clearly emerged: either to participate in bourgeois cabinets in order to obtain the maximum number of social measures favourable to working-class sectors; or else, to enter into opposition and thereby to double one's impotence. The pressure-group character of trade union interests, typical of social democracy, nearly always imposed the first alternative.

There was, however, a second reason for the paralysis of social democracy with regard to any structural change: and this was the persistence of the Second International's economism, the view that the economy constituted a homogeneous space dominated by necessary laws, not susceptible to conscious regulation. A. Sturmthal perceptively comments: 'Oddly enough, the Radical Marxist tradition, still alive in Herman Müller and other right-wing leaders, increased their stubborn support of *laissez-faire*. The belief that "capitalism cannot be reformed" was part of the Marxist credo, designed at the beginning of the Socialist party to separate it from all middle-class reform movements. Capitalism was supposed to follow its own laws; only a Socialist revolution . . . would permit banishment of the evil social consequences of the old system. The obvious implication of this theory was the belief in revolutionary rather than democratic methods, but even when the socialist movement accepted democracy it did not completely abandon the basic ideology of its original theory. Capitalist government had to be administered according to this view, within the traditional framework of capitalist economy . . . Thus Herman Müller had the support of the Radicals, who otherwise held him in deep mistrust.'[25]

It was the Great Depression which forced a change in this perspective and, at the same time, gave a new basis for the redefinition of social-democratic politics. The 'planism' of the 1930s was the first expression of the new type of attitude. While creating a new welfare-state economic alternative, the implementation of Keynesianism allowed a universalist status to be granted to the interests of the workers, inasmuch as a high-wages policy became a stimulus for economic growth by contributing to the expansion of aggregate demand.[26]

Planism at its height — as it was formulated in the works of its main exponent Henri De Man[27] — was, however, more than a simple economic proposal: it was an attempt to recast the objectives of the socialist movement in a radically new, anti-economist version. All the elements we saw emerging in the crisis of the economist and reductionist version of Marxism are present in De Man: the critique of the rationalist conception of subjectivity based on economic 'interests' — he was one of the first socialists seriously to study psychoanalysis; the critique of class reductionism; the necessity of a mass bloc broader than the working class; the need to put forward socialism as a *national* alternative, as an organic reconstitution of the nation on a new basis; the requirement of a myth — in the Sorelian sense — which would cement the diverse components of a collective socialist will. The 'Plan' was, therefore, not a simple economistic instrument; it was the very axis for the reconstitution of a historical bloc which would make it possible to combat the decline of bourgeois society and to counter the advance of fascism. (The pro-fascist position which De Man personally adopted after 1938, and the similar evolution of Marcel Déat's socialists in France, should not make us forget the significance of planism as a real effort to regain the political initiative for socialism in the transformed social climate following the war and the Depression. Many of its themes became the common patrimony of social democracy after 1945 — particularly its economic-technocratic aspects; while its more radical and renovating political insights tended in the main to be cast aside.)

In this respect, it is instructive to recall a frequently noted ambiguity[28] which goes to the heart of the limitations of social-democratic politics after World War II. The project of the left-wing supporters of planism was to establish a mixed economy in which the capitalist sector would gradually disappear; thus, it was in effect a road of transition to socialism. For a more technocratic variant, however, the point was merely to create an area of state intervention which would correct — particularly through the control of credit — the imbalances inherent in the course of capitalism. The terms of this alternative show very clearly that both the left and right alternatives related to *economic policy*; while projects for radical democratization and the construction of a new collective will were either absent or occupied a marginal position. Before 1945 it was the inveterate classism of the social-democratic movements which barred any attempt at hegemonic articulation. After 1945 — with the creation of the Welfare State — this classism slackened considerably, not of course in the direction of a deepening of the democratic process, but simply through the expansion of a Keynesian State in which the interests of the different sectors were no longer defined along clear-cut class lines. In this sense, social democracy became a politico-economic alternative *within* a given State form, and not a radical alternative to that form. (Here we are evidently referring not to a 'revolutionary' alternative, involving the violent overthrow of the existing State, but to a deepening and articulation of a variety of antagonisms, within both the State and civil society, which allows a 'war of position' against the dominant hegemonic forms.) As a result of this absence of a hegemonic alternative, social democracy reduced itself to a combination of, on the one hand, privileged pragmatic relations with the trade unions and, on the other, more or less left-wing technocratic policies, which in any case made everything dependent upon solutions implemented at a State level. This is the root of the absurd notion according to which the degree of 'leftness' of a programme is gauged by the number of companies it proposes to nationalize.

The Last Redoubt of Essentialism: the Economy

Our earlier analysis can be seen from two different perspectives which are, strictly speaking, complementary. From a first point of view, the picture we have presented is of a process of splits and fragmentations through which the disaggregation of the orthodox paradigm took place. But the space occupied by this paradigm does not remain empty: from a second point of view, the same process can be seen as the emergence and expansion of the new articulatory and recomposing logic of hegemony. We saw, however, that this expansion met a limit. Whether the working class is considered as the political leader in a class alliance (Lenin) or as the articulatory core of a historical bloc (Gramsci), its fundamental identity is constituted in a terrain different from that in which the hegemonic practices operate. Thus, there is a threshold which none of the strategic-hegemonic conceptions manages to cross. If the validity of the economist paradigm is maintained in a certain instance — last though decisive, as it is the rational substratum of history — it is accorded a necessity such that hegemonic articulations can be conceived only as mere contingency. This final rational stratum, which gives a tendential sense to all historical processes, has a specific location in the topography of the social: at the economic level.

The economic level, however, must satisfy three very precise conditions in order to play this role of constituting the subjects of hegemonic practices. *Firstly*, its laws of motion must be strictly endogenous and exclude all indeterminacy resulting from political or other external interventions — otherwise, the constitutive function could not refer exclusively to the economy. *Secondly*, the unity and homogeneity of social agents, constituted at the economic level, must result from the very laws of motion of this level (any fragmentation and dispersion of positions requiring an instance of recomposition external to the economy is excluded). *Thirdly*, the position of these agents in the relations of production must endow them with 'historical interests', so that the presence of such agents at other social levels — through mechanisms of 'representation' or 'articulation' — must ultimately be explained on the basis of economic interests. The latter are, therefore, not restricted to a determinate social sphere, but are the anchorage for a globalizing perspective on society.

Even those Marxist tendencies which struggled hardest to overcome economism and reductionism mantained, in one way or another, that essentialist conception of the structuring of economic space which we have just described. Thus, the debate between economist and anti-economist tendencies within Marxism was necessarily reduced to the secondary problem of the weight that should be attached to the superstructures in the determination of historical processes. Yet the most 'superstructuralist' of conceptions retained a naturalist vision of the economy — even when it attempted to limit the area of its effects. In the remainder of this chapter we will probe this last redoubt of orthodox essentialism. Referring to certain contemporary debates, we will attempt to demonstrate that the space of the economy is itself structured as a political space, and that in it, as in any other 'level' of society, those practices we characterized as hegemonic are fully operative. Before we embark on this task, however, it is necessary to distinguish two very different problems which have frequently been confused in the critique of economism: the first refers to the nature and constitution of the economic space; the second, *which has no relation whatsoever with the first,* concerns the relative weight of the economic space in the determination of social processes external to itself. The first is the decisive problem, and constitutes the ground for a radical break with essentialist paradigms. The second, for reasons we will attempt to clarify in this book, cannot be determined at the level of a general theorization of the social. (To assert that what occurs at *all* levels of society *in a given conjuncture* is absolutely determined by what happens at the level of the economy, is not — strictly speaking — logically incompatible with an anti-economist response to our first question.)

Our three conditions for the ultimate constitution of hegemonic subjects by the economic level correspond to three basic theses of classical Marxist theory: the condition regarding the endogenous character of the laws of motion of the economy corresponds to the thesis of the neutrality of the productive forces; the condition of the unity of social agents at the economic level, to the thesis of the growing homogenization and impoverishment of the working class; and the condition that the relations of production should be the *locus* of 'historical interests' transcending the economic sphere, to the thesis that the working class has a fundamental interest in socialism. We will now attempt to demonstrate that these three theses are false.

For Marxism, the development of the productive forces plays the key role in the historical evolution towards socialism, given that 'the past development of the productive forces makes socialism possible, and their future development makes socialism necessary.'[29] They are at the root of the formation of an ever more numerous and exploited proletariat, whose historical mission is to take possession of, and collectively manage, highly socialized and developed productive forces. At present, the capitalist relations of production constitute an insurmountable obstacle to the advance of these productive forces. The contradiction between bourgeoisie and proletariat is, therefore, the social and political expression of a primal economic contradiction, one which combines a general law of development of the productive forces with the laws of development specific to the capitalist mode of production. According to this view, if history has a sense and a rational substratum, it is due to the general law of development of the productive forces. Hence, the economy may be understood as a mechanism of society acting upon objective phenomena independently of human action.

Now, in order that this general law of development of the productive forces may have full validity, it is necessary that all the elements intervening in the productive process be submitted to its determinations. To ensure this, Marxism had to resort to a fiction: it conceived of labour-power as a commodity. Sam Bowles and Herbert Gintis have shown how this fiction would make Marxism blind to a whole series of characteristics of labour-power as an element of the process of capitalist production. Labour-power differs from the other necessary elements of production in that the capitalist must do more than simply purchase it; he must also make it produce labour. This essential aspect, however, escapes the conception of labour-power as a commodity whose use-value is labour. For if it were merely a commodity like the others, its use-value could obviously be made automatically effective from the very moment of its purchase. 'The designation of labour as the use-value of labour-power to capital obscures the absolutely fundamental distinction between productive inputs *embodied in people capable of social practices* and all those remaining inputs for whom ownership by capital is sufficient to secure the "consumption" of their productive services.'[30] A large part of the capitalist organization of labour can be understood only as a result of the necessity to extract labour from the labour-power purchased by the capitalist. The evolution of the productive forces becomes unintelligible if this need of the capitalist to exercise his domination at the very heart of the labour process is not understood. This, of course, calls into question the whole idea of the development of the productive forces as a natural, spontaneously progressive phenomenon. We can therefore see that both elements of the economist viewpoint — labour power as a commodity, and the development of the productive forces as a neutral process — reinforce each other. Little wonder that the study of the labour process was for long depreciated within the Marxist tradition.

It was the publication of Braverman's *Labour and Monopoly Capital*[31] which finally triggered off the debate. It defends the thesis that the guiding principle of technology under capitalism is the separation of conception and execution, producing ever more degraded and 'deskilled' labour. Taylorism is the decisive moment in this struggle of the capitalists to dominate the workers and control the labour process. Braverman postulates that it is the law of capital accumulation which lies behind the need of capital to wrest control of the labour process from the direct producer; he, however, fails to provide a real explanation why this is expressed through an unceasing effort to destroy the skills of the workers and to reduce them to mere performers. Above all, he presents this logic of domination as an omnipotent force — operating apparently without trammels — as if the economic forces available to capital did not permit the working class to resist and influence the course of development. Here, the old notion of labour-power as commodity, entirely subject to the logic of capital, continues to produce its effects.

Contrary to Braverman's argument, the critique of the notion of labour-power as a commodity whose use-value is labour allows us to understand capital's need to control the labour process. The fact is that once labour-power is purchased, the maximum possible labour has to be extracted from it. Hence the labour process cannot exist without a series of relations of domination. Hence, too, well before the advent of monopoly capitalism, the capitalist organization of labour had to be both a technique of production and a technique of domination. This aspect has been stressed in a number of works, such as those by Stephen Marglin and Katherine Stone,[32] who argue that the fragmentation and specialization of labour bear no relation whatsoever to a supposed need for efficiency, but are instead the effect of capital's need to exercise its domination over the labour process. Since the worker is capable of social practices, he could resist the imposed control mechanisms and force the capitalist to use different techniques. Thus, it is not a pure logic of capital which determines the evolution of the labour process; the latter is not merely the place where capital exerts its domination, but the ground of a struggle.

A number of recent studies, undertaken in Western Europe and the United States, have analysed the evolution of the labour process from the point of view of the relation of forces between workers and capitalists, and of the workers' resistance. These reveal the presence of a 'politics of production', and challenge the idea that the development of capitalism is the effect solely of the laws of competition and the exigencies of accumulation. Richard Edwards, in *Contested Terrain*,[33] distinguishes three main forms of control: simple control based on vigilance; technical control, corresponding to the subordination of the worker to the rhythm of the machine as found on the assembly line; and finally, bureaucratic control — manifesting itself through the institutionalization of hierarchical power — by which control depends no longer on the physical structure of the labour process, as in the previous case, but on its social structure. He maintains that the workers' resistance explains the need for capital to experiment with new forms. Similarly, Jean-Paul Gaudemar isolates four cycles of technological domination in the case of France: '*a "panoptic" cycle; a cycle of extensive disciplining* (in the factory *and* outside the factory); a cycle founded on a twofold process involving internalization of discipline within a labour process remodelled on mechanization, a cycle which I propose to call *cycle of mechanist discipline;* finally, *a cycle of contractual discipline,* in which the internalization of discipline proceeds by formal and real modes of a partial delegation of power.'[34] For its part, the Italian *operaista* current of the sixties demonstrated how the development of capital, far from blindly imposing its logic on the working class, is subordinated to the latter's struggle. Mario Tronti,[35] for example, points out that working-class struggles have forced capital to modify its internal composition and forms of domination — for, by imposing a limit on the working day, they have compelled capital to pass from absolute to relative surplus value. This leads Panzieri to uphold the thesis that production is a 'political mechanism', and that it is necessary to analyse 'technology and the organization of labour as establishing a relation of forces among classes.'[36] The idea common to these works is that specific historical forms of capitalist control have to be studied as part of overall social relations, given that the changing organizational forms of the labour process cannot be understood merely in terms of the difference between absolute and relative surplus value. Moreover, a comparative historical analysis reveals important differences among the various countries. The strength of trade unions in Britain, for example, has made possible a greater resistance to change than elsewhere.

Workers' struggles, understood in these terms, obviously cannot be explained by an endogenous logic of capitalism, since their very dynamism cannot be subsumed under the 'commodity' form of labour-power. But if this split between a logic of capital and a logic of workers' resistance influences the organization of the capitalist labour process, it must also crucially affect the character and rhythm of expansion of the productive forces. Thus, the thesis that the productive forces are neutral, and that their development can be conceived as natural and unilinear, is entirely unfounded. This also removes the only ground on which the economy could be understood as an autonomous and self-regulated universe. The first condition, therefore, of the exclusive privilege granted to the economic sphere in the constitution of social agents, is not fulfilled.

This conclusion should already make us suspect that the second condition is also not fulfilled, as the economy could hardly constitute subjects unified by a single logic which it does not itself possess. Nevertheless, it is important to explore the variegated decentring of the diverse positions of the 'working class' subject. In the first place, the very concept of working class in Marx covers two distinct relations with their own laws of motion: the wage relation established through the sale of labour-power — which turns the worker into a proletarian; and that resulting from the worker's location in the labour process — which makes him a manual worker. This dichotomy underpins the pregnant distinction drawn by Michael Burawoy[37] between relations *of* production and relations *in* production. If for Marx the distinction is not evident, it is not only because the two sets of relations tended to coincide in his immediate historical experience; but also because, seeing labour-power as a simple commodity, he tended to withdraw all autonomy and relevance from the relations established in the labour process. It does, however, remain clear that both relations have evolved in a different manner, making problematic the common 'working class' label which united them: whereas the wage form has become generalized in advanced capitalism, the class of industrial workers has declined in numbers and importance. This dysymmetry is at the root of the ambiguities which have dominated recent debate on the limits of the working class.

Once the theory of impoverishment proved untenable as a specific mechanism for the constitution of working-class unity, two new attempts were made to find an economic basis for such unity: one centred on the phenomenon of 'deskilling' (Braverman), while the other sought to identify a more restricted core of workers who would constitute the 'true' working class (Poulantzas). Braverman, starting from his analysis of Taylorism, argues that the degradation of labour resulting from the separation between conception and execution brings ever broader strata of workers — be they employed by the commodity-producing sectors or not — within the category of the proletarianized working class.[38] According to him, the polarization foreseen by Marx is therefore in the process of fulfilment, and the ongoing degradation of its labour conditions will push the working class to organize itself and struggle politically against the system. However, few studies dealing with the North American working class share Braverman's homogenization thesis. On the contrary, the general tendency is to insist on the division and fragmentation of the working class. The works of Edwards, Gordon and Reich[39] demonstrate, for example, how the forms of control in the labour process, combined with racism and sexism, have created a segmentation of the labour market which has crystallized in the fractioning of the working class.[40] Similar work in Western Europe[41] also vitiates the thesis of a progressive simplification of the social structure and confirms that the current general tendency is towards a polarization between two sectors of the economy: a well-paid and protected general sector, and a peripheral sector of unskilled or semi-skilled workers for whom no security exists. If we add a third sector, that of the structurally unemployed whose number is constantly growing, it becomes apparent that the thesis of homogenization truly cannot be sustained. Furthermore, deskilling does not display the general character attributed to it by Braverman: although it is increasing in some sectors, there is also a parallel process of the creation of new skills.

Furthermore, the creation of a dual labour-power market must be related to the different capitalist strategies to combat shopfloor resistance and cannot be seen as a simple effect of capitalist development. Thus Andrew Friedman has shown how in the British case, capitalists employ various strategies according to the capacity of the different groups of workers to resist their authority.[42] Within a given country and within the same company, a distinction may be drawn between central and peripheral workers, belonging to different labour markets, whose wages and working conditions reflect their unequal capacity for resistance. Women and immigrants are generally situated in the unprotected market. Friedman, however, sees this segmentation not as the result of a conspiracy to divide the working class, but as the consequence of relations of force in which the unions themselves play an important role. The divisions within the working class are therefore more deeply rooted than many wish to allow; and they are, to a certain extent, the result of the workers' own practices. They are political, and not merely economic divisions.

It is impossible to talk today about homogeneity of the working class, and a fortiori to trace it to a mechanism inscribed in the logic of capitalist accumulation. In order to maintain the idea of a workers' identity around common interests, derived from a class insertion in the relations of production, the second tendency we mentioned earlier has therefore attempted to locate the *true* working class by means of a more restricted definition. The reality of fragmentation is fully accepted, and the unitary identity is attributed to one of the fragments. In this respect, it is instructive to examine the debate which opposed Erik Olin Wright to Nicos Poulantzas.[43] According to Poulantzas, productive labour is the criterion for identifying the limits of the working class,[44] and unproductive waged workers constitute a 'new petty bourgeoisie'. The heterogeneity of the sectors included in this category does not create a special problem for Poulantzas. Since, in his view, classes cannot be defined only at the economic level, and since the old and the new petty bourgeoisie occupy the same ideological position with regard to the proletariat and the bourgeoisie, he feels quite justified in bracketing them in the same class category. This approach has been criticized by Eric Olin Wright, who rejects not only Poulantzas's definition of productive labour, but also the very idea that such a criterion could serve to define the limits of the working class. His argument is that the distinction between productive and unproductive labour does not in any way imply that unproductive workers have different class interests and are not concerned with socialism. He states: 'For two positions within the social division of labour to be placed in different classes on the basis of economic criteria implies that they have fundamentally different class *interests* at the economic level.'[45] The solution he offers is to make a distinction between 'ambiguous' and 'non-ambiguous' class positions. The latter characterize the proletariat, the bourgeoisie and the petty bourgeoisie.[46] Together with these three non-ambiguous positions, Wright distinguishes what he calls 'contradictory class locations', half-way between the two non-ambiguous positions. Where the economic criteria are contradictory, ideological and political struggle will play a determinant role in the definition of class interests.

The reason for this Diogenes-like search for the 'true' working class is, of course, political: the object is to determine that category of workers whose *economic* interests link them directly to a socialist perspective, and who are therefore destined to lead the anti-capitalist struggle. The problem, however, with these approaches which start from a restricted definition of the working class, is that they are still based on the concept of 'objective interest' — a concept which lacks any theoretical basis whatsoever, and involves little more than an arbitrary attribution of interests, by the analyst, to a certain category of social agents. In the classical view, class unity was constructed around interests, but it was not a datum of the social structure; it was a *process* of unification, resulting from the impoverishment and proletarianization which went hand in hand with the development of the productive forces. Braverman's homogenization through *deskilling* belongs to the same explanatory level. The *objective* interests were *historical* interests, insofar as they depended upon a rational and necessary movement of history accessible to scientific knowledge. What cannot be done is to abandon the eschatological conception of history, and to retain a notion of 'objective interest' which only has sense within the former. Both Poulantzas and Wright seem to assume that the fragmentation of the working class is a fragmentation of positions *among diverse* social agents. Neither pays heed to a more substantial reality of which classical Marxism was well aware: namely, that a fragmentation of positions exists *within* the social agents themselves, and that these therefore lack an ultimate rational identity. The tension between economic and political struggle — and theoretical analyses of working-class 'embourgeoisement' or Bernstein's assertion that through the progress of democracy the worker ceases to be a proletarian and becomes a citizen, etc. — implied that the working class was dominated by a plurality of weakly integrated and frequently contradictory subject positions. Here, the alternative is clear: either one has a theory of history according to which this contradictory plurality will be eliminated and an absolutely united working class will become transparent to itself at the moment of proletarian chiliasm — in which case its 'objective interests' can be determined from the very beginning; or else, one abandons that theory and, with it, any basis for privileging certain subject positions over others in the determination of the 'objective' interests of the agent as a whole — in which case this latter notion becomes meaningless. In our view, in order to advance in the determination of social antagonisms, it is necessary to analyse the plurality of diverse and frequently contradictory positions, and to discard the idea of a perfectly unified and homogenous agent, such as the 'working class' of classical discourse. The search for the 'true' working class and its limits is a false problem, and as such lacks any theoretical or political relevance.

Evidently, this implies not that working class and socialism are incompatible, but the very different statement that fundamental interests in socialism cannot be *logically* deduced from determinate positions in the economic process. The opposite view — that such a link is provided by the workers' interest in preventing capitalist absorption of the economic surplus — would only be valid if one further assumed (a) that the worker is a homo *oeconomicus* who tries to maximize the economic surplus just as much as the capitalist; or b) that he is a spontaneously cooperative being, who aspires to the social distribution of his labour product. Even then, however, neither of these barely plausible hypotheses would supply the requisite proof, for there is no logical connection whatsoever between positions in the relations of production and the mentality of the producers. The workers' resistance to certain forms of domination will depend upon the position they occupy within the ensemble of social relations, and not only in those of production. At this point, it is obvious that our last two conditions for the agents of hegemony to be exclusively constituted by the economic sphere — that they should be fully constituted as subjects within that space, and that they should be endowed with 'historical interests' derived from their class positions — are not fulfilled either.

Facing the Consequences

Let us draw the conclusions. It is not the case that the field of the economy is a self-regulated space subject to endogenous laws; nor does there exist a constitutive principle for social agents which can be fixed in an ultimate class core; nor are class positions the necessary location of historical interests. From this point, the implications quickly follow. Since Kautsky, Marxism knew that the socialist determination of the working class does not arise spontaneously but depends upon the political mediation of intellectuals. Such mediation, however, was not conceived as *articulation* — that is to say, as a *political construction* from dissimilar elements. It had an epistemological basis: socialist intellectuals *read* in the working class its objective destiny. In Gramsci politics is finally conceived as articulation, and through his concept of historical bloc a profound and radical complexity is introduced into the theorization of the social. Yet even for Gramsci, the ultimate core of the hegemonic subject's identity is constituted at a point external to the space it articulates: the logic of hegemony does not unfold all of its deconstructive effects on the theoretical terrain of classical Marxism. We have witnessed, however, the fall of this last redoubt of class reductionism, insofar as the very unity and homogeneity of class subjects has split into a set of precariously integrated positions which, once the thesis of the neutral character of the productive forces is abandoned, cannot be referred to any necessary point of future unification. The logic of hegemony, as a logic of articulation and contingency, has come to determine the very identity of the hegemonic subjects. A number of consequences follow from this, representing as many starting points for our subsequent analysis.

   1. Unfixity has become the condition of every social identity. The fixity of every social element in the first theorizations of hegemony

proceeded, as we saw, from the indissoluble link between the hege-monized task and the class that was supposed to be its natural agent; while the bond between the task and the class which hegemonized it was merely factual or contingent. But, insofar as the task has ceased to have any *necessary* link with a class, its identity is given to it solely by its articulation within a hegemonic formation. Its identity, then, has become purely relational. And as this system of relations has itself ceased to be fixed and stable — thereby making hegemonic practices possible — the sense of every social identity appears con-stantly deferred. The moment of the 'final' suture never arrives. With this, however, not only does the very category of necessity fall, but it is no longer possible to account for the hegemonic relation in terms of pure contingency, as the space which made intelligible the necessary/contingent opposition has dissolved. The idea that the hegemonic link could be grasped theoretically through a mere nar-rative exercise proves to have been a mirage. The link must instead be defined in terms of new theoretical categories whose status, insofar as they attempt to apprehend a type of relation that never manages to be identical to itself, constitutes a problem.

2. Let us briefly refer to the *dimensions* in which this unfixity of the social produces its effects. The first belongs to the terrain of political subjectivity. We have seen that in Rosa Luxemburg, the symbolic dimension linking the different antagonisms and political points of rupture was the matrix of new social forces — the ones Gramsci was to call 'collective wills'. This logic of the symbolic constitution of the social encountered precise limits in the persistence, at a morpho-logical level, of the economist conception of history. Once this has been dissolved, however, the overflowing of class bounds by the various forms of social protest can freely operate. (*Freely,* that is, of any a priori class character of struggles or demands — obviously not in the sense that *every* articulation is possible in a given conjuncture.) If this is the case, however, three important consequences can be derived for our analysis. **The first** refers to the link between socialism and concrete social agents. We have demonstrated that there is no logical and necessary relation between socialist objectives and the positions of social agents in the relations of production; and that the articulation between them is external and does not proceed from any *natural* movement of each to unite with the other. In other words, their articulation must be regarded as a hegemonic relation. It follows that, from the socialist point of view, the direction of the workers' struggle is not uniformly progressive: it depends, *just as with any other social struggle,* upon its forms of articulation within a

given hegemonic context. For the same reason, a variety of other points of rupture and democratic antagonisms can be articulated to a socialist 'collective will' *on an equal footing* with workers' demands. The era of 'privileged subjects' — in the ontological, not practical sense — of the anti-capitalist struggle has been definitively superseded. **The second consequence** refers to the nature of the 'new social movements', which have been so much discussed during the last decade. Here, the two dominant tendencies of thought are incompatible with our theoretical position. The first approaches the nature and efficacy of these movements within a problematic of the privileged subject of socialist change: thus, they are considered either as marginal or peripheral with regard to the working class (the fundamental subject in the orthodox view) or as a revolutionary substitute for a working class which has been integrated into the system (Marcuse). Everything we have said so far, however, indicates that there are no privileged points for the unleashing of a socialist political practice; this hinges upon a 'collective will' that is laboriously constructed from a number of dissimilar points. Nor can we agree, therefore, with the other dominant tendency in the discussion of new social movements, which consists in a priori affirmation of their progressive nature. The political meaning of a local community movement, of an ecological struggle, of a sexual minority movement, is not given from the beginning: it crucially depends upon its hegemonic articulation with other struggles and demands. **The third consequence** refers to the form of conceiving the relation among different subject positions, which our analysis has tended to de-totalize. However, were the decentring operation to be concluded at this point, we would only have managed to affirm a new form of fixity: that of the various decentred subject positions. If these themselves are not fixed, it is clear that a logic of de-totalization cannot simply affirm the *separation* of different struggles and demands, and that the articulation cannot just be conceived as the linkage of dissimilar and fully constituted elements. It is here that the radicalization of the concept of 'overdetermination' will give us the key to the specific logic of social articulations.

3. The logic of our analysis would seem, however, to imply that the very notion of 'hegemony' should be put into question. The discursive areas of the emergence and validity of this category were originally limited to the theoretical terrain of a split. A class constituted at the level of essences was confronted with historical contingencies forcing it to take on tasks alien to its own nature. But we have seen, on the one hand, that this split could not survive the

collapse of the distinction between these two planes; and, on the other, that insofar as there was an advance in a democratic direction, the hegemonized task altered the identity of the hegemonic subject. Does this mean that 'hegemony' was merely a transitional concept, a moment in the dissolution of the essentialist discourse, and unable to outlive it? In the next two chapters we will attempt to show that this is not an adequate answer, and that the tensions inherent in the concept of hegemony are also inherent in every political practice and, strictly speaking, every social practice.

Notes to Chapter Two

1. The concept of 'suture', which we will be using frequently, is taken from psychoanalysis. Its explicit formulation is attributed to Jacques-Alain Miller ('Suture elements of the logic of the signifier', *Screen,* Winter 1977/78, vol. 18, no. 4, pp. 24–34), although it implicity operates in the whole of Lacanian theory. It is used to designate the production of the subject on the basis of the chain of its discourse; that is, of the non-correspondence between the subject and the Other — the symbolic — which prevents the closure of the latter as a full presence. (Hence, the constitution of the unconscious as *edge* operating the junction/division between the subject and the Other.) 'Suture names the relation of the subject to the chain of its discourse; we shall see that it figures there as the element which is lacking, in the form of a stand-in. For while there lacking, it is not purely and simply absent. Suture, by extension — the general relation of lack to the structure of which it is an element, inasmuch as it implies the position of a taking-the-place of' (Miller, pp. 25-6). This moment of lack is, however, only one aspect. In a second aspect, suture implies a filling-in. As Stephen Heath points out, 'suture names not just a structure of lack but also an availability of the subject, a certain closure . . . It is not surprising . . ., therefore, that Lacan's own use of the term "suture" . . . gives it sense of a "pseudo-identification", defines it as "function of the imaginary and the symbolic". . . . The stake is clear: the "I" is a division but joins all the same, the stand-in is the lack in the structure, but nevertheless simultaneously, the possibility of a coherence, of the *filling* in' (S. Heath, 'Notes on Suture', *Screen,* pp. 55-6). It is this double movement that we will attempt to stress in our extension of the concept of suture to the field of politics. Hegemonic practices are suturing insofar as their field of operation is determined by the openness of the social, by the ultimately unfixed character of every signifier. This original lack is precisely what the hegemonic practices try to fill in. A *totally* sutured society would be one where this filling-in would have reached its ultimate consequences and would have, therefore, managed to identify itself with the transparency of a closed symbolic order. Such a closure of the social is, as we will see, impossible.
2. In the sense in which Jacques Derrida has talked about a 'logic of the supplement'. The supplementary of the 'indeterminate' disappears, of course, if the link between the specificity and the necessity of the 'determinate' is broken. We have seen that this is what happens with Sorel's myth. In that case, however, the only terrain that made possible the emergence of the dualism, also disappears.
3. P. Anderson, pp. 15ff.
4. Concerning the initial formulation of Trotsky's thesis of permanent revolution,

see A. Brossat, *Aux origines de la révolution permanente: la pensée politique du jeune Trotsky*, Paris 1974; and Michael Löwy, *The Politics of Combined and Uneven Development*, London 1981, chapter 2.

5. L. Trotsky, *1905*, London 1971, pp. 333, 339.

6. 'There are no miracles in nature or history, but every abrupt turn in history, and this applies to every revolution, presents such a wealth of content, unfolds such unexpected and specific combinations of forms of struggle and alignment of forces of the contestants, that to the lay mind there is much that must appear miraculous . . . That the revolution succeeded so quickly and — seemingly, at the first superficial glance — so radically, is only due to the fact that, as extremely unique historical situation, *absolutely dissimilar currents, absolutely heterogeneous* class interests, *absolutely contrary* political and social strivings have *merged* and in a strikingly "harmonious" manner.' Lenin, *Letters from Afar*, First Letter. The First Stage of the First Revolution', *Collected Works*, vol. 23, pp. 297, 302.

7. 'The mechanics of political democracy works in the same direction. Nothing in our times can be done without elections; nothing can be done without the masses. And in this era of printing and parliamentarism it is *impossible* to gain the following of the masses without a widely ramified, systematically managed, well-equipped system of flattery, lies, fraud, juggling with fashionable and popular catchwords, and promising all manner of reforms and blessings to the workers right and left — as long as they renounce the revolutionary struggle for the overthrow of the bourgeoisie. I would call this system Lloyd-Georgism after the English minister Lloyd George, one of the foremost and most dexterous representatives of this system in the classic land of the "bourgeois labour party". A first-class bourgeois manipulator, an astute politician, a popular orator who will deliver any speeches you like, even revolutionary ones, to a labour audience, and a man who is capable of obtaining sizeable sops for docile workers in the shape of social reforms (insurance, etc.), Lloyd George serves the bourgeoisie splendidly, and serves it precisely *among* the workers, brings its influence *precisely* to the proletariat, to where the bourgeoisie needs it most and where it finds it most difficult to subject the masses morally.' Lenin, 'Imperialism and the Split of Socialism', *Collected Works*, vol. 23, p. 117-8.

8. *Pyatyi vsemirnyi Kongress Komunisticheskogo Internatsionala. 17 iuniya-8 iuliya 1924 g. Stenograficheskii otchet*, Moscow-Leningrad 1925, I, pp. 482-3. Quoted in M. Hájek, 'La bolscevizzazione dei partiti comunisti', in E.J. Hobsbawm et al., eds., *Storia*, Turin 1980, vol. 3, p. 468.

9. Cf. E. Laclau, *Politics and Ideology in Marxist Theory*, London 1977, pp. 138ff.

10. Cf. especially Ch. Buci-Glucksmann, *Gramsci and the State*, London 1980.

11. B. de Giovanni, 'Lenin and Gramsci: State, Politics and Party', in Ch. Mouffe, ed., *Gramsci and Marxist Theory*, London 1979, pp. 259-288. For a critique of de Giovanni's conception, see Ch. Mouffe's introduction to that volume.

12. A. Gramsci, 'Notes on the Southern Question', in *Selections from Political Writings 1921-26*, ed. and trans. Q. Hoare, London 1978, p. 443.

13. With regard to the relationship between hegemony, ideology and state in Gramsci, see Ch. Mouffe, 'Hegemony and Ideology in Gramsci', in *Gramsci and Marxist Theory*, pp. 168-204; and Ch. Mouffe, 'Hegemony and the Integral State in Gramsci: Towards a New Concept of Politics', in G. Bridges and R. Brunt, eds., *Silver Linings: Some Strategies for the Eighties*, London 1981.

14. A. Gramsci, *Quaderni dal Carcere*, ed. V. Gerratana, Turin 1975, vol. 2, p. 349.

15. Ibid., p. 1058.

16. Ibid., vol. 3, p. 1875.

17. See the essays contained in the volume *Clausewitz en el pensamiento marxista*,

Mexico 1979, in particular the work by Clemente Ancona, 'La influencia de *De la Guerra* de Clausewitz en el pensamiento marxista de Marx a Lenin', pp. 7-38. These essays refer, however, more to the relationship between war and politics than to the political metaphorization of military notions.

18. In a literal sense, which includes armed confrontations themselves. From Mao onwards, 'people's war' is conceived as a process of constitution of a mass 'collective will', wherein the military aspects are subordinate to the political ones. 'War of position', therefore, transcends the alternative armed struggle/peaceful struggle.

19. Althusser has wrongly assimilated Gramscian 'absolute historicism' to the other forms of 'leftism' of the twenties, such as the works of Lukács and Korsch. Elsewhere, we have argued (see E. Laclau, 'Togliatti and Politics', *Politics and Power* 2, London 1980, pp. 251-258) that this assimilation rests on a misunderstanding, insofar as what Gramsci calls 'absolute historicism' is precisely the radical rejection of any essentialism and of any a priori teleology, and it is, therefore, incompatible with the notion of 'false consciousness'. On the specificity of Gramsci's intervention in this regard, see C. Buci-Glucksmann, op. cit.

20. An adequate study of the positions adopted by Kautsky after the war, particularly with regard to the October revolution, can be found in A. Bergounioux and B. Manin, *La social-démocratie ou le compromis*, Paris 1979, pp. 73-104.

21. This is why the critique undertaken by M. Salvadori ('Gramsci and the PCI: Two Conceptions of Hegemony', in *Gramsci and Marxist Theory*, pp. 237-258) to the theoreticians of the Italian Communist Party, is so unconvincing. According to this critique, Eurocommunism could not legitimately claim the Gramscian tradition as the source of its democratic strategy, for Gramsci's thought continues to attribute an essential importance to the moment of rupture and seizure of power. Gramsci would, thus, constitute the highest moment of a Leninism adapted to the conditions of Western Europe. There is no doubt that for Gramsci 'war of position' is merely a prelude to 'war of movement'; yet, this does not justify talking about a 'structural Leninism' in Gramsci. This would only be justified if the alternative reform/ revolution, peaceful/violent road, was the only relevant distinction; but, as we have seen, the totality of Gramscian thought moves in the direction of withdrawing the importance and eliminating the absolute character of this alternative. In more important aspects, neither the Gramscian conception of political subjectivity, nor its form of conceptualizing the hegemonic links, is compatible with the Leninist theory of 'class alliance'.

22. A. Sturmthal, *The Tragedy of European Labour, 1918-1939*, London 1944, p. 23. This early work is a highly penetrating attempt to establish a relation between the limits of Social Democratic politics and the corporative mentality of the unions.

23. Vienna 1919.

24. A. Przeworski, 'Social Democracy as a Historical Phenomenon', *New Left Review*, no. 122, July-August 1980, p. 48.

25. A. Sturmthal, pp. 39-40.

26. A. Przeworski, 'Social Democracy', p. 52.

27. Cf. particularly *Au-delà du marxisme* (1927) and *L'Idée socialiste* (1933).

28. See, for example, A. Bergounioux and B. Manin, pp. 118-120.

29. G.A. Cohen, *Karl Marx's Theory of History*, Oxford 1978, p. 206.

30. S. Bowles and H. Gintis, 'Structure and Practice in the Labour Theory of Value', *Review of Radical Political Economics*, vol. 12, no. 4, p. 8. This idea had already been criticized by Castoriadis in a 1961 article, 'Le mouvement révolutionnaire sous le capitalisme moderne', *Capitalisme moderne et révolution*, Paris 1979, vol. 1.

31. H.B. Braverman, *Labour and Monopoly Capital. The Degradation of Work in the*

Twentieth Century, New York 1974.

32. S. Marglin, 'What do Bosses Do?', *Review of Radical Political Economics*, vol. 6, no. 2, 1974; K. Stone, 'The Origins of Job Structure in the Steel Industry', *Review*, vol. 6, no. 2, 1974.

33. R. Edwards, *Contested Terrain: the Transformation of the Workplace in the Twentieth Century*, New York 1979.

34. Jean P. de Gaudemar, *L'ordre et la production. Naissance et formes de la discipline d'usine*, Paris 1982, p. 24.

35. M. Tronti, *Ouvriers et capital*, Paris 1977, p. 106.

36. Panzieri, quoted by B. Coriat, 'L'operaïsme italien', *Dialectiques*, no. 30, p. 96.

37. M. Burawoy, 'Terrains of Contest: Factory and State under Capitalism and Socialism', *Socialist Review*, no. 58.

38. Braverman, passim.

39. D. Gordon, R. Edwards and M. Reich, *Segmented Work, Divided Workers*, Cambridge 1982.

40. They distinguish the existence of three labour markets corresponding to three different sections of the working class. The first includes most occupations of a professional type. It is the domain of the middle sectors who enjoy stable employment with possibilities of promotion and of relatively high salaries. These characteristics can also be found in the first subordinate market, with the difference that the workers of this sector — the 'traditional' working class together with the semi-skilled workers of the tertiary sector — only possess specific skills acquired in the enterprise, and that their work is repetitive and tied to the rhythm of the machines. Thirdly, we encounter the 'secondary market' with its unskilled workers, having no possibilities of promotion, without employment security and with low wages. These workers are not unionized, the turnover is quick and the proportion of blacks and women is very high.

41. See, for example, M. Paci, *Mercato del Lavoro e classi sociali in Italia: Ricerche sulla composizione del proletariato*, Bologna 1973. For a more general perspective on industrial societies, see S. Berger and M. Piore, *Dualism and Discontinuity in Industrial Societies*, Cambridge 1980.

42. A.L. Friedman, *Industry & Labour. Class Struggle at Work and Monopoly Capitalism*, London 1977.

43. N. Poulantzas, *Classes in Contemporary Capitalism*, NLB, London 1975; E. Olin Wright, *Class, Crisis and the State*, London 1978.

44. The concept of 'productive labour' is more restricted in Poulantzas than in Marx, as he defines it as 'labour that produces surplus-value while *directly reproducing the material elements that serve as the substratum of the relation of exploitation: labour that is directly involved in material production by producing use-values that increase material wealth*' (p. 216).

45. Wright, p. 48.

46. The criteria for belonging to the proletariat are: 1) absence of control over the physical means of production; 2) absence of control over investments and the process of accumulation; 3) absence of control over other people's labour-power. The bourgeoisie is, on the contrary, defined by its exercise of control over the three items, while the petty bourgeoisie controls investments, the process of accumulation and the physical means of production — it does not exercise control over other people's labour-power.

3
Beyond the Positivity of the Social: Antagonisms and Hegemony

We now have to construct theoretically the concept of hegemony. Our analysis has so far provided us with something more and something less than a precise discursive location from which to embark. Something more, inasmuch as the space of hegemony is not merely that of a localized 'unthought': it is rather a space in which bursts forth a whole conception of the social based upon an intelligibility which reduces its distinct moments to the interiority of a closed paradigm. Something less, inasmuch as the diverse surfaces of emergence of the hegemonic relation do not harmoniously come together to form a theoretical void that a new concept is required to fill. On the contrary, some of them would seem to be surfaces of *dissolution* of the concept: for the relational character of every social identity implies a breaking-up of the differentiation of planes, of the unevenness between articulator and articulated, on which the hegemonic link is founded. To construct the concept of hegemony therefore involves not a simple speculative effort within a coherent context, but a more complex strategic movement requiring negotiation among mutually contradictory discursive surfaces.

From everything said so far, it follows that the concept of hegemony supposes a theoretical field dominated by the category of *articulation*; and hence that the articulated elements can be separately identified. (Later, we will examine how it is possible to specify 'elements' independently of the articulated totalities.) In any case, if articulation is a practice, and not the name of a *given* relational complex, it must imply some form of separate presence of the elements which that practice articulates or recomposes. In the type of theorization we wish to analyse, the elements on which articulatory practices operate were originally specified as fragments of a lost structural or organic totality. In the eighteenth century, the German Romantic generation took the experience of fragmentation and division as the starting-point of its theoretical reflection. Since the seventeenth century the collapse of the view of the cosmos as a meaningful order within which man occupied a precise and determined place — and the replacement of this view by a self-defining conception of the subject, as an entity maintaining relations of exteriority with the rest of the universe (the Weberian disenchantment of the world) — led the Romantic generation of the *Sturm und Drang* to an eager search for that lost unity, for a new synthesis that would permit the division to be overcome. The notion of man as the expression of an integral totality attempts to break with all dualisms — body/soul, reason/ feeling, thought/senses — established by rationalism since the seventeenth century.[1] It is well known that the Romantics conceived this experience of dissociation as strictly linked to functional differentiation and the division of society into classes, to the growing complexity of a bureaucratic State establishing relations of exteriority with the other spheres of social life.

Given that the elements to be rearticulated were specified as *fragments* of a lost unity, it was clear that any recomposition would have an *artificial* character, as opposed to the *natural* organic unity peculiar to Greek culture. Hölderlin stated: 'There are two ideals of our existence: one is the condition of the greatest simplicity, where our needs accord with each other, with our powers and with everything we are related to, *just through the organization of nature,* without any action on our part. The other is a condition of the highest cultivation, where this accord would come about between infinitely diversified and strengthened needs and powers, through the organization which we are able to give to ourselves.'[2] Now, everything depends on how we conceive this 'organization which we are able to give to ourselves' and which gives the elements a new form of unity: either that organization is contingent and, therefore, external to the fragments themselves; or else, both the fragments and the organization are necessary moments of a totality which transcends them. It is clear that only the first type of 'organization' can be conceived as an *articulation;* the second is, strictly speaking, a *mediation.* But it is also evident that, in philosophical discourses, the distances between the one and the other have been presented more as a nebulous area of ambiguities than as a clear watershed.

From our present perspective, this is the ambiguity which Hegel's thought presents in its approach to the dialectic of unity and fragmentation. His work is at once the highest moment of German Romanticism and the first modern — that is to say, post-Enlightenment — reflection on society. It is not a critique of society from utopia, nor a description and theorization of the mechanisms which make possible an order that is accepted as certain and given; rather, Hegel's reflection starts from the opaqueness of the social vis-à-vis elusive forms of a rationality and intelligibility detectable only by reference to a cunning of reason which leads separation back to unity. Hegel thus appears as located in a watershed between two epochs. In a first sense, he represents the highest point of rationalism: the moment when it attempts to embrace within the field of reason, without dualisms, the totality of the universe of differences. History and society, therefore, have a rational and intelligible structure. But, in a second sense, this synthesis contains all the seeds of its dissolution, as the rationality of history can be affirmed only at the price of introducing contradiction into the field of reason. It would, therefore, be sufficient to show that this is an impossible operation requiring constant violation of the method that it itself postulates — as was already demonstrated in the nineteenth century by Trendelenburg[3] — for the Hegelian discourse to become something very different: a series of contingent and not logical transitions. It is precisely here that Hegel's modernity lies: for him, identity is never positive and closed in itself, but is constituted as transition, relation, difference. If, however, Hegel's logical relations become contingent transitions, the connections between them cannot be fixed as moments of an underlying or sutured totality. This means that they are articulations. In the Marxist tradition, this area of ambiguity is displayed in the contradictory uses of the concept of 'dialectics'. On the one hand, this has been uncritically introduced whenever an attempt has been made to escape the logic of fixation — that is, to think articulation. (Consider, for example, Mao Tse-tung's picturesque notion of dialectics: his very incomprehension of the logical character of dialectical transitions enables a logic of articulation to be introduced, in a dialectical disguise, at the politico–discursive level.) On the other hand, 'dialectics' exerts an effect of closure in those cases where more weight is attached to the necessary character of an a priori transition, than to the discontinuous moment of an open articulation. We should not reproach Marxists too much for these ambiguities and imprecisions if, as Trendelenburg already pointed out, they were present . . . in Hegel himself.

Now, this area of ambiguity constituted by the discursive uses of 'dialectics' is the first that has to be dissolved. In order to place ourselves firmly within the field of articulation, we must begin by renouncing the conception of 'society' as founding totality of its partial processes. We must, therefore, consider the openness of the social as the constitutive ground or 'negative essence' of the existing, and the diverse 'social orders' as precarious and ultimately failed attempts to domesticate the field of differences. Accordingly, the multiformity of the social cannot be apprehended through a system of mediations, nor the 'social order' understood as an underlying principle. There is no sutured space peculiar to 'society', since the social itself has no essence. Three remarks are important here. First, the two conceptions imply different logics of the social: in the case of 'mediations', we are dealing with a system of logical transitions in which relations between objects are conceived as following a relation between concepts; in the second sense, we are dealing with contingent relations whose nature we have to determine. Secondly, in criticizing the conception of society as an ensemble united by necessary laws, we cannot simply bring out the non-necessary character of the *relations* among elements, for we would then retain the necessary character of the *identity* of the elements themselves. A conception which denies any essentialist approach to social relations, must also state the precarious character of every identity and the impossibility of fixing the sense of the 'elements' in any ultimate literality. Thirdly, it is only in contrast to a discourse postulating their unity, that an ensemble of elements appears as fragmented or dispersed. Outside any discursive structure, it is obviously not possible to speak of fragmentation, nor even to specify elements. Yet, a discursive structure is not a merely 'cognitive' or 'contemplative' entity; it is an *articulatory practice* which constitutes and organizes social relations. We can thus talk of a growing complexity and fragmentation of advanced industrial societies — not in the sense that, *sub specie aeternitatis,* they are more complex than earlier societies; but in the sense that they are constituted around a fundamental asymmetry. This is the asymmetry existing between a growing proliferation of differences — a surplus of meaning of 'the social' — and the difficulties encountered by any discourse attempting to fix those differences as moments of a stable articulatory structure.

We must, therefore, begin by analysing the category of *articulation,* which will give us our starting-point for the elaboration of the concept of hegemony. The theoretical construction of this category requires us to take two steps: to establish the possibility of specifying the elements which enter into the articulatory relation; and to determine the specificity of the relational moment comprising this articulation. Although this task could be broached from a number of different points, we prefer to begin with a *détour.* We shall first analyse in detail those theoretical discourses in which some of the concepts we will elaborate are present, but in which their development is still inhibited by the basic categories of an essentialist discourse. Let us, in this sense, consider the evolution of the Althusserian school: by radicalizing *some* of its themes in a way that will explode its basic concepts, we will attempt to constitute a ground that will allow us to construct an adequate concept of 'articulation'.

Social Formation and Overdetermination

Althusser began his theoretical trajectory by trying drastically to differentiate his conception of society as a 'complex structured whole', from the Hegelian notion of totality. The Hegelian totality could be very complex, but its complexity was always that of a plurality of moments in a single process of self-unfolding. 'The *Hegelian totality* is the alienated development of the Idea; so, strictly speaking, it is the phenomenon, the self-manifestation of this simple principle which persists in all its manifestations, and therefore even in the alienation which prepares its restoration.'[4] This conception, which reduces the real to the concept by identifying differences with necessary mediations in the self-unfolding of an essence, is of a very different order from the Althusserian complexity, which is the one inherent in a process of *overdetermination*. Given the indiscriminate and imprecise use subsequently made of this key Althusserian concept, it is necessary to specify its original meaning and the theoretical effects it was called upon to produce in Marxist discourse. The concept comes from psychoanalysis, and its extension had more than a superficially metaphoric character. In this regard, Althusser is very clear: 'I did not invent this concept. As I pointed out, it is borrowed from two existing disciplines: specifically, from linguistics and psychoanalysis. In these disciplines it has an objective dialectical "connotation", and — particularly in psychoanalysis — one sufficiently related formally to the content it designates here for the loan not to be an arbitrary one.'[5] For Freud, overdetermination is no ordinary process of 'fusion' or 'merger' — which would at most be a metaphor established by analogy with the physical world, compatible with any form of multi-causality; on the contrary, it is a very precise type of fusion entailing a symbolic dimension and a plurality of meanings. The concept of overdetermination is constituted in the field of the symbolic, and has no meaning whatsoever outside it. Consequently, the most profound *potential* meaning of Althusser's statement that everything existing in the social is overdetermined, is the assertion that the social constitutes itself as a symbolic order. The symbolic — i.e., overdetermined — character of social relations therefore implies that they lack an ultimate literality which would reduce them to necessary moments of an immanent law. There are not *two* planes, one of essences and the other of appearances, since there is no possibility of fixing an *ultimate* literal sense for which the symbolic would be a second and derived plane of signification. Society and social agents lack any essence, and their regularities merely consist of the relative and precarious forms of fixation which accompany the establishment of a certain order. This analysis seemed to open up the possibility of elaborating a new concept of articulation, which would start from the overdetermined character of social relations. But this did not occur. The concept of overdetermination tended to disappear from Althusserian discourse, and a growing closure led to the installation of a new variant of essentialism. This process, already started in 'On the Materialist Dialectic', was to culminate in *Reading Capital*.

If the concept of overdetermination was unable to produce the totality of its deconstructive effects within Marxist discourse, this was because, from the very beginning, an attempt was made to render it compatible with another central moment in Althusserian discourse that is, strictly speaking, incompatible with the first: namely, determination in the last instance by the economy. Let us consider the implications of this concept. If this ultimate determination were a truth valid *for every society,* the relationship between such determination and the conditions making it possible would not develop through a contingent historical articulation, but would constitute an a priori necessity. It is important to note that the problem under discussion is not that the economy should have its conditions of existence. This is a tautology, for if something exists, it is because given conditions render its existence possible. The problem is that if the 'economy' is determinant in the last instance *for every type of society,* it must be defined independently of any specific type of society; and the conditions of existence of the economy must also be defined separately from any concrete social relation. In that case, however, the only reality of those conditions of existence would be that of assuring the existence and determining role of the economy — in other words, they would be an internal moment of the economy as such; the difference would not be constitutive.[6]

There is, however, something more. Althusser starts by affirming the need not to hypostatize the abstract, given that there is no reality which is not overdetermined. In this sense, he approvingly quotes both Mao's analysis of contradiction and Marx's rejection, in the

1857 Introduction, of abstractions like 'production', which only have meaning in terms of a concrete system of social relations. Yet, Althusser lapses into the very defect he criticizes: there is an abstract universal object, the 'economy', which produces concrete effects (determination in the last instance here and now); and there is another equally abstract object (conditions of existence) whose forms vary historically, but which are unified by the pre-established essential role of assuring the reproduction of the economy; finally, as the economy and its centrality are invariables of any possible social arrangement, the possibility opens up of providing a *definition* of society. Here the analysis has turned full circle. If the economy is an object which can determine any type of society in the last instance, this means that, at least with reference to that instance, we are faced with simple determination and not overdetermination. If society has a last instance which determines its laws of motion, then *the relations between the overdetermined instances and the last instance must be conceived in terms of simple, one-directional determination by the latter.* We can deduce from this that the field of overdetermination is extremely limited: it is the field of contingent variation as opposed to essential determination. And, if society does have a last and essential determination, the difference is not constitutive and the social is unified in the sutured space of a rationalist paradigm. Thus, we are confronted with exactly the same dualism that we found reproduced since the end of the nineteenth century in the field of Marxist discursiveness.

This is the point where the disarticulation of Althusser's rationalism will begin. It is important to note that the inconsistent dualism of the starting-point will be transmitted to those very theoretical forms which will preside over the disaggregation of the original schema. In effect, two possibilities arose: the first was to develop all the implications of the concept of overdetermination, showing the impossibility of a concept such as 'determination in the last instance by the economy' and affirming the precarious and relational character of every identity. The second possibility was to demonstrate the *logical inconsistency* of the necessary links postulated among the *elements* of the social totality, and thus to show, by a different path, the impossibility of the object 'society' as a rationally unified totality. The course actually followed was the latter. In consequence, the critique of the initial rationalism took place in a terrain which accepted the analytical assumptions of rationalism, while denying the possibility of a rationalist conception of the social. The result of this deconstructive escalation was that the concept of articulation became strictly unthinkable. It is the critique of this line of thought which will provide us with a different basis for constructing our concept of articulation.

The attempt to break the logical connections among the different moments of the Althusserian rationalist paradigm started with a self-criticism by Balibar,[7] and it was carried to its ultimate consequences in certain currents of British Marxism.[8] The pattern of Balibar's self-criticism involved the introduction of hiatuses at various points in the argument of *Reading Capital* — hiatuses in which the logical transitions were shown to have had a spurious character. He filled these, however, by diversifying the entities which were supposed to effect the transition from abstract to concrete. Thus, the understanding of the transition from one mode of production to another necessitated an expansion of the terrain of class struggle, whose unevenness prevented its reduction to the simple logic of a single mode of production. It was argued that reproduction required superstructural processes which could not be reduced to that logic; and that the unevenness of the diverse aspects of a conjuncture had to be understood in terms of a combination, in which the abstract unity of the participating elements dissolved. It is clear, however, that these analyses only succeeded in reproducing on an enlarged scale the difficulties of the initial formulation. What actually are these classes whose struggles must account for the processes of transition? If they are social agents constituted around interests determined by the relations of production, the rationality of their action and the forms of their political calculation can be determined by the logic of the mode of production. If, on the contrary, this does not exhaust the identity of classes, then where is their identity constituted? Similarly, to know that the superstructures intervene in the process of reproduction does not lead us very far, if we also know from the start that they are *superstructures,* that they have a place assigned to them within the topography of the social. A further step along this deconstructive line can be found in the work of Barry Hindess and Paul Hirst, where the concepts of 'determination in the last instance' and 'structural causality' were subjected to a devastating critique. Having established the non-necessary character of the correspondence between productive forces and relations of production, they concluded that the concept of mode of production had to be discarded as a legitimate object of Marxist discourse. Once any totalizing perspective was abandoned, the type of articulation existent in a concrete social formation was posed in the following terms: 'The social formation is not a totality governed by an organizing principle, determination in the last instance, structural causality, or whatever. It should be conceived as consisting of a definite set of relations of production together with economic, political and cultural forms in which their conditions of existence are secured. But there is no necessity for those conditions of existence to be secured and no necessary structure of the social formation in which those relations and forms must be combined. As for classes . . . if they are conceived as economic classes, as categories of economic agents occupying definite positions of possession of or separation from the means of production, then they cannot also be conceived as, or represented by, political forces and ideological forms.'[9]

We are here presented with a conception of social formation which specifies *certain* objects of classical Marxist discourse — relations of production, productive forces, etc. — and reconceptualizes the articulation between those objects in terms of 'securing the conditions of existence'. We will attempt to prove: a) that the criterion for specifying objects is illegitimate; b) that the conceptualization of the relation among them in terms of mutually 'securing their conditions of existence', does not provide any concept of articulation.

Regarding the first point, Cutler et al. start with the unobjectionable statement that — unless we fall into a dogmatically rationalist attempt to determine at the conceptual level a general mechanism of reproduction of the social formation — it is impossible to derive from the conditions of existence of a certain conceptually specified relation, the necessity that those conditions be fulfilled or that specific forms be adopted by them. This is followed, however, by an entirely illegitimate assertion: namely, that the relations of production of a given social formation can be specified separately from the concrete forms securing their conditions of existence. Let us examine the problem with attention. The conditions of existence of capitalist relations of production — for example, the legal conditions which secure private property — are *logical* conditions of existence, in so far as it would be contradictory to affirm the possibility of existence of those relations of production if such conditions were not fulfilled. It is also a *logical* conclusion that nothing in the concept of 'capitalist relations of production' implies that they should secure their own conditions of existence. Indeed, at the level of the same discourse which constitutes the former as an object, it follows that the latter would be *externally* secured. But, precisely because of this, it is inappropriate to say that it is not known how, in each case, these relations of production are to be secured, given that the distinction relations of production/conditions of existence is a logical distinction within a discourse about the abstract concept of relation of production, which does not diversify into a variety of concrete cases. Thus, if it is stated that in Britain the conditions of existence of capitalist relations of production are secured by these or those institutions, a doubly illegitimate discursive transposition is brought into play. On the one hand, it is asserted that certain concrete discourses and institutional practices secure the conditions of existence of an abstract entity — the capitalist relations of production — belonging to another discursive order; on the other hand, if the abstract term 'capitalist relations of production' is used to designate the relations of production in Britain, it is evident that an object specified in a certain discourse is being used as a *name* to point out, as referents, the objects constituted by other discourses and practices — those comprising the ensemble of British productive relations. In this case, however, as these are not merely 'capitalist relations of production in general' but the locus of a multiplicity of practices and discourses, there is no longer any terrain in which the exteriority of the relations of production to their conditions of existence can be established a priori. Moreover, as the possibility of specifying distinctions among objects was based on a logical criterion, what is in question is the very pertinence of this criterion. If, as Cutler et al. argue, a *relation* between concepts does not imply a relation between the objects specified in those concepts, nor is it the case that a *separation* between objects can be derived from a separation between concepts. Cutler et al. maintain the specific identity and separation of the objects, but only by specifying one of the objects in a certain discourse and the other in a different discourse.

Let us now move on to our second problem. Can the link called 'securing the conditions of existence' be understood as an articulation of elements? Whatever conception one might have of a relation of articulation, this must include a system of differential positions; and, given that this system constitutes a *configuration*, the problem necessarily arises of the relational or non-relational character of the identity of the elements involved. Is it possible to consider that the 'securing of the conditions of existence' constitutes an adequate analytical terrain for posing the problems raised by this relational moment? Evidently not. To secure a *condition* of existence is to fill a logical requirement of an object's existence, but it does not constitute a *relation of existence* between two objects. (For example, certain juridical forms can contribute the conditions of existence of certain relations of production, even if the latter do not actually exist.) If, on the other hand, we consider the relations — and not simply the logical compatibility — existing between an object and the instance or instances that secure its conditions of existence, it is evident that those relations cannot be conceptualized on the basis that these instances secure the object's conditions of existence, simply because the securing does not constitute a *relation*. Consequently, it is necessary to move to a different terrain, if one wishes to think the specificity of the relation of articulation.

Hirst and Wooley contend: 'He (Althusser) conceives social relations as *totalities,* as a whole governed by a single determinative principle. This whole must be consistent with itself and must subject all agents and relationships within its purview to its effects. We on the other hand consider social relations as aggregates of institutions, forms of organization, practices and agents which do not answer to any single causal principle or logic of consistency, which can and do differ in form and which are not essential to one another.'[10] This paragraph reveals all the problems posed by a purely logicist deconstruction. The notion of totality is here rejected by reference to the non-essential character of the links uniting the elements of the presumed totality. In this, we have no disagreements. But, once elements such as 'institutions', 'forms of organization' or 'agents' have been specified, a question immediately arises. If these aggregates — by contrast with the totality — are considered legitimate objects of social theorization, must we conclude that the relations among the internal components of each of them are essential and necessary? If the answer is yes, we have clearly moved from an essentialism of the totality to an essentialism of the elements; we have merely replaced Spinoza with Leibnitz, except that the role of God is no longer to establish harmony among the elements, but simply to secure their independence. If, on the contrary, the relations among those internal elements are neither essential nor necessary, then, besides having to specify the nature of relations characterized in a purely negative manner, we are compelled to explain why these non-necessary relations among internal components of the 'legitimate' objects cannot exist *among the legitimate objects themselves.* Should this prove possible, a certain notion of totality could be reintroduced, with the difference that it would no longer involve an underlying principle that would unify 'society', but an ensemble of totalizing effects in an open relational complex. But if we move solely within the alternative 'essential relations or non-relational identities', all social analysis will involve a pursuit of the infinitely receding mirage of logical atoms irreducible to any subsequent division.

The problem is that this entire debate concerning the *separation* among elements and objects has evaded a prior and fundamental issue: that of the *terrain* where the separation occurs. In this way, a very classical alternative has surreptitiously crept into the analysis: either the objects are separated as conceptually discrete elements — in which case we are dealing with a logical separation; or else, they are separated as empirically given objects — in which case it is impossible to elude the category of 'experience'. Thus, by failing to specify the terrain in which the unity or separation among objects takes place, we once again fall back into the 'rationalism or empiricism' alternative which the Hindess and Hirst current tries by all possible means to avoid. This unsatisfactory situation was, in fact, predetermined from the beginning: from the moment when the critique of Althusser's rationalism adopted the form of a critique of the logical connections postulated among different elements of the 'totality'. For, a logical deconstruction can only be implemented if the disconnected 'elements' are conceptually specified and fixed; that is, if a full and unequivocal identity is attributed to them. The only path that is then left open is a logical pulverization of the social, coupled with a theoretically agnostic descriptivism of the 'concrete situations'.

In the original Althusserian formulation, however, a very different theoretical undertaking was foreshadowed: that of a break with orthodox essentialism not through the logical disaggregation of its categories — with a resultant *fixing* of the identity of the disaggregated elements — but through the critique of every type of fixity, through an affirmation of the incomplete, open and politically negotiable character of every identity. This was the logic of over-determination. For it, the sense of every identity is overdetermined inasmuch as all literality appears as constitutively subverted and exceeded; far from there being an essentialist *totalization,* or a no less essentialist *separation* among objects, the presence of some objects in the others prevents any of their identities from being fixed. Objects appear articulated not like pieces in a clockwork mechanism, but because the presence of some in the others hinders the suturing of the identity of any of them. Our examination of the history of Marxism has, in this sense, shown a very different spectacle from that depicted by the näive positivism of 'scientific' socialism: far from a rationalist game in which social agents, perfectly constituted around interests, wage a struggle defined by transparent parameters, we have seen the difficulties of the working class in constituting itself as a historical subject, the dispersion and fragmentation of its positionalities, the emergence of forms of social and political reaggregation — 'historical bloc', 'collective will', 'masses', 'popular sectors' — which define new objects and new logics of their conformation. Thus, we are in the field of the overdetermination of some entities by others, and the relegation of any form of paradigmatic fixity to the ultimate horizon of theory. It is this specific logic of articulation that we must now attempt to determine.

Articulation and Discourse

In the context of this discussion, we will call *articulation* any practice establishing a relation among elements such that their identity is modified as a result of the articulatory practice. The structured totality resulting from the articulatory practice, we will call *discourse*. The differential positions, insofar as they appear articulated within a discourse, we will call *moments*. By contrast, we will call *element* any difference that is not discursively articulated. In order to be correctly understood, these distinctions require three main types of specification: with regard to the characteristic coherence of the discursive formation; with regard to the dimensions and extensions of the discursive; and with regard to the openness or closure exhibited by the discursive formation.

1. A discursive formation is not unified either in the logical coherence of its elements, or in the a priori of a transcendental subject, or in a meaning-giving subject à la Husserl, or in the unity of an experience. The type of coherence we attribute to a discursive formation is — with the differences we will indicate later — close to that which characterizes the concept of 'discursive formation' formulated by Foucault: regularity in dispersion. In the *Archaeology of Knowledge,* Foucault rejects four hypotheses concerning the unifying principle of a discursive formation — reference to the same object, a common style in the production of statements, constancy of the concepts, and reference to a common theme. Instead, he makes dispersion itself the principle of unity, insofar as it is governed by rules of formation, by the complex conditions of existence of the dispersed statements.[11] A remark is necessary at this point. A dispersion governed by rules may be seen from two symmetrically opposed perspectives. In the first place, as *dispersion*: this requires

determination of the point of reference with respect to which the elements can be thought of as dispersed. (In Foucault's case, one can evidently speak of dispersion only by reference to the type of absent unity constituted around the common object, the style, the concepts and the theme.) But the discursive formation can also be seen from the perspective of the *regularity* in dispersion, and be thought, in that sense, as an ensemble of differential positions. This ensemble is not the expression of any underlying principle external to itself — it cannot, for instance, be apprehended either by a hermeneutic reading or by a structuralist combinatory — but it constitutes a configuration, which in certain contexts of exteriority can be *signified* as a totality. Given that our principal concern is with articulatory practices, it is this second aspect which interests us in particular.

Now, in an articulated discursive totality, where every element occupies a differential position — in our terminology, where every *element* has been reduced to a *moment* of that totality — all identity is relational and all relations have a necessary character. Benveniste, for example, states with reference to Saussure's principle of value: 'To say that the values are "relative" means that they are relative *to each other*. Now, is that not precisely the proof of their *necessity? . . .* Whoever says system says arrangement or conformity of parts in a structure which transcends and explains its elements. Everything is so *necessary* in it that modifications of the whole and of the details reciprocally condition one another. The relativity of values is the best proof that they depend closely upon one another in the synchrony of a system which is always being threatened, always being restored. The point is that all values are values of opposition and are defined only by their difference . . . If language is something other than a fortuitous conglomeration of erratic notions and sounds uttered at random, it is because necessity is inherent in its structure as in all structure.'[12] Necessity derives, therefore, not from an underlying intelligible principle but from the regularity of a system of structural positions. In this sense, no relation can be contingent or external, since the identity of its elements would then be specified outside the relation itself. But this is no more than to affirm that in a discursive-structural formation constituted in this way, the practice of articulation would be impossible: the latter involves working on *elements,* while here we would be confronted only with *moments* of a closed and fully constituted totality where every moment is subsumed from the beginning under the principle of repetition. As we shall see, if contingency and articulation are possible, this is because no discursive formation is a sutured totality and the transformation of the elements into moments is never complete.

2. Our analysis rejects the distinction between discursive and non-discursive practices. It affirms: a) that every object is constituted as an object of discourse, insofar as no object is given outside every discursive condition of emergence; and b) that any distinction between what are usually called the linguistic and behaviourial aspects of a social practice, is either an incorrect distinction or ought to find its place as a differentiation within the social production of meaning, which is structured under the form of discursive totalitites. Foucault, for example, who has maintained a distinction — in our opinion inconsistent — between discursive and non-discursive practices,[13] attempts to determine the relational totality that founds the regularity of the dispersions of a discursive formation. But he is only capable of doing this in terms of a discursive practice: '[Clinical medicine must be regarded] as the establishment of a relation, in medical discourse, between a number of distinct elements, some of which concerned the status of doctors, others the institutional and technical site from which they spoke, others their position as subjects perceiving, observing, describing, teaching, etc. It can be said that this relation between different elements (some of which are new, while others were already in existence) is effected by clinical discourse: it is this, as a practice, that establishes between them all a system of relations that is not "really" given or constituted *a priori*; and if there is a unity, if the modalities of enunciation that it uses, or to which it gives place, are not simply juxtaposed by a series of historical contingencies, it is because it makes constant use of this group of relations.'[14] Two points have to be emphasized here. Firstly, if the so-called non-discursive complexes — institutions, techniques, productive organization, and so on — are analysed, we will only find more or less complex forms of differential positions among objects, which do not arise from a necessity external to the system structuring them and which can only therefore be conceived as discursive articulations. Secondly, the very logic of Foucault's argument concerning the articulatory nature of clinical discourse implies that the identity of the articulated elements must be at least partially modified by that articulation: that is, the category of dispersion only partially permits us to think the specificity of the regularities. The status of the dispersed entities is constituted in some intermediate region between the elements and the moments.[15]

We cannot enter here into all the complexities of a theory of discourse as we understand it, but we should at least indicate the following basic points in order to obviate the more common mis-understandings.

(a) The fact that every object is constituted as an object of discourse has *nothing to do* with whether there is a world external to thought, or with the realism/idealism opposition. An earthquake or the falling of a brick is an event that certainly exists, in the sense that it occurs here and now, independently of my will. But whether their specificity as objects is constructed in terms of 'natural phenomena' or 'expressions of the wrath of God', depends upon the structuring of a discursive field. What is denied is not that such objects exist externally to thought, but the rather different assertion that they could constitute themselves as objects outside any discursive condition of emergence.

(b) At the root of the previous prejudice lies an assumption of the *mental* character of discourse. Against this, we will affirm the *material* character of every discursive structure. To argue the opposite is to accept the very classical dichotomy between an objective field constituted outside of any discursive intervention, and a discourse consisting of the pure expression of thought. This is, precisely, the dichotomy which several currents of contemporary thought have tried to break.[16] The theory of speech acts has, for example, underlined their performative character. Language games, in Wittgenstein, include within an indissoluble totality both language and the actions interconnected with it: 'A is building with building-stones: there are blocks, pillars, slabs, and beams. B has to pass the stones, and that in the order in which A needs them. For this purpose they use a language consisting of the words "block", "pillar", "slab", "beam". A calls them out; B brings the stone which he has learnt to bring at such and such a call.'[17] The conclusion is inevitable: 'I shall also call the whole, consisting of language and the actions into which it is woven, the "language-game".'[18] It is evident that the very material properties of objects are part of what Wittgenstein calls language game, which is an example of what we have called discourse. What constitutes a differential position and therefore a relational identity with certain linguistic elements, is not the idea of building-stone or slab, but the building-stone or the slab as such. (The connection with the idea of 'building-stone' has not, as far as we know, been sufficient to construct any building.) The linguistic and non-linguistic elements are not merely juxtaposed, but constitute a differential and structured system of positions — that is, a discourse. The differential positions include, therefore, a dispersion of very diverse material elements.[19]

It might be argued that, in this case, the discursive unity is the teleological unity of a project; but this is not so. The objective world is structured in relational sequences which do not necessarily have a finalistic sense and which, in most cases, do not actually require any meaning at all: it is sufficient that certain regularities establish differential positions for us to be able to speak of a discursive formation. Two important conclusions follow from this. The first is that the material character of discourse cannot be unified in the experience or consciousness of a founding subject; on the contrary, diverse *subject positions* appear dispersed within a discursive formation. The second consequence is that the practice of articulation, as fixation/dislocation of a system of differences, cannot consist of purely linguistic phenomena; but must instead pierce the entire material density of the multifarious institutions, rituals and practices through which a discursive formation is structured. The recognition of this complexity, and of its discursive character, began to beat an obscure path in the terrain of Marxist theorization. Its characteristic form was the progressive affirmation, from Gramsci to Althusser, of the material character of *ideologies,* inasmuch as these are not simple systems of ideas but are embodied in institutions, rituals and so forth. What did, however, become an obstacle for the full theoretical unfolding of this intuition was that, in all cases, it was referred to the field of *ideologies*; that is, to formations whose identity was thought under the concept of 'superstructure'. It was an a priori unity vis-à-vis the dispersion of its materiality, so that it required an appeal either to the unifying role of a class (Gramsci), or to the functional requirements of the logic of reproduction (Althusser). But once this essentialist assumption is abandoned, the category of articulation acquires a different theoretical status: articulation is now a discursive practice which does not have a plane of constitution prior to, or outside, the dispersion of the articulated elements.

(c) Finally, we must consider the meaning and productivity of the centrality we have assigned to the category of discourse. Through this centrality, we obtain a considerable enlargement of the field of objectivity, and the conditions are created which permit us to think numerous relations placed before us by the analysis of the preceding chapters. Let us suppose that we attempted to analyse social relations on the basis of the type of objectivity constructed by the discourse of natural sciences. This immediately sets strict limits both on the objects that it is possible to construct within that discourse, and on the relations that can be established among them. Certain relations and certain objects are excluded in advance. Metaphor, for example, is impossible as an objective relation between two entities. But this excludes the possibility of conceptually specifying a wide range of relations among objects in the social and political field. What we characterized as 'communist enumeration', for example, is based on a relation of *equivalence* among different class sectors within a social space divided into two antagonistic camps. But this equivalence supposes the operation of the principle of analogy among literally diverse contents — and what is this but a metaphorical transposition? It is important to observe that the equivalence constituted through communist enumeration is not the discursive *expression* of a real movement constituted outside discourse; on the contrary, this enumerative discourse *is* a real force which contributes to the moulding and constitution of social relations. Something similar occurs with a notion such as 'contradiction' — to which we will return below. If we consider social relations from the perspective of a naturalist paradigm, contradiction is excluded. But if we consider social relations as discursively constructed, contradiction becomes possible. For, whereas the classical notion of 'real object' excludes contradiction, a relation of contradiction can exist between two objects of discourse. The main consequence of a break with the discursive/extra-discursive dichotomy is the abandonment of the thought/reality opposition, and hence a major enlargement of the field of those categories which can account for social relations. Synonymy, metonymy, metaphor are not forms of thought that add a second sense to a primary, constitutive literality of social relations; instead, they are part of the primary terrain itself in which the social is constituted. Rejection of the thought/reality dichotomy must go together with a rethinking and interpenetration of the categories which have until now been considered exclusive of one or the other.

3. Now, the transition to the relational totality that we have called 'discourse', would hardly be able to solve our initial problems if the relational and differential logic of the discursive totality prevailed without any limitation. In that case, we would be faced with pure relations of necessity, and, as we earlier pointed out, any articulation would be impossible given that every 'element' would *ex definitione* be 'moment'. This conclusion can impose itself, however, only if we allow that the relational logic of discourse be carried through to its ultimate consequences, without limitation by any exterior.[20] If we accept, on the contrary, that a discursive totality never exists in the form of a simply *given and delimited* positivity, the relational logic will be incomplete and pierced by contingency. The transition from the 'elements' to the 'moments' is never entirely fulfilled. A no-

man's-land thus emerges, making the articulatory practice possible. In this case, there is no social identity fully protected from a discursive exterior that deforms it and prevents it becoming fully sutured. Both the identities and the relations lose their necessary character. As a systematic structural ensemble, the relations are unable to absorb the identities; but as the identities are purely relational, this is but another way of saying that there is no identity which can be fully constituted.

This being so, all discourse of fixation becomes metaphorical: literality is, in actual fact, the first of metaphors.

Here we arrive at a decisive point in our argument. The incomplete character of every totality necessarily leads us to abandon, as a terrain of analysis, the premise of *'society'* as a sutured and self-defined totality. 'Society' is not a valid object of discourse. There is no single underlying principle fixing — and hence constituting — the whole field of differences. The irresoluble interiority/exteriority tension is the condition of any social practice: necessity only exists as a partial limitation of the field of contingency. It is in this terrain, where neither a total interiority nor a total exteriority is possible, that the social is constituted. For the same reason that the social cannot be reduced to the interiority of a fixed system of differences, pure exteriority is also impossible. In order to be *totally* external to each other, the entities would have to be totally internal with regard to themselves: that is, to have a fully constituted identity which is not subverted by any exterior. But this is precisely what we have just rejected. *This field of identities which never manage to be fully fixed, is the field of overdetermination.*

Thus, neither absolute fixity nor absolute non-fixity is possible. We will now consider these two successive moments, beginning with non-fixity. We have referred to 'discourse' as a system of differential entities — that is, of moments. But we have just seen that such a system only exists as a partial limitation of a 'surplus of meaning' which subverts it. Being inherent in every discursive situation, this 'surplus' is the necessary terrain for the constitution of every social practice. We will call it the *field of discursivity*. This term indicates the form of its relation with every concrete discourse: it determines at the same time the necessarily discursive character of any object, and the impossibility of any given discourse to implement a final suture. On this point, our analysis meets up with a number of contemporary currents of thought which — from Heidegger to Wittgenstein — have insisted on the impossibility of fixing ultimate meanings. Derrida, for example, starts from a radical break in the history of the concept of structure, occurring at the moment in which the centre — the *transcendental signified* in its multiple forms: eidos, arché, telos, energeia, ousia, alétheia, etc. — is abandoned, and with it the possibility of fixing a meaning which underlies the flow of differences. At this point, Derrida generalizes the concept of discourse in a sense coincident with that of our text. 'It became necessary to think both the law which somehow governed desire for a centre in the constitution of structure, and the process of signification which orders the displacements and substitutions for this law of central presence — but as a central presence which has never been itself, has always already been exiled from itself into its own substitute. The substitute does not substitute itself for anything which has somehow existed before it, henceforth, it was necessary to begin thinking that there was no centre, that the centre could not be thought in the form of a present-being, that the centre had no natural site, that it was not a fixed locus but a function, a sort of non-locus in which an infinite number of sign-substitutions came into play. This was the moment when language invaded the universal problematic, the moment when, in the absence of a centre or origin, everything became discourse — provided we can agree on this word — that is to say, a system in which the central signified, the original or transcendental signified, is never absolutely present outside a system of differences. The absence of the transcendental signified extends the domain and the play of signification infinitely.'[21]

Let us move on to our second dimension. The impossibility of an ultimate fixity of meaning implies that there have to be partial fixations — otherwise, the very flow of differences would be impossible. Even in order to differ, to subvert meaning, there has to be *a* meaning. If the social does not manage to fix itself in the intelligible and instituted forms of a *society*, the social only exists, however, as an effort to construct that impossible object. Any discourse is constituted as an attempt to dominate the field of discursivity, to arrest the flow of differences, to construct a centre. We will call the privileged discursive points of this partial fixation, *nodal points*. (Lacan has insisted on these partial fixations through his concept of *points de capiton*, that is, of privileged signifiers that fix the meaning of a signifying chain. This limitation of the productivity of the signifying chain establishes the positions that make predication possible — a discourse incapable of generating any fixity of meaning is the discourse of the psychotic.)

Saussure's analysis of language considered it as a system of differences without positive terms; the central concept was that of *value*, according to which the meaning of a term was purely relational and determined only by its opposition to all the others. But this shows us that we are presented with the conditions of possibility of a *closed* system: only within it is it possible to fix in such a manner the meaning of every element. When the linguistic model was introduced into the general field of human sciences, it was this effect of systematicity that predominated, so that structuralism became a new form of essentialism: a search for the underlying structures constituting the inherent law of any possible variation. The critique of structuralism involved a break with this view of a fully constituted structural space; but as it also rejected any return to a conception of unities whose demarcation was given, like a nomenclature, by its reference to an object, the resulting conception was of a relational space unable to constitute itself as such — of a field dominated by the desire for a structure that was always finally absent. The sign is the name of a split, of an impossible suture between signified and signifier.[22]

We now have all the necessary analytical elements to specify the concept of articulation. Since all identity is relational — even if the system of relations does not reach the point of being fixed as a stable system of differences — since, too, all discourse is subverted by a field of discursivity which overflows it, the transition from 'elements' to 'moments' can never be complete. The status of the 'elements' is that of floating signifiers, incapable of being wholly articulated to a discursive chain. And this floating character finally penetrates every discursive (i.e. social) identity. But if we accept the non-complete character of all discursive fixation and, at the same time, affirm the relational character of every identity, the ambiguous character of the signifier, its non-fixation to any signified, can only exist insofar as there is a proliferation of signifieds. It is not the poverty of signifieds but, on the contrary, polysemy that disarticulates a discursive structure. That is what establishes the overdetermined, symbolic dimension of every social identity. Society never manages to be identical to itself, as every nodal point is constituted within an intertextuality that overflows it. *The practice of articulation, therefore, consists in the construction of nodal points which partially fix meaning; and the partial character of this fixation proceeds from the openness of the social, a result, in its turn, of the constant overflowing of every discourse by the infinitude of the field of discursivity.*

Every social practice is therefore — in one of its dimensions — articulatory. As it is not the internal moment of a self-defined totality, it cannot simply be the expression of something already acquired, it cannot be *wholly* subsumed under the principle of repetition; rather, it always consists in the construction of new differences. The social *is* articulation insofar as 'society' is impossible. Earlier we said that, for the social, necessity only exists as a partial effort to limit contingency. This implies that the relations between 'necessity' and 'contingency' cannot be conceived as relations between two areas that are delimited and external to each other — as, for example, in Labriola's morphological prediction — because the contingent only exists within the necessary. This presence of the contingent in the necessary is what we earlier called *subversion,* and it manifests itself as symbolization, metaphorization, paradox, which deform and question the literal character of every necessity. Necessity, therefore, exists not under the form of an underlying principle, of a ground, but as an effort of literalization which fixes the differences of a relational system. The necessity of the social is the necessity proper to purely relational identities — as in the linguistic principle of value[23] — not natural 'necessity' or the necessity of an analytical judgement. 'Necessity', in this sense, is simply equivalent to a 'system of differential positions in a sutured space'.

This way of approaching the problem of articulation would seem to contain all the necessary elements to resolve the apparent antinomies with which the logic of hegemony confronted us: on the one hand, the open and incomplete character of every social identity permits its articulation to different historico-discursive formations — that is, to 'blocs' in the sense of Sorel and Gramsci; on the other hand, the very identity of the articulatory force is constituted in the general field of discursivity — this eliminates any reference to a transcendental or originative subject. However, before formulating our concept of hegemony, we need to tackle two further questions. The first concerns the precise status in our analysis of the category of 'subject'; the second concerns the concept of *antagonism,* whose importance stems from the fact that, in one of its key dimensions, the specificity of a *hegemonic* articulatory practice is given by its confrontation with other articulatory practices of an antagonistic character.

The Category of 'Subject'

Discussion of this category requires us to distinguish two very different problems, which have frequently been confused in recent debates: the problem of the discursive or pre-discursive character of the category of subject; and the problem of the relationship among different subject positions.

The first problem has received more consistent attention, and has led to a growing questioning of the 'constitutive' role that both rationalism and empiricism attribute to 'human individuals'. This critique has essentially borne upon three conceptual targets: the view of the subject as an agent both rational and transparent to itself; the supposed unity and homogeneity of the ensemble of its positions; and the conception of the subject as origin and basis of social relations (the problem of constitutivity in the strict sense). We do not need to refer in detail to the main dimensions of this critique, as its classical moments — Nietzsche, Freud, Heidegger — are well enough known. More recently, Foucault has shown how the tensions of the 'analytic of finitude', characteristic of what he has called the 'Age of Man', are resolved into a set of oppositions — the empirical/the transcendental, the Cogito/the unthought, withdrawal/return of the origin — which are insurmountable insofar as the category of 'Man' is maintained as a unified subject.[24] Other analyses have pointed out the difficulties in breaking with the category of 'originative subject', which continues to creep into the very conceptions that seek to implement the rupture with it.[25]

With regard to this alternative, and to its diverse constitutive elements, our position is clear. Whenever we use the category of 'subject' in this text, we will do so in the sense of 'subject positions' within a discursive structure. Subjects cannot, therefore, be the origin of social relations — not even in the limited sense of being endowed with powers that render an experience possible — as all 'experience' depends on precise discursive conditions of possibility.[26] This, however, is only an answer to our first problem, which in no way anticipates the solution that will be given to the second. From the discursive character of all subject positions, nothing follows concerning the type of relation that could exist among them. As every subject position is a discursive position, it partakes of the open character of every discourse; consequently, the various positions cannot be totally fixed in a closed system of differences. We can see why these very different problems were confused. Since the affirmation of the discursive character of every subject position was linked to the rejection of the notion of subject as an originative and founding totality, the analytic moment that had to prevail was that of dispersion, detotalization or decentring of certain positions with regard to others. Every moment of articulation or relation among them broke the cognitive effects of the dispersion metaphor, and led to the suspicion of a retotalization which would surreptitiously reintroduce the category of subject as a unified and unifying essence. From here, it was but one step to transform that *dispersion* of subject positions into an effective *separation* among them. However, the transformation of dispersion into separation obviously creates all the analytical problems we signalled earlier — especially those inherent in the replacement of the essentialism of the totality with an essentialism of the elements. If every subject position is a discursive position, the analysis cannot dispense with the forms of overdetermination of some positions by others — of the contingent character of all necessity which, as we have seen, is inherent in any discursive difference.

Let us consider two cases which have recently given rise to important discussions: that relating to the status of apparently abstract categories (above all, 'Man'); and that relating to the 'subject' of feminism. The first is at the centre of the entire recent debate on humanism. If the status of 'Man'[27] were that of an *essence*, its location with regard to other characteristics of 'human beings' would be inscribed on a logical scale proceeding from the abstract to the concrete. This would open the way for all the familiar tricks of an analysis of concrete situations in terms of 'alienation' and 'misrecognition'. But if, on the contrary, 'Man' is a discursively constructed subject position, its presumed abstract character in no way anticipates the form of its articulation with other subject positions. (The range is here infinite, and it challenges the imagination of any 'humanist'. For example, it is known how, in the colonial countries, the equivalence between 'rights of Man' and 'European values' was a frequent and effective form of discursively constructing the acceptability of imperialist domination.) The confusion created by E.P. Thompson in his attack on Althusser[28], rests precisely on this point. When referring to 'humanism', Thompson believes that if humanist values are denied the status of an essence, then they are deprived of all historical validity. In reality, however, what is important is to try to show how 'Man' has been produced in modern times, how the 'human' subject — that is, the bearer of a human identity without distinctions — appears in certain religious discourses, is embodied in juridical practices and is diversely constructed in other spheres. An understanding of this dispersion can help us to grasp the fragility of 'humanist' values themselves, the possibility of their perversion through equivalential articulation with other values, and their restriction to certain categories of the population — the property-owning class, for example, or the male population. Far from considering that 'Man' has the status of an essence — presumably a gift from heaven — such an analysis can show us the historical conditions of its emergence and the reasons for its current vulnerability, thus enabling us to struggle more efficiently, and without illusions, in defence of humanist values. But it is equally evident that the analysis cannot simply remain at the moment of *dispersion*, given that 'human identity' involves not merely an ensemble of dispersed positions but also the forms of overdetermination existing among them. 'Man' is a fundamental nodal point from which it has been possible to proceed, since the eighteenth century, to the 'humanization' of a number of social practices. To insist on the dispersion of the positions from which 'Man' has been produced, constitutes only a first moment; in a second stage, it is necessary to show the relations of overdetermination and totalization that are established among these. The non-fixation or openness of the system of discursive differences is what makes possible these effects of analogy and interpenetration.

Something similar may be said about the 'subject' of feminism. The critique of feminist essentialism has been carried out in particular by the English journal *m/f*: a number of important studies have rejected the notion of a preconstituted category 'women's oppression' — whether its cause is located in the family, the mode of production or elsewhere — and have attempted to study 'the particular historical moment, the institutions and practices through which the category of woman is produced'.[29] Once it is denied that there is a single mechanism of women's oppression, an immense field of action opens up for feminist politics. One can then perceive the importance of punctual struggles against any oppressive form of constructing sexual differences, be it at the level of law, of the family, of social policy, or of the multiple cultural forms through which the category of 'the feminine' is constantly produced. We are, therefore, in the field of a dispersion of subject positions. The difficulty with this approach, however, arises from the one-sided emphasis given to the moment of dispersion — so one-sided that we are left with only a heterogeneous set of sexual differences constructed through practices which have no relation to one another. Now, while it is absolutely correct to question the idea of an orginal sexual division represented a posteriori in social practices, it is also necessary to recognize that overdetermination among the diverse sexual differences produces a systematic effect of sexual *division*.[30] Every construction of sexual differences, whatever their multiplicity and heterogeneity, invariably constructs the feminine as a pole subordinated to the masculine. It is for this reason that it is possible to speak of a sex/gender system.[31] The ensemble of social practices, of institutions and discourses which produce woman as a category, are not completely isolated but mutually reinforce and act upon one another. This does not mean that there is a single cause of feminine subordination. It is our view that once female sex has come to connote a feminine gender with specific characteristics, this 'imaginary signification' produces concrete effects in the diverse social practices. Thus, there is a close correlation between 'subordination', as a general category informing the ensemble of significations constituting 'femininity', and the autonomy and uneven development of the diverse practices which construct the concrete forms of subordination. These latter are not the *expression* of an immutable feminine essence; in their construction, however, the symbolism which is linked to the feminine condition in a given society, plays a primordial role. The diverse forms of concrete subordination react, in turn, by contributing to the maintenance and reproduction of this symbolism.[32] It is therefore possible to criticize the idea of an original antagonism between men and women, constitutive of the sexual division, without denying that in the various forms of construction of 'femininity', there is a common element which has strong overdetermining effects in terms of the sexual division.

Let us now move on to consider the different forms which the determination of social and political subjects has adopted within the Marxist tradition. The starting-point and constant leitmotiv is clear: the subjects are social classes, whose unity is constituted around interests determined by their position in the relations of production. More important than insisting on this common theme, however, is to study the precise ways in which Marxism has politically and theoretically responded to the diversification and dispersion of subject positions with regard to the paradigmatic forms of their unity. A first type of response — the most elementary — consists of an illegitimate passage through the referent. It involves, for example, the assertion that the workers' political struggle and economic struggle are unified by the concrete social agent — the working class — which conducts them both. This type of reasoning — common not only in Marxism but also in the social sciences as a whole — is based on a fallacy: the expression 'working class' is used in two different ways, to define a specific subject position in the relations of production, and to *name* the agents who occupy that subject position. The resulting ambiguity allows the logically illegitimate conclusion to slip through that the other positions occupied by these agents are also 'working-class positions'. (They are obviously 'working-class' in the second sense, but not necessarily in the first.) The implicit assumption of the unity and transparency of the consciousness of every social agent serves to consolidate the ambiguity — and hence the confusion.

This subterfuge, however, can only operate when one tries to affirm the unity among *empirically given* positions; not when one tries to explain — as has been most frequently the case in the Marxist tradition — the essential heterogeneity of some positions with regard to the others (that is, the characteristic splits of 'false consciousness'). In this case, as we have seen, the unity of the class is conceived as a future unity; the way in which that unity manifests itself is through the category of representation, the split between real workers and their objective interests requiring that the latter be represented by the vanguard party. Now, every relation of representation is founded on a fiction: that of the presence at a certain level of something which, strictly speaking, is absent from it. But because it is *at the same time* a fiction and a principle organizing actual social relations, representation is the terrain of a game whose result is not predetermined from the beginning. At one end of the spectrum of possibilities we would have a dissolution of the fictitious character of representation, so that the means and the field of representation would be totally transparent vis-à-vis what is represented; at the other end, we would have total opaqueness between representative and represented: the fiction would become a fiction in a strictly literal sense. It is important to note that neither of these extremes constitutes an impossible situation, as both have well-defined conditions of possibility: a representative can be subjected to such conditions of control that what becomes a fiction is the very fictitiousness of the representation; and, on the contrary, a total absence of control can make the representation literally fictitious. The Marxist conception of the vanguard party shows this peculiarity: that the party represents not a concrete agent but its historical interests, and that there is no fiction since representative and represented are constituted by the same discourse and on the same plane. This tautological relation, however, exists in its extreme form only in tiny sects which proclaim themselves to be the vanguard of the proletariat, without the proletariat ever realizing, of course, that it has a vanguard. In every political struggle of a certain significance, there is on the contrary a very clear effort to win the allegiance of concrete social agents to their supposed 'historical interests'. If the tautology of a single discourse constituting both represented and representative is abandoned, it is necessary to conclude that represented and representative are constituted at different levels. A first temptation would then be to make total that separation of planes, and to derive the impossibility of the relation of representation from its fictitious character. Thus, it has been stated: 'To deny economism is to reject the classical conception of the economic-political-ideological unity of classes. It is to maintain that political and ideological struggles cannot be conceived as the struggles of economic classes. There is no middle way . . . Class "interests" are not given to politics and ideology by the economy. They arise within the political practice, and they are determined as an effect of definite modes of political practice. Political practice does not recognize class interests and then represent them: it constitutes the interests which it represents.'[33]

This assertion could, however, only be upheld if political practice was a perfectly delimited field, whose frontiers with the economy could be drawn *more geometrico* — that is, if we excluded as a matter of principle any overdetermination of the political by the economic or vice versa. But we know that this separation can only be established a priori in an essentialist conception, which derives a real separation among elements from a conceptual separation, transforming the conceptual specification of an identity into a fully and absolutely differentiated discursive position. Yet, if we accept the overdetermined character of every identity, the situation changes. *There is* a different way which — although we do not know whether it is middle — is in any case a third way. The 'winning over of agents to their historical interests' is, quite simply, an articulatory practice which constructs a discourse wherein the concrete demands of a group — the industrial workers — are conceived as steps towards a total liberation involving the overcoming of capitalism. Undoubtedly, there is no essential necessity for these demands to be articulated in this way. But nor is there an essential necessity for them to be articulated in any other way, given that, as we have seen, the relation of articulation is not a relation of necessity. What the discourse of 'historical interests' does is to *hegemonize* certain demands. On this point, Cutler et al. are absolutely right: political practice constructs the interests it represents. But if we observe closely, we will note that, far from being consolidated, the separation between the economic and the political is hereby *eliminated*. For, a reading in socialist terms of immediate economic struggles discursively articulates the political and the economic, and thus does away with the exteriority existing between the two. The alternative is clear: either the separation between the political and the economic takes place on an extra-discursive plane which secures it a priori; or else that separation is the result of discursive practices, and it is not possible to immunize it a priori from every discourse constructing their unity. If the dispersion of positions is a condition of any articulatory practice, there is no reason why that dispersion should *necessarily* take the form of a separation between the political and the economic identity of social agents. Were economic identity and political identity to be sutured, the conditions of any relation of representation would evidently disappear: we would have returned to the tautological situation in which representative and represented are moments of a single relational identity. Let us accept instead that neither the political identity nor the economic identity of the agents crystallizes as differential moment of a unified discourse, and that the relation between them is the precarious unity of a tension. We already know what this means: the subversion of each of the terms by a polysemy which prevents their stable articulation. In this case, the economic *is* and *is not* present in the political and vice versa; the relation is not one of literal differentiations but of unstable analogies between the two terms. Now, this form of presence through metaphorical transposition is the one that the *fictio iuris* of representation attempts to think. Representation is therefore constituted not as a definite type of relation; but as the field of an unstable oscillation whose vanishing point is, as we saw, either the literalization of the fiction through the breaking of every link between representative and represented, or the disappearance of the separate identity of both through their absorption as moments of a single identity.

All this shows us that the specificity of the category of subject cannot be established either through the absolutization of a dispersion of 'subject positions', or through the equally absolutist unification of these around a 'transcendental subject'. The category of subject is penetrated by the same ambiguous, incomplete and polysemical character which overdetermination assigns to every discursive identity. For this reason, the moment of closure of a discursive totality, which is not given at the 'objective' level of that totality, cannot be established at the level of a 'meaning-giving subject', since the subjectivity of the agent is penetrated by the same precariousness and absence of suture apparent at any other point of the discursive totality of which it is part. 'Objectivism' and 'subjectivism'; 'holism' and 'individualism' are symmetrical expressions of the *desire* for a fullness that is permanently deferred. Owing to this very absence of a final suture, the dispersion of subject positions cannot constitute a solution: given that none of them manages ultimately to consolidate itself as a *separate position,* there is a game of overdetermination among them that reintroduces the horizon of an impossible totality. It is this game which makes hegemonic articulation possible.

Antagonism and Objectivity

The impossibility of closure (i.e., the impossibility of 'society') has up to this point been presented as the precariousness of every identity, which manifests itself as a continuous movement of differences. We must now, however, ask ourselves: are there not some 'experiences', some discursive forms, in which what is manifested is no longer the continuous deferment of the 'transcendental signified', but the very vanity of this deferring, the final impossibility of any stable difference and, thus, of any 'objectivity'?. The answer is yes. This 'experience' of the limit of all objectivity does have a form of precise discursive presence, and this is *antagonism.*

Antagonisms have been widely studied in historical and sociological literature. From Marxism to the various forms of 'conflict theory', a whole range of explanations have been given as to how and why antagonisms emerge in society. This theoretical diversity does, however, display a common feature: the discussion has centred almost exclusively on the description of antagonisms and their original causes. Only rarely has an attempt been made to address the core of our problem: what is an antagonistic relation? what type of relation among objects does it suppose? Let us begin with one of the few discussions which have broached this question: namely, that initiated by Lucio Colletti's analysis of the specificity of social antagonisms, and of the claims which the categories 'real opposition' and 'contradiction' can make to account for that specificity.[34]

Colletti starts from the Kantian distinction between real opposition (*Realrepugnanz*) and logical contradiction. The first coincides with the principle of contrariety and responds to the formula 'A — B': each of its terms has its own positivity, independent of its relation with the other. The second is the category of contradiction and responds to the formula 'A — not A': the relation of each term with the other exhausts the reality of both. Contradiction occurs in the terrain of the proposition; it is only possible to enter into contradictions at a logico–conceptual level. The first type of opposition occurs, on the contrary, in the terrain of real objects, for no *real* object exhausts its identity by its opposition to another object; it has a reality of its own, independent of that opposition.[35] Colletti then concludes that whereas Hegel, as an idealist philosopher who reduced reality to the concept, could introduce contradiction into the real, this is incompatible with a materialist philosophy like Marxism which starts from the extra-mental character of the real. According to this view, Marxists fell into a lamentable confusion by considering antagonisms as contradictions. Colletti's programme is to re-interpret the former in terms of real oppositions.

Let us note that Colletti starts from an exclusive alternative: *either* something is a real opposition, *or* it is a contradiction. This derives from the fact that his universe has room for only two types of entities, real objects and concepts; and that the starting-point and permanent assumption of all his analysis is the separation between thought and reality. There follow a number of consequences which, as we shall try to show, destroy the credentials of both 'real opposition' and 'contradiction' as categories capable of accounting for antagonisms. First of all, it is clear that an antagonism cannot be a *real* opposition. There is nothing antagonistic in a crash between two vehicles: it is a material fact obeying positive physical laws. To apply the same principle to the social terrain would be tantamount to saying that what is antagonistic in class struggle is the physical act by which a policeman hits a worker militant, or the shouts of a group in Parliament which prevent a member of an opposing sector from speaking. 'Opposition' is here a concept of the physical world which has been metaphorically extended to the social world, or vice versa; but there is evidently little point in pretending that there is a common core of meaning which is sufficient to explain the type of relation implicit in both cases. This is even clearer if, in order to refer to the social, we replace 'opposed forces' with 'enemy forces' — for in this case, the metaphorical transposition to the physical world, at least in a post-Homeric universe, has not taken place. It may be objected that it is not the *physical* character of the opposition that counts but only its *extra-logical* character. But it is even less clear how a theory of the specificity of social antagonisms can be grounded upon the mere opposition to logical contradiction that is shared by a clash between two social forces and a collision between two stones.[36]

Furthermore, as Roy Edgley[37] and Jon Elster[38] have pointed out, two different assertions are mixed together in this problem: (a) that the real is contradictory, and (b) that contradictions exist in reality. Regarding the first, there can be no doubt that the statement is self-defeating. Popper's famous critique of the dialectic[39] is, from this point of view, unobjectionable. The second assertion, however, is undeniable: it is a fact that in reality there are situations which can only be described in terms of logical contradiction. Propositions are also a part of the real and, insofar as contradictory propositions exist empirically, it is evident that contradictions exist *in* the real. People argue and, inasmuch as a set of social practices — codes, beliefs, etc. — can adopt a propositional structure, there is no reason why they should not give rise to contradictory propositions. (At this point, however, Edgley falls into the obvious fallacy of believing that the possible real existence of contradictory propositions proves the correctness of the dialectic. The dialectic is a doctrine about the essentially contradictory nature of the real, not about the empirical existence of contradictions in reality.)

It would thus seem that the category of contradiction has an assured place within the real, and that it provides the basis from which to account for social antagonisms. But a moment's reflection is sufficient to convince us that this is not so. We all participate in a number of mutually contradictory belief systems, and yet no antagonism emerges from these contradictions. Contradiction does not, therefore, necessarily imply an antagonistic relation.[40] But if we have excluded both 'real opposition' and 'contradiction' as categories accounting for antagonism, it would seem that the latter's specificity cannot be apprehended. The usual descriptions of antagonisms in the sociological or historical literature confirm this impression: they explain the *conditions* which made antagonisms possible, but not the antagonisms as such. (The description proceeds through expressions such as 'this *provoked* a reaction' or 'in that situation X or Z *found itself* forced to react'. In other words, there is a sudden jump from explanation to an appeal for our common sense or experience to complete the meaning of the text: that is to say, the explanation is interrupted.)

Let us attempt to unravel the meaning of this interruption. First, we must ask ourselves whether the impossibility of assimilating antagonism to real opposition or to contradiction, is not the impossibility of assimilating it to something shared by these types of relation. They do, in fact, share something, and that is the fact of being *objective relations* — between conceptual objects in the second case, and between real objects in the first. But in both cases, it is something that the objects *already are* which makes the relation intelligible. That is, in both cases we are concerned with full identities. In the case of contradiction, it is because A *is fully* A that being-not-A is a contradiction — and therefore an impossibility. In the case of real opposition, it is because A is also fully A that its relation with B produces an objectively determinable effect. But in the case of antagonism, we are confronted with a different situation: the presence of the 'Other' prevents me from being totally myself. The relation arises not from full totalities, but from the impossibility of their constitution. The presence of the Other is not a logical impossibility: it exists; so it is not a contradiction. But neither is it subsumable as a positive differential moment in a causal chain, for in that case the relation would be given by what each force is and there would be no negation of this being. (It is because a physical force *is* a physical force that another identical and countervailing force leads to rest; in contrast, it is because a peasant *cannot be* a peasant that an antagonism exists with the landowner expelling him from his land.) Insofar as there is antagonism, I cannot be a full presence for myself. But nor is the force that antagonizes me such a presence: its objective being is a symbol of my non-being and, in this way, it is overflowed by a plurality of meanings which prevent its being fixed as full positivity. Real opposition is an *objective* relation — that is, determinable, definable — among things; contradiction is an equally definable relation among concepts; antagonism constitutes the limits of every objectivity, which is revealed as partial and precarious *objectification*. If language is a system of differences, antagonism is the failure of difference: in that sense, it situates itself within the limits of language and can only exist as the disruption of it — that is, as metaphor. We can thus understand why sociological and historical narratives must interrupt themselves and call upon an 'experience', transcending their categories, to fill their hiatuses: for every language and every society are constituted as a repression of the consciousness of the impossibility that penetrates them. Antagonism escapes the possibility of being apprehended through language, since language only exists as an attempt to fix that which antagonism subverts.

Antagonism, far from being an objective relation, is a relation wherein the limits of every objectivity are *shown* — in the sense in which Wittgenstein used to say that what cannot be *said* can be *shown*. But if, as we have demonstrated, the social only exists as a partial effort for constructing society — that is, an objective and closed system of differences — antagonism, as a witness of the impossibility of a final suture, is the 'experience' of the limit of the social. Strictly speaking, antagonisms are not *internal* but *external* to society; or rather, they constitute the limits of society, the latter's impossibility of fully constituting itself. This statement may seem paradoxical, but only if we surreptitiously introduce certain assumptions which must be carefully excluded from our theoretical perspective. In particular, two such assumptions would make absurd our thesis concerning the theoretical location of antagonism. The first is the identification of 'society' with an ensemble of *physically* existing agents who live within a given territory. If this criterion is accepted, it is obvious that antagonisms occur *among* those agents and are not external to them. But it does not necessarily follow, from the 'empirical' coexistence of the agents, that the relations among them should be shaped according to an objective and intelligible pattern. (The price of identifying 'society' with the referent would be to empty it of any rationally specifiable content.) However, accepting that 'society' is an intelligible and objective ensemble, we would introduce another assumption incompatible with our analysis if we attributed to that *rational totality* the character of an underlying principle of the social conceived as an *empirical totality*. For there would then no longer be any aspect of the second which could not be reabsorbed as a moment of the first. In that case antagonisms, like everything else, would have to be *positive internal* moments of society, and we would have returned to the Hegelian cunning of reason. But if we maintain our conception of the social as a non-sutured space, as a field in which all positivity is metaphorical and subvertible, then there is no way of referring the *negation* of an objective position to an underlying positivity — be it causal or of any other type — which would account for it. Antagonism as the negation of a given order is, quite simply, the limit of that order, and not the moment of a broader totality in relation to which the two poles of the antagonism would constitute differential — i.e. objective — partial instances. (Let us be understood: the conditions which made the antagonism possible may be described as positivities, but the antagonism as such is not reducible to them.)

We must consider this 'experience' of the limit of the social from two different points of view. On the one hand, as an experience of failure. If the subject is constructed through language, as a partial and metaphorical incorporation into a symbolic order, any putting into question of that order must necessarily constitute an identity crisis. But, on the other hand, this experience of failure is not an access to a diverse ontological order, to a something beyond differences, simply because . . . there is no beyond. The limit of the social cannot be traced as a frontier separating two territories — for the perception of a frontier supposes the perception of something beyond it that would have to be objective and positive — that is, a new difference. The limit of the social must be given within the social itself as something subverting it, destroying its ambition to constitute a full presence. Society never manages fully to be society, because everything in it is penetrated by its limits, which prevent it from constituting itself as an objective reality. We must now consider the way in which this subversion is discursively constructed. As we have seen, this will require us to determine the forms assumed by the presence of the antagonistic as such.

Equivalence and Difference

How does this subversion occur? As we have seen, the condition for a full presence is the existence of a closed space where each differential position is fixed as a specific and irreplaceable moment. So, the first condition for the subversion of that space, for the prevention of closure, is that the specificity of each position should be dissolved. It is at this point that our earlier remarks about the relation of equivalence acquire all their relevance. Let us give an example. In a colonized country, the presence of the dominant power is every day made evident through a variety of contents: differences of dress, of language, of skin colour, of customs. Since each of these contents is equivalent to the others in terms of their common differentiation from the colonized people, it loses its condition of differential *moment,* and acquires the floating character of an *element.* Thus, equivalence creates a second meaning which, though parasitic on the first, subverts it: the differences cancel one other out insofar as they are used to express something identical underlying them all. The problem is to determine the content of that 'identical something' present in the various terms of the equivalence. If, through the chain of equivalence, *all* the differential objective determinations of its terms have been lost, then identity can only be given either by a positive determination underlying them all, or by their common reference to something external. The first of these possibilities is excluded: a common positive determination is expressed in a direct way, without requiring a relation of equivalence. But the common external reference cannot be to something positive, for in that case the relation between the two poles could also be constructed in a direct and positive way, and this would make impossible the complete cancellation of differences implied by a relation of total equivalence. This is the case, for example, in Marx's analysis of the relation of equivalence. The *non-materiality* of labour as substance of value is expressed through the equivalence among *materially* diverse commodities. However, the materiality of commodities and the non-materiality of value are not equivalent to each other. It is because of this that the use-value/exchange-value distinction can be conceived in terms of differential and, hence, positive positions. But if *all* the differential features of an object have become equivalent, it is impossible to express anything *positive* concerning that object; this can only imply that through the equivalence something is expressed which the object *is not*. Thus, a relation of equivalence absorbing *all* the positive determinations of the colonizer in opposition to the colonized, does not create a system of positive differential positions between the two, simply because it dissolves all positivity: the colonizer is discursively constructed as the anti-colonized. In other words, the identity has come to be purely negative. It is because a negative identity cannot be represented in a direct manner — i.e., positively — that it can only be represented indirectly, through an equivalence between its differential moments. Hence the ambiguity penetrating every relation of equivalence: two terms, to be equivalent, must be different — otherwise, there would be a simple identity. On the other hand, the equivalence exists only through the act of subverting the differential character of those terms. This is exactly the point where, as we said earlier, the contingent subverts the necessary by preventing it from fully constituting itself. This non-constitutivity — or contingency — of the system of differences is *revealed* in the unfixity which equivalences introduce. The *ultimate* character of this unfixity, the *ultimate* precariousness of all difference, will thus show itself in a relation of total equivalence, where the differential positivity of all its terms is dissolved. This is precisely the formula of antagonism, which thus establishes itself as the limit of the social. We should note that in this formula it is not the case that a pole defined as positivity confronts a negative pole: as *all* the differential determinations of a pole have dissolved through their negative-equivalential reference to the other pole, each one of them shows exclusively what it is not.

Let us insist once again: to be something is always not to be something else (to be A implies not to be B). This banality is not what we are asserting, as it is situated in a *logical* terrain entirely dominated by the principle of contradiction: *not being* something is simply the logical consequence of being something different; the positivity of being dominates the totality of the discourse. What we affirm is something different: *that certain discursive forms, through equivalence, annul all positivity of the object and give a real existence to negativity as such*. This impossibility of the real — negativity — has attained a form of presence. As the social is penetrated by negativity — that is, by antagonism — it does not attain the status of transparency, of full presence, and the objectivity of its identities is permanently subverted. From here onward, the impossible relation between objectivity and negativity has become constitutive of the social. Yet the impossibility of the relation remains: it is for this reason that the coexistence of its terms must be conceived not as an objective relation of frontiers, but as reciprocal subversion of their contents.

This last point is important: if negativity and objectivity exist only through their reciprocal subversion, this means that neither the conditions of total equivalence nor those of total differential objectivity are ever fully achieved. The condition of total equivalence is that the discursive space should strictly divide into two camps. Antagonism does not admit *tertium quid*. And it is easy to see why. For if we could differentiate the chain of equivalences with regard to something other than that which it opposes, its terms could not be exclusively defined in a negative manner. We would have adjudicated to it a specific position in a system of relations: that is, we would have endowed it with a new objectivity. The logic of the subversion of differences would here have found a limit. But, just as the logic of difference never manages to constitute a fully sutured space, neither does the logic of equivalence ever achieve this. The dissolution of the differential character of the social agent's positions through the equivalential condensation, is never complete. If society is not totally possible, neither is it totally impossible. This allows us to formulate the following conclusion: if society is never transparent to itself because it is unable to constitute itself as an objective field, neither is antagonism entirely transparent, as it does not manage totally to dissolve the objectivity of the social.

At this point, we must move on to consider the structuring of political spaces, from the points of view of the opposed logics of equivalence and difference. Let us take certain polar examples of situations in which one or the other predominates. An extreme example of the logic of equivalence can be found in millennarian movements. Here the world divides, through a system of paratactical equivalences, into two camps: peasant culture representing the identity of the movement, and urban culture incarnating evil. The second is the negative reverse of the first. A maximum separation has been reached: no element in the system of equivalences enters into relations other than those of opposition to the elements of the other system. There are not one but two societies. And when the millennarian rebellion takes place, the assault on the city is fierce, total and indiscriminate: there exist no discourses capable of establishing differences within an equivalential chain in which each and every one of its elements symbolizes evil. (The only alternative is massive emigration towards another region in order to set up the City of God, totally isolated from the corruption of the world.)

Now let us consider an opposite example: the politics of Disraeli in the nineteenth century. Disraeli as a novelist had started from his conception of the two nations, that is, of a clear-cut division of society into the two extremes of poverty and wealth. To this we must add the equally clear-cut division of European political space between the *'anciens régimes'* and the 'people'. (The first half of the nineteenth century, under the combined effects of the industrial revolution and the democratic revolution, was the era of the frontal chains of equivalence.) This was the situation Disraeli wanted to change, and his first objective was to overcome the paratactical division of social space — that is, the impossibility of constituting society. His formula was clear: 'one nation'. For this it was necessary to break the system of equivalences which made up the popular revolutionary subjectivity, stretching from republicanism to a varied ensemble of social and political demands. The method of this rupture: the differential absorption of demands, which segregated them from their chains of equivalence in the popular chain and transformed them into objective differences within the system — that is, transformed them into 'positivities' and thus displaced the frontier of antagonism to the periphery of the social. This constitution of a pure space of differences would be a tendential line, which was later expanded and affirmed with the development of the Welfare State. This is the moment of the positivist illusion that the ensemble of the social can be absorbed in the intelligible and ordered framework of a society.

We, thus, see that the logic of equivalence is a logic of the simplification of political space, while the logic of difference is a logic of its expansion and increasing complexity. Taking a comparative example from linguistics, we could say that the logic of difference tends to expand the syntagmatic pole of language, the number of positions that can enter into a relation of combination and hence of continuity with one another; while the logic of equivalence expands the paradigmatic pole — that is, the elements that can be substituted for one another — thereby reducing the number of positions which can possibly be combined.

Until now, when we have spoken of antagonism, we have kept it in the singular in order to simplify our argument. But it is clear that antagonism does not necessarily emerge at a single point: any position in a system of differences, insofar as it is negated, can become the locus of an antagonism. Hence, there are a variety of possible antagonisms in the social, many of them in opposition to each other. The important problem is that the chains of equivalence will vary radically according to which antagonism is involved; and that they may affect and penetrate, in a contradictory way, the identity of the subject itself. This gives rise to the following conclusion: the more unstable the social relations, the less successful will be any definite system of differences and the more the points of antagonism will proliferate. This proliferation will make more difficult the construction of any centrality and, consequently, the establishment of unified chains of equivalence. (This is, approximately, the situation described by Gramsci under the term 'organic crisis'.)

It would thus seem that our problem may be reduced, in the analysis of the political spaces which are the foundation of antagonisms, to one of determining the points of rupture and their possible modes of articulation. But here we enter a dangerous terrain in which slight displacements in our reasoning can lead to radically mistaken conclusions. We shall therefore start from an impressionistic description and then attempt to determine the conditions of validity of that descriptive picture. It would appear that an important differential characteristic may be established between advanced industrial societies and the periphery of the capitalist world: in the former, the proliferation of points of antagonism permits the multiplication of democratic struggles, but these struggles, given their diversity, do not tend to constitute a 'people', that is, to enter into equivalence with one another and to divide the political space into two antagonistic fields. On the contrary, in the countries of the Third World, imperialist exploitation and the predominance of brutal and centralized forms of domination tend from the beginning to endow the popular struggle with a centre, with a single and clearly defined enemy. Here the division of the political space into two fields is present from the outset, but the diversity of democratic struggles is more reduced. We shall use the term *popular subject position* to refer to the position that is constituted on the basis of dividing the political space into two antagonistic camps; and *democratic subject position* to refer to the locus of a clearly delimited antagonism which does not divide society in that way.

Now, this descriptive distinction confronts us with a serious difficulty. For if a democratic struggle *does not divide* the political space into two camps, into two paratactical series of equivalences, it follows that the democratic antagonism occupies a precise location in a system of relations with other elements; that a system of positive relations is established among them; and that there is a lessening of the charge of negativity attaching to the antagonism. From here it is but one step to affirm that democratic struggles — feminism, anti-racism, the gay movement, etc. — are secondary struggles and that the struggle for the 'seizure of power' in the classical sense is the only truly radical one, as it supposes just such a division of the political space into two camps. The difficulty arises, however, from the fact that the notion of 'political space' has not been given a precise definition in our analysis, so that it has surreptitiously been made to coincide with the empirically given social formation. This is, of course, an illegitimate identification. Any democratic struggle emerges within an ensemble of positions, within a *relatively* sutured political space formed by a multiplicity of practices that do not exhaust the referential and empirical reality of the agents forming part of them. The relative closure of that space is necessary for the discursive construction of the antagonism, given that the delimitation of a certain interiority is required to construct a totality permitting the division of this space into two camps. In this sense, the autonomy of social movements is something more than a requirement for certain struggles to develop without interference: it is a requirement for the antagonism as such to emerge. The political space of the feminist struggle is constituted within the ensemble of practices and discourses which create the different forms of the subordination of women; the space of the anti-racist struggle, within the overdetermined ensemble of practices constituting racial discrimination. But the antagonisms within each of these relatively autonomized spaces divide them into two camps. This explains the fact that, when social struggles are directed not against objects constituted within their own space but against simple empirical referents — for example, men or white people as biological referents — they find themselves in difficulties. For, such struggles ignore the specificity of the political spaces in which the other democratic antagonisms emerge. Take, for example, a discourse which presents men, qua biological reality, as the enemy. What will happen to a discourse of this kind when it is necessary to develop antagonisms like the struggle for the freedom of expression or the struggle against the monopolization of economic power, both of which affect men and women? As to the terrain where those spaces become autonomous from one another, in part it is constituted by the discursive formations which have institutionalized the various forms of subordination, and in part it is the result of the struggles themselves.

Once we have constructed the theoretical terrain which permits the radical antagonistic character of democratic struggles to be explained, what remains of the specificity of the 'popular' camp? Does not the non-correspondence between 'political space' and 'society' as an empirical referent annul the sole differential criterion between 'the popular' and 'the democratic'? The answer is that the political space of the popular emerges in those situations where, through a chain of democratic equivalences, a political logic *tends* to bridge the gap between political space and society as an empirical referent. Conceived in this manner, popular struggles only occur in the case of relations of extreme exteriority between the dominant groups and the rest of the community. In the case of millenarianism, to which we previously referred, the point is evident: between the peasant community and the dominant urban community there are practically no elements in common; and, in this sense, *all* the features of urban culture can be symbols of the anti-community. If we turn to the cycle of expansion and constitution of popular spaces in Western Europe, we notice that all such cases have coincided with the phenomenon of externality or externalization of power. The beginnings of populist patriotism in France appeared during the Hundred Years War, that is, in the midst of a division of the political space resulting from something so external as the presence of a foreign power. The symbolic construction of a *national* space through the action of a plebeian figure like Joan of Arc is, in Western Europe, one of the first moments of emergence of the 'people' as a historical agent. In the case of the *ancien régime* and the French Revolution, the frontier of the popular has become an internal frontier, and its condition is the separation and parasitism of the nobility and the monarchy vis-à-vis the rest of the nation. But, through the process we have pointed out, in the countries of advanced capitalism since the middle of the nineteenth century, the multiplication and 'uneven development' of democratic positions have increasingly diluted their simple and automatic unity around a popular pole. Partly because of their very success, democratic struggles tend less and less to be unified as 'popular struggles'. The conditions of political struggle in mature capitalism are increasingly distant from the nineteenth-century model of a clear-cut 'politics of frontiers' and tend to adopt a new pattern which we will attempt to analyse in the next chapter. The production of 'frontier effects' — which are the condition of expansion of the negativity pertaining to antagonisms — ceases thus to be grounded upon an *evident and given* separation, in a referential framework acquired once and for all. The production of this framework, the constitution of the very identities which will have to confront one another antagonistically, becomes now *the first of political problems*. This widens immensely the field of articulatory practices, and transforms any frontier into something essentially ambiguous and unstable, subject to constant displacements. Having reached this point, we have all the necessary theoretical elements to determine the specificity of the concept of hegemony.

Hegemony

We must now see how our different theoretical categories link up to produce the concept of 'hegemony'. The general field of the emergence of hegemony is that of articulatory practices, that is, a field where the 'elements' have not crystallized into 'moments'. In a closed system of relational identities, in which the meaning of each moment is absolutely fixed, there is no place whatsoever for a hegemonic practice. A fully successful system of differences, which excluded any floating signifier, would not make possible any articulation; the principle of repetition would dominate every practice within this system and there would be nothing to hegemonize. It is because hegemony supposes the incomplete and open character of the social, that it can take place only in a field dominated by articulatory practices.

This, however, immediately poses the problem: who is the articulating subject? We have already seen the answer that the Marxism of the Third International gave to this question: from Lenin to Gramsci it maintained — with all the nuances and differences we analysed earlier — that the ultimate core of a hegemonic force consists of a fundamental class. The difference between hegemonic and hegemonized forces is posed as an ontological difference between the planes of constitution of each of them. Hegemonic relations are syntactic relations founded upon morphological categories which precede them. But it is clear that this cannot be our answer, for it is precisely that differentiation of planes which all our previous analysis has attempted to dissolve. In point of fact, we are once again confronted with the interiority/exteriority alternative, and with the two equally essentialist solutions which we would face if we accepted it as exclusive. The hegemonic subject, as the subject of any articulatory practice, must be partiallly exterior to what it articulates — otherwise, there would not be any articulation at all. On the other hand, however, such exteriority cannot be conceived as that existing between two different ontological levels. Consequently, it would seem that the solution is to reintroduce our distinction between discourse and general field of discursivity: in that case, both the hegemonic force and the ensemble of hegemonized elements would constitute themselves on the same plane — the general field of discursivity — while the exteriority would be that corresponding to different discursive formations. No doubt this is so, but it must be further specified that this exteriority cannot correspond to two fully constituted discursive formations. For, what characterizes a discursive formation is the regularity in dispersion, and if that exteriority were a regular feature in the relation between the two formations, it would become a new difference and the two formations would not, strictly speaking, be external to each other. (And with this, once again, the possibility of any articulation would disappear.) Hence, if the exteriority supposed by the articulatory practice is located in the general field of discursivity, it cannot be that corresponding to two systems of fully constituted differences. It must therefore be the exteriority existing between subject positions located within certain discursive formations and 'elements' which have no precise discursive articulation. It is this ambiguity which makes possible articulation as a practice instituting nodal points which partially fix the meaning of the social in an organized system of differences.

We must now consider the specificity of the hegemonic practice within the general field of articulatory practices. Let us start from two situations which we would *not* characterize as hegemonic articulations. At one extreme we could refer, as an example, to a reorganization of an ensemble of bureaucratic administrative functions according to criteria of efficiency or rationality. Here are present central elements of any articulatory practice: constitution of an organized system of differences — of moments, therefore — starting from disaggregated and dispersed elements. And here, however, we would not speak of hegemony. The reason is that in order to speak of hegemony, the articulatory moment is not sufficient. It is also necessary that the articulation should take place through a confrontation with antagonistic articulatory practices — in other words, that hegemony should emerge in a field criss-crossed by antagonisms and therefore suppose phenomena of equivalence and frontier effects. But, conversely, not every antagonism supposes hegemonic practices. In the case of millennarianism, for example, we have an antagonism in its most pure form, and yet there is no hegemony because there is no articulation of floating elements: the distance between the two communities is something immediately given and acquired from the beginning, and it does not suppose any articulatory construction. The chains of equivalence do not construct the communitarian space; rather, they operate on pre-existing communitarian spaces. Thus, the two conditions of a hegemonic articulation are the presence of antagonistic forces and the instability of the frontiers which separate them. Only the presence of a vast area of floating elements and the possibility of their articulation to opposite camps — which implies a constant redefinition of the latter — is what constitutes the terrain permitting us to define a practice as hegemonic. Without equivalence and without frontiers, it is impossible to speak strictly of hegemony.

At this point it is clear how we may recover the basic concepts of Gramscian analysis, although it will be necessary to radicalize them in a direction that leads us beyond Gramsci. A conjuncture where there is a generalized weakening of the relational system defining the identities of a given social or political space, and where, as a result there is a proliferation of floating elements, is what we will call following Gramsci, a conjuncture of *organic crisis*. It does not emerge from a single point, but it is the result of an overdetermination of circumstances; and it reveals itself not only in a proliferation of antagonisms but also in a generalized crisis of social identites. A social and political space relatively unified through the instituting of nodal points and the constitution of *tendentially* relational identities, is what Gramsci called a *historical bloc*. The type of link joining the different elements of the historical bloc — not unity in any form of historical a priori, but regularity in dispersion — coincides with our concept of discursive formation. Insofar as we consider the historical bloc from the point of view of the antagonistic terrain in which it is constituted, we will call it *hegemonic formation*.

Finally, inasmuch as the hegemonic formation implies a phenomenon of frontiers, the concept of *war of position* reveals its full significance. Through this concept Gramsci brings about two important theoretical effects. The first is to confirm the impossibility of any closure of the social: since the frontier is internal to the social, it is impossible to subsume the social formation as an empirical referent under the intelligible forms of a society. Every 'society' constitutes its own forms of rationality and intelligibility by dividing itself; that is, by expelling outside itself any surplus of meaning subverting it. But, on the other hand, insofar as that frontier varies with the fluctuations in the 'war of position', the identity of the actors in confrontation also changes, and it is therefore impossible to find in them that final anchorage not offered to us by any sutured totality. Earlier we said that the concept of war of position led to a demilitarization of war; it actually does something more: it introduces a radical ambiguity into the social which prevents it from being fixed in any transcendental signified. This is, however, the point at which the concept of war of position displays its limits. War of position *supposes* the division of the social space into two camps and presents the hegemonic articulation as a logic of mobility of the frontier separating them. However, it is evident that this assumption is illegitimate: the existence of two camps may in some cases be an *effect* of the hegemonic articulation but not its a priori condition — for, if it were, the terrain in which the hegemonic articulation operated would not itself be the product of that articulation. The Gramscian war of position supposes the type of division of the political space which earlier we characterized as specific to *popular* identities. Its advance over the nineteenth-century conception of the 'people' consists in the fact that for Gramsci such a popular identity is no longer something simply given, but has to be constructed — hence the articulatory logic of hegemony; there still remains, however, from the old conception, the idea that such a construction *always* operates on the basis of expanding the frontier within a dichotomically divided political space. This is the point where the Gramscian view becomes unacceptable. As we pointed out earlier, the proliferation of these political spaces, and the complexity and difficulty of their articulation, are a central characteristic of the advanced capitalist social formations. We will thus retain from the Gramscian view the logic of articulation and the political centrality of the frontier effects, but we will eliminate the assumption of a single political space as the *necessary* framework for those phenomena to arise. We will therefore speak of *democratic* struggles where these imply a plurality of political spaces, and of *popular* struggles where certain discourses *tendentially* construct the division of a single political space in two opposed fields. But it is clear that the fundamental concept is that of 'democratic struggle', and that popular struggles are merely specific conjunctures resulting from the multiplication of equivalence effects among the democratic struggles.

It is clear from the above that we have moved away from two key aspects of Gramsci's thought: (a) his insistence that hegemonic subjects are necessarily constituted on the plane of the fundamental classes; and (b) his postulate that, with the exception of interregna constituted by organic crises, every social formation structures itself around a single hegemonic centre. As we pointed out earlier, these are the two last elements of essentialism remaining in Gramscian thought. But, as a result of abandoning them, we must now confront two successive series of problems that did not arise for Gramsci.

The first problem concerns the separation of planes, the external moment which hegemony, like any articulatory relation, supposes. As we have seen, this does not present any problems for Gramsci, as the final class core of a 'collective will' is not, in his analysis, the result of hegemonic articulations. But how do things stand once the ontological privilege of this final core has been dissolved? If, in the case of a successful hegemony, the articulatory practices have managed to construct a structural system of differences, of relational identities, does not the external character of the hegemonic force also disappear? Does it not become a new difference within the historical bloc? The answer must undoubtedly be affirmative. A situation in which a system of differences had been so welded together would imply the end of the hegemonic form of politics. In that case there would be relations of subordination or power, but not, strictly speaking, hegemonic relations. For, with the disappearance of the separation of planes, of the moment of exteriority, the field of articulatory practices would also have disappeared. The hegemonic dimension of politics only expands as the open, non-sutured character of the social increases. In a medieval peasant community the area open to differential articulations is minimal and, thus, there are no hegemonic forms of articulation: there is an abrupt transition from repetitive practices within a closed system of differences to frontal and absolute equivalences when the community finds itself threatened. This is why the hegemonic form of politics only becomes dominant at the beginning of modern times, when the reproduction of the different social areas takes place in permanently changing conditions which constantly require the construction of new systems of differences. Hence the area of articulatory practices is immensely broadened. Thus the conditions and the possibility of a pure fixing of differences recede; every social identity becomes the meeting point for a multiplicity of articulatory practices, many of them antagonistic. In these circumstances, it is not possible to arrive at a complete interiorization that totally bridges the gap between articulated and articulator. But, it is important to emphasize, neither is it possible for the identity of the articulating force to remain separate and unchanged. Both are subjected to a constant process of subversion and redefinition. This is so much the case that not even a system of equivalences is immune to the danger of being transformed into a new difference: it is known how the frontal opposition of many groups to a system can cease to be exterior to it and become simply a contradictory but internal location within that system — that is, another difference. A hegemonic formation also embraces what opposes it, insofar as the opposing force accepts the system of basic articulations of that formation as something it negates, but the *place of the negation* is defined by the internal parameters of the formation itself. So, the theoretical determination of the conditions of extinction of the hegemonic form of politics, also explains the reasons for the constant expansion of this form in modern times.

The second problem refers to the singleness of the hegemonic centre. Once we reject the ontological plane, which would inscribe hegemony as *centre* of the social and hence as its essence, it is evidently not possible to maintain the idea of the singleness of the nodal hegemonic point. Hegemony is, quite simply, a political *type of relation,* a *form,* if one so wishes, of politics; but not a determinable location within a topography of the social. In a given social formation, there can be a variety of hegemonic nodal points. Evidently some of them may be highly overdetermined: they may constitute points of condensation of a number of social relations and, thus, become the focal point of a multiplicity of totalizing effects. But insofar as the social is an infinitude not reducible to any underlying unitary principle, the mere idea of a centre of the social has no meaning at all. Once the status of the concept of hegemony and the characteristic plurality of the social has been redefined in these terms, we must ask ourselves about the forms of relation existing between them. This irreducible plurality of the social has frequently been conceived as an autonomization of spheres and forms of struggle. This requires that we briefly analyse some of the problems related to the concept of 'autonomy'. In recent years there has been considerable debate concerning, for example, the concept of 'relative autonomy of the State',[41] but it has mostly been posed in terms that have led it into a dead end. In general, such attempts to explain the 'relative autonomy of the State' were made in a framework that accepted the assumption of a sutured society — for example, through determination in the last instance by the economy — and so the problem of relative autonomy, be it of the State or of any other entity, became insoluble. For, either the structural framework constituted by the basic determinations of society explains not only the limits of autonomy but also the nature of the autonomous entity — in which case that entity is another structural determination of the system and the concept of 'autonomy' is redundant; or else the autonomous entity is not determined by the system, in which case it is necessary to explain where it is constituted, and the premise of a sutured society would also have to be discarded. It is precisely the wish to combine this premise with a concept of autonomy inconsistent with it, that has marred most contemporary Marxist debate on the State — the work of Poulantzas in particular. If, however, we renounce the hypothesis of a final closure of the social, it is necessary to start from a plurality of political and social spaces which do not refer to any ultimate unitarian basis. Plurality is not the phenomenon to be explained, but the starting point of the analysis. But if, as we have seen, the identity of each of these spaces is always precarious, it is not possible simply to affirm the equation between autonomy and dispersion. Neither total autonomy nor total subordination is, consequently, a plausible solution. This clearly indicates that the problem cannot be resolved in the terrain of a stable system of differences; that both autonomy and subordination — and their different degrees of relativity — are concepts which only acquire their meaning in the field of articulatory practices and, insofar as these operate in political fields crisscrossed by antagonisms, of hegemonic practices. Articulatory practices take place not only *within* given social and political spaces, but *between* them. The autonomy of the State as a whole — assuming for a moment that we can speak of it as a unity — depends on the construction of a political space which can only be the result of hegemonic articulations. And something similar can be said for the degree of unity and autonomy existing among the different branches and apparatuses of the State. That is, the autonomization of certain spheres is not the necessary structural effect of anything, but rather the result of precise articulatory practices constructing that autonomy. *Autonomy, far from being incompatible with hegemony, is a form of hegemonic construction.*

Something similar can be said for the other important use made of the concept of autonomy in recent years: autonomy linked to the pluralism required by the expansion of the new social movements. Here we are in the same situation. If the identity of the subjects or social forces that become autonomous was constituted once and for all, the problem would be posed *only* in terms of autonomy. But if these identities depend on certain precise social and political conditions of existence, autonomy itself can only be defended and expanded in terms of a wider hegemonic struggle. The feminist or ecological political subjects, for example, are up to a certain point, *like any other social identity*, floating signifiers, and it is a dangerous illusion to think that they are assured once and for all, that the terrain which has constituted their discursive conditions of emergence cannot be subverted. The question of a hegemony which would come to threaten the autonomy of certain movements is, therefore, a badly posed problem. Strictly speaking, this incompatibility would *only* exist if the social movements were monads, disconnected one from another; but if the identity of each movement can never be acquired once and for all, then it cannot be indifferent to what takes place outside it. That, in certain circumstances, the class political subjectivity of white workers in Britain is overdetermined by racist or anti-racist attitudes, is evidently important for the struggle of the immigrant workers. This will bear upon certain practices of the trade union movement, which will in turn have consequences in a number of aspects of State policy and ultimately rebound upon the political identity of the immigrant workers themselves. Here there clearly is a hegemonic struggle, insofar as the articulation between the trade union militancy of white workers and racism or anti-racism is not defined from the beginning; but the forms of this struggle undertaken by anti-racist movements will in part pass through the autonomization of certain activities and organizational forms, partly through systems of alliances with other forces, and partly through the construction of systems of equivalence among contents of the different movements. For, nothing can consolidate anti-racist struggles more than the construction of stable forms of overdetermination among such contents as anti-racism, anti-sexism and anti-capitalism which, left to themselves, do not necessarily tend to converge. Once again, autonomy is not opposed to hegemony, but is an internal moment of a wider hegemonic operation. (Evidently, this operation does not necessarily pass through the 'party' form, nor through a single institutional form, nor through any other type of a priori arrangement.)

If hegemony is a *type of political relation* and not a topographical concept, it is clear that it cannot either be conceived as an irradiation of effects from a privileged point. In this sense, we could say that hegemony is basically metonymical: its effects always emerge from a surplus of meaning which results from an operation of displacement. (For example, a trade union or a religious organization may take on organizational functions in a community, which go beyond the traditional practices ascribed to them, and which are combated and resisted by opposing forces.) This moment of dislocation is essential to any hegemonic practice: we have witnessed it from the very emergence of the concept in Russian Social Democracy, under the form of the exteriority of class identity to the hegemonic tasks; and our conclusion is that no social identity is ever totally acquired — a fact which gives the articulatory-hegemonic moment the full measure of its centrality. The condition of this centrality is, therefore, the collapse of a clear demarcation line between the internal and the external, between the contingent and the necessary. But this leads to an inescapable conclusion: no hegemonic logic can account for the totality of the social and constitute its centre, for in that case a new suture would have been produced and the very concept of hegemony would have eliminated itself. The openness of the social is, thus, the precondition of every hegemonic practice. Now, this necessarily leads to a second conclusion: the hegemonic formation, as we have conceived it, cannot be referred to the specific logic of a single social force. Every historical bloc — or hegemonic formation — is constructed through regularity in dispersion, and this dispersion includes a proliferation of very diverse elements: systems of differences which partially define relational identities; chains of equivalences which subvert the latter but which can be transformistically recovered insofar as the place of opposition itself becomes regular and, in that way, constitutes a new difference; forms of overdetermination which concentrate either power, or the different forms of resistance to it; and so forth. The important point is that every form of power is constructed in a pragmatic way and *internally* to the social, through the opposed logics of equivalence and difference; power is never *foundational*. The problem of power cannot, therefore, be posed in terms of the search for *the* class or *the* dominant sector which constitutes the centre of a hegemonic formation, given that, by definition, such a centre will always elude us. But it is equally wrong to propose as an alternative, either pluralism or the total diffusion of power within the social, as this would blind the analysis to the presence of nodal points and to the partial concentrations of power existing in every concrete social formation. This is the point at which many of the concepts of classical analysis — 'centre', 'power', 'autonomy', etc. — can be reintroduced, if their status is redefined: all of them are contingent *social logics* which, as such, acquire their meaning in precise conjunctural and relational contexts, where they will always be limited by other — frequently contradictory — logics; but none of them has absolute validity, in the sense of defining a space or structural moment which could not in its turn be subverted. It is, therefore, impossible to arrive at a theory of the social on the basis of absolutizing any of those concepts. If society is not sutured by any single unitary and *positive* logic, our understanding of it cannot provide that logic. A 'scientific' approach attempting to determine the 'essence' of the social would, in actual fact, be the height of utopianism.

One important point before we conclude. In the foregoing argument we spoke of 'social formation' as an empirical referent, and of 'hegemonic formation' as an articulated totality of differences. The same term — 'formation' — is used, therefore, in two totally different senses, and we must attempt to eliminate the resulting ambiguity. The problem in its more general form may be formulated as follows: if an ensemble of empirically given agents (in the case of a social formation) or an ensemble of discursive moments (in the case of a hegemonic formation) are included in the totality implied by the notion of formation, it is because through that totality it is possible to distinguish them with regard to something external to the latter. Thus, it is on the basis of its own limits that a formation is shaped as a totality. If we pose the problem of the construction of these limits in the case of a hegemonic formation, we will have to distinguish two levels: that related to the abstract conditions of possibility of every 'formation', and that related to the specific difference which the logic of hegemony introduces into it. Let us begin from the internal space of a formation as a relatively stable system of differences. It is clear that the logic of difference is not sufficient to construct limits, for if it were exclusively dominant, what lay beyond it could only be other differences, and the regularity of these would transform them into a part of the formation itself. If we remain in the field of differences, we remain in the field of an infinitude which makes it impossible to think any frontier and which, consequently, dissolves the concept of 'formation'. That is, limits only exist insofar as a systematic ensemble of differences can be cut out as *totality* with regard to something *beyond* them, and it is only through this cutting out that the totality constitutes itself as formation. If, from what has been said, it is clear that that beyond cannot consist in something positive — in a new difference — then the only possibility is that it will consist in something negative. But we already know that the logic of equivalence is the one that introduces negativity into the field of the social. This implies that a formation manages *to signify itself* (that is, to constitute itself as such) only by transforming the limits into frontiers, by constituting a chain of equivalences which constructs what is beyond the limits as that which it *is not*. It is only through negativity, division and antagonism that a formation can constitute itself as a totalizing horizon.

The logic of equivalence, however, is merely the most abstract and general condition of existence of every formation. In order to be able to speak of hegemonic formation, we have to introduce another condition provided by our previous analysis: namely, that continuous redefinition of the social and political spaces and those constant processes of displacement of the limits constructing social division, which are proper to contemporary societies. It is only under these conditions that the totalities shaped through the logic of equivalence acquire a hegemonic character. But this would seem to imply that, insofar as this precariousness tends to make unstable the internal frontiers of the social, the category of formation itself is threatened. And this is exactly what occurs: if every frontier disappears, this does not simply mean that the formation is more difficult to *recognize*. As the totality is not a datum but a construction, when there is a breaking of its constitutive chains of equivalence, the totality does something more than conceal itself: *it dissolves*.

It follows from this that the term 'social formation', when used to designate a referent, is meaningless. Social agents do not, as referents, constitute any formation. If the term 'social formation' attempts, for example, in an apparently neutral way, to designate the social agents living in a given territory, the problem is immediately posed of the limits of that that territory. And here it is necessary to define political boundaries — that is, configurations constituted at a level different from that of the simple referential entity of the agents. Here there are two options: either the political limits are considered as a simple external datum — in which case terms such as 'French social formation' or 'English social formation' designate hardly more than 'France' or 'England', and the term 'formation' is clearly excessive; or else the agents are reintegrated into the various formations constituting them — and in that case there is no reason why these should coincide with national frontiers. Certain articulatory practices will make them coincide with the limits of the formation as such. But in either case this is an open process which will depend on the multiple hegemonic articulations shaping a given space, and operating within it at the same time.

Through this chapter we have attempted to show, at several points in our argument, the openness and indeterminacy of the social, which gives a primary and founding character to negativity and antagonism, and assures the existence of articulatory and hegemonic practices. We must now once again take up the line of our political argument of the first two chapters, and show how the indeterminacy of the social and the articulatory logic which follows from it, allows the question of the relation between hegemony and democracy to be posed in new terms.

Notes to Chapter 3

1. C. Taylor, *Hegel*, Cambridge 1975, p. 23 and, in general, chapter 1.
2. Hölderlin, *Hyperion Fragment,* quoted in C. Taylor, p. 35.
3. A. Trendelenburg, *Logische Untersuchungen*, Hildesheim 1964 (first edition 1840).
4. L. Althusser, *For Marx*, London 1969, p. 203.
5. Ibid., p. 206 (footnote).
6. As can be observed, our critique coincides on some points with that of the Hindess and Hirst school in England. We do, however, have some fundamental disagreements with their approach, to which we will refer later in the text.
7. E. Balibar, 'Sur la dialectique historique. (Quelques remarques critiques à propos de *Lire le Capital*)', in *Cinq études du matérialisme historique*, Paris 1984.
8. B. Hindess and P. Hirst, *Pre-capitalist Modes of Production*, London 1975; B. Hindess and P. Hirst, *Mode of Production and Social Formation*, London 1977; A. Cutler, B. Hindess, P. Hirst and A. Hussein, *Marx's Capital and Capitalism Today*, London 1977, 2 vols.
9. Cutler et al., vol. 1, p. 222.
10. P. Hirst and P. Wooley, *Social Relations and Human Attributes*, London 1982, p. 134.
11. M. Foucault, *Archaeology of Knowledge*, London 1972, pp. 31-39.
12. E. Benveniste, *Problems in General Linguistics*, Miami 1971, pp. 47-8.
13. In an insightful study on the limits of Foucault's archaeological method, B. Brown and M. Cousins ('The linguistic fault: the case of Foucault's archaeology', *Economy and Society*, August 1980, vol. 9, no. 3) state: '(Foucault) makes no distribution of phenomena into two classes of being, Discourse and the Non-Discursive. For him the question is always the identity of particular discursive formations. What falls outside a particular discursive formation merely falls outside it. It does not thereby join the ranks of a general form of being, the Non-Discursive.' This is undoubtedly true regarding a possible 'distribution of phenomena into two classes of being', that is, with regard to a discourse that would establish regional divisions within a totality. But this does not eliminate the problem concerning the form of conceiving the discursive. The acceptance of non-discursive entities does not merely have a topographical relevance; it also modifies the concept of discourse.
14. M. Foucault, pp. 53-4. H.L. Dreyfus and P. Rabinow, in their book on Foucault (*Michel Foucault. Beyond Structuralism and Hermeneutics*, Chicago 1982, pp. 65-6), realize the potential importance of this passage, but reject it rather hastily in favour of a conception of institutions as 'non-discursive'.
15. What is strictly implied here, is the very concept of 'formation'. The problem can be formulated, in its most general form, as follows: if what characterizes a formation is regularity in dispersion, how then is it possible to determine the limits of

that formation? Let us suppose that there is a discursive entity or difference which is exterior to the formation, but which is absolutely regular in this exteriority. If the sole criterion at stake is dispersion, how is it possible to establish the 'exteriority' of that difference? The first question to be decided must, in that case, be whether or not the determination of the limits depends upon a concept of 'formation' which super-imposes itself on the archaeological fact. If we accept the first possibility, we are simply introducing an entity of the same type as those which had been methodo-logically excluded at the beginning — 'oeuvre', 'tradition', et cetera. If we accept the second possibility, it is clear that within the archaeological material itself, there must exist certain logics which produce effects of totality capable of constructing the limits, and thus of constituting the formation. As we will argue further on in the text, this is the role fulfilled by the logics of equivalence.

16. Starting from phenomenology, Merleau-Ponty conceived the project of an existential phenomenology as the attempt to overcome the dualism between 'in-itself' and 'for-itself', and to set up a terrain which would allow the overcoming of oppo-sitions considered insurmountable by a philosophy such as that of Sartre. The *pheno-menon* is thus conceived as the point where the link is established between 'the thing' and 'the mind', and perception as a more primary founding level than the *Cogito*. The limits of the conception of meaning inherent in every phenomenology, insofar as it is based on the irreducibility of 'the lived', must not make us forget that in some of its formulations — and particularly in the work of Merleau-Ponty — we find some of the most radical attempts to break with the essentialism inherent in every form of dualism.

17. L. Wittgenstein, *Philosophical Investigations*, Oxford 1983, p. 3.

18. Ibid., p. 5.

19. To the objection of a certain type of Marxism, which argues that such a view of the primacy of the discursive would call 'materialism' into question, we would simply suggest a glimpse through the texts of Marx. And in particular *Capital*: not only the famous passage about the bee and the architect at the beginning of the chapter on the labour process, but also the whole analysis of the value form, where the very logic of the process of commodity production — the foundation of capitalist accumu-lation — is presented as a strictly social logic which only imposes itself through establishing a relation of equivalence among materially distinct objects. From the first page it is stated — as a comment on the assertion of Barbon: ' "Things have an intrinsik vertue" (this is Barbon's special term for use-value) "which in all places have the same vertue; as the loadstone to attract iron" (op. cit. p. 6). The magnet's property of attracting iron only became useful once it had led to the discovery of magnetic polarity.'

20. With this 'exterior' we are not reintroducing the category of the extra-discursive. The exterior is constituted by other discourses. It is the discursive nature of this exterior which creates the conditions of vulnerability of every discourse, as nothing finally protects it against the deformation and destabilization of its system of differences by other discursive articulations which act from outside it.

21. J. Derrida, *Writing and Difference*, London 1978, p. 280.

22. A number of recent works have extended this conception concerning the impossibility of suturation and, therefore, of the ultimate internal intelligibility of every relational system, to the very system traditionally presented as a model of a pure structural logic: that is, language. F. Gadet and M. Pêcheux, for example, have pointed out concerning Saussure: 'Regarding the theories which isolate the poetic as a location of special effects, from language as a whole, the work of Saussure . . . makes the poetic a slipping inherent to every language: what Saussure has established is not a

property of Saturnian verse, nor even of poetry, but a property of language itself' (*La langue introuvable*, Paris 1981, p. 57). Cf. F. Gadet, 'La double faille', *Actes du Colloque de Sociololinguistique de Rouen*, 1978; C. Normand, 'L'arbitraire du signe comme phénomène de déplacement', *Dialectiques*, 1972, no. 1-2; J.C. Milner, *L'amour de la langue*, Paris 1978.

23. Cf. what we said before regarding Benveniste's critique of Saussure.

24. Cf. M. Foucault, *The Order of Things*, London 1970.

25. Cf. with regard to this B. Brewster, 'Fetishism in *Capital* and *Reading Capital*', *Economy and Society*, 1976, vol. 5, no. 3; and P. Hirst, 'Althusser and the Theory of Ideology', *Economy and Society*, 1976, vol. 5, no. 4.

26. Cf. ibid.

27. The ambiguity arising from the use of 'Man' to refer at the same time to 'human being' and 'male member of the species' is symptomatic of the discursive ambiguities which we are attempting to show.

28. E.P. Thompson, *The Poverty of Theory*, London 1978. We should not, however, jump to the conclusion that Thompson has simply misread Althusser. The problem is considerably more complex, for if Thompson proposed a false alternative by opposing a 'humanism' based on the postulate of a human essence and an anti-humanism founded on the negation of the latter, it is equally true that Althusser's approach to humanism leaves little room for anything other than its relegation to the field of ideology. For, if history has an intelligible structure given by the succession of modes of production, and if it is this structure which is accessible to a 'scientific' practice, this can only be accompanied by a notion of 'humanism' as something constituted on the plane of ideology — a plane which, though not conceived as false consciousness, is ontologically different and subordinate to a mechanism of social reproduction established by the logic of the mode of production. The way out of the blind alley to which these two essentialisms — constituted around 'Man' and 'mode of production' — lead, is the dissolution of the differentiation of planes wherein the appearance/reality distinction is founded. In that case, humanist discourses have a status which is neither privileged a priori nor subordinated to other discourses.

29. *m/f*, 1978, no. 1, editorial note.

30. Cf. C. Mouffe, 'The Sex/Gender System and the Discursive Construction of Women's Subordination', in S. Häninen and L. Paldan, eds., *Rethinking Ideology: A Marxist Debate*, Berlin 1983. A historical introduction to feminist politics from this viewpoint can be found in Sally Alexander, 'Women, Class and Sexual Difference', *History Workshop* 17, Spring 1984. On the more general question of sexual politics, see Jeffrey Weeks, *Sex, Politics and Society*, London 1981.

31. This concept has been developed by Gayle Rubin, 'The Traffic in Women: Notes on the "Political Economy" of Sex', in R.R. Reiter, ed., *Toward an Anthropology of Women*, New York/London 1975, pp. 157-210.

32. This aspect is not totally ignored by the editors of *m/f*. Thus, P. Adams and J. Minson state: 'there are certain forms of "all-purpose" responsability which cover a multitude of social relations – that persons are held "responsible" in general, in a multiplicity of evaluations (being held "irresponsible" in the negative pole). But however diffuse this all-purpose responsability appears to be it is nonetheless still subject to the satisfaction of definite social conditions and "all-purpose" responsibility must be construed as a heterogeneous bundle of statuses'. 'The "Subject" of Feminism', *m/f*, 1978, no. 2, p. 53.

33. A Cutler et al., vol. 1. p.236-237.

34. L. Colletti, 'Marxism and the Dialectic', *New Left Review*, September/October 1975, no. 93, pp. 3-29; and *Tramonto dell'ideologia*, pp. 87-161.

35. Kant summarizes in the following four principles the characteristics of real opposition in its difference with contradiction. 'In the first place, the determinations which oppose each other must be found in the same subject: if we, in effect, pose that a determination is in one thing, and another determination, whatever it may be, is in another thing, a real opposition does not follow. Secondly: in a real opposition one of the opposed determinations cannot ever be the contradictory contrary of the other, as in that case the contrast would be of a logical nature, and as we saw earlier, impossible. Thirdly: a determination cannot ever negate anything different from that which is posed by the other, as in the latter there would not be any opposition whatsoever. Fourthly: if they are in contrast neither of them can be negative, as in the latter case neither of them would pose something that was annulled by the other. It is because of this that in every real opposition both predicates must be positive, but in such a manner that in their union within the same subject the consequences reciprocally annul each other. Thus, in the case of those things which are considered each the negative of the other, when they combine in the same subject, the result is zero.' (I. Kant, 'Il concetto delle quantità negative', in *Scritti precritici*, Bari 1953, pp. 268–9). The positivity of its two terms is thus the defining characteristic of real opposition.

36. It is interesting to point out that Hans Kelsen, in his polemic with Max Adler, clearly perceived the need to move outside the exclusive alternative real opposition/ contradiction in characterizing antagonisms belonging to the social world. Cf. with regard to this the summary of Kelsen's position in R. Racinaro, 'Hans Kelsen e il dibattito su democrazia e parlamentarismo negli anni Venti-Trenta', Introduction to H. Kelsen, *Socialismo e Stato. Una ricerca sulla teoria politica del marxismo*, Bari 1978, pp. cxxii–cxxv.

37. R. Edgley, 'Dialectic: the Contradictions of Colletti', *Critique*, 1977, no. 7.

38. J. Elster, *Logic and Society: Contradictions and Possible Worlds*, Chichester 1978.

39. 'What is Dialectic?', in *Conjectures and Refutations*, London, 1969, p. 312-335.

40. On this point, our opinion differs with that expressed by one of the authors of this book in an earlier work, in which the concept of antagonism is assimilated to that of contradiction (E. Laclau, 'Populist Rupture and Discourse', *Screen Education*, Spring 1980). In rethinking our earlier position, the critical commentaries made by Emilio De Ipola in a number of conversations, have proved most useful.

41. Concerning the various ways of approaching the problem of relative autonomy of the State in different contemporary Marxist theorizations, see B. Jessop, *The Capitalist State*, New York and London 1982.

4

Hegemony and Radical Democracy

In November 1937, in exile in New York, Arthur Rosenberg was concluding his reflections upon contemporary European history since the French Revolution.[1] These reflections, which brought to a close his life as a militant intellectual, were centred upon a fundamental theme: the relationship between socialism and democracy, or, better, the failure of attempts to constitute organic forms of unity between the two. This double failure — of democracy and of socialism — appeared to him as a process of progressive estrangement, dominated by a radical break. Initially 'democracy', conceived as a field of popular action, is the great protagonist in the historic confrontations which dominate the life of Europe between 1789 and 1848. It is the 'people' (in the sense of *plebs* rather than *populus*), the barely organized and differentiated masses, who dominate the barricades of 1789 and 1848, the Chartist agitation in England and the Mazzinian and Garibaldian mobilizations in Italy. Later comes the major break constituted by the long reaction of the 1850s; and when this comes to an end and popular protest is renewed, the protagonists have changed. It will be the unions or nascent social-democratic parties, first in Germany and England and then in the rest of Europe, which establish themselves with increasing solidity in the last third of the century.

This break has frequently been interpreted as the transition to a moment of higher political rationality on the part of the dominated sectors: in the first half of the century the amorphous character of 'democracy', its lack of roots in the economic bases of society, made it essentially vulnerable and unstable, and prevented it from constituting itself into a steadfast and permanent trench in the struggle against the established order. Only with the disintegration of this amorphous 'people', and its replacement with the solid social base of the working class, would popular movements achieve the maturity that allowed them to undertake a long-term struggle against the dominant classes. Nevertheless, this mythical transition to a higher stage of social maturity resulting from industrialization, and to a higher level of political efficacy in which the anarchic outbursts of the 'people' would be replaced by the rationality and solidity of class politics, could only appear as a bad joke to Rosenberg, who wrote his book while Spain burned, Hitler was preparing for the *Anschluss*, and Mussolini was invading Ethiopia. For Rosenberg, this closing up along class lines constituted on the contrary the great historical sin of the European labour movement. The workers' inability to constitute the 'people' as an historical agent was for him the essential fault of social democracy, and the Ariadne's thread which allowed him to unravel the whole of the tortuous political process which began in 1860. The constitution of a unified popular pole, far from becoming more simple, grew increasingly difficult as the growing complexity and institutionalization of capitalist society — the 'trenches and fortifications of civil society' of which Gramsci spoke — led to the corporatization and separation of those sectors which should ideally have been united 'among the people'. This process of growing social complexity was already in evidence between 1789 and 1848:

> The task of democracy in 1789 consisted of leading in a unitary manner the struggle of the dependent peasantry against the land-owning nobility and the struggle of the poor citizens against capital. At this time this was much easier than it would be in 1848. In effect, between the two periods the industrial proletariat, for all that the greater part of it was still working in small-scale industry, had grown so much in importance that it made every political problem culminate in the confrontation between proletarian and capitalist . . . This required on the part of the democratic party an exceptional tactical skill in order to achieve convergence between the workers' movement and that of the peasants. If it wished to pass over the heads of the peasant owners to reach the mass of small tenants and labourers, it required tactics which were absolutely realistic and complex into the bargain. Thus the task of social democracy fifty years after Robespierre had become increasingly difficult, while at the same time the democrats were less intellectually capable of resolving the problems.[2]

And of course, the growing difficulty of constituting a popular anti-system pole had only increased after 1848. In reality, Rosenberg was seeking to orient himself upon a new terrain, dominated by a radical mutation of which he was only half conscious: the decline of a form of politics for which the division of the social into two antagonistic camps is *an original and immutable datum, prior to all hegemonic construction,*[3] and the transition towards a new situation, characterized by the essential instability of political spaces, in which the very identity of the forces in struggle is submitted to constant shifts, and calls for an incessant process of redefinition. In other words, in a manner at once far-sighted and hesitant, Rosenberg is describing to us the process of generalization of the hegemonic form of politics — which imposes itself as a condition for the emergence of every collective identity once articulatory practices have succeeded in determining the very principle of social division — and showing us at the same time the vanity of the aspiration that the 'class struggle' should constitute itself, *in an automatic and a priori manner,* in the foundation of this principle.

In all rigour, the opposition people/ancien régime was the last moment in which the antagonistic limits between two forms of society presented themselves — with the qualification noted — in the form of clear and empirically *given* lines of demarcation. From then on the demarcating line between the internal and the external, the dividing line from which the antagonism was constituted in the form of two opposing systems of equivalences, became increasingly fragile and ambiguous, and its construction came to be the crucial problem of politics. That is to say, from then on there was no politics without hegemony. This permits us to understand the specificity of Marx's intervention: his reflection took place in a moment at which the division of the political space in terms of the dichotomy people/ancien régime seemed to have exhausted its productivity, and was in any case incapable of constructing a vision of the political which would recapture the complexity and the plurality peculiar to the social in industrial societies. Marx seeks, then, to think the primary fact of social division on the basis of a new principle: the confrontation between classes. The new principle, however, is undermined from the start by a radical insufficiency, arising from the fact that class opposition is incapable of dividing the totality of the social body into two antagonistic camps, of reproducing itself *automatically* as a line of demarcation in the political sphere. It is for this reason that the affirmation of the class struggle as the fundamental principle of political division always had to be accompanied by supplementary hypotheses which relegated its full applicability to the future: historical-sociological hypotheses — the simplifcation of the social structure, which would lead to the coincidence of real political struggles and struggles between the classes as agents constituted at the level of relations of production; hypotheses regarding the consciousness of the agents — the transition from the class in itself to the class for itself. What is important, in any case, is that this change introduced by Marxism into the political principle of social division maintains unaltered an essential component of the Jacobin imaginary: the postulation of *one* foundational moment of rupture, and of a *unique* space in which the political is constituted. Only the temporal dimension has changed, as this division, at once social and political, into two camps is relegated to the future, at the same time that we are provided with a set of sociological hypotheses regarding the process which would lead to it.

In this chapter we shall defend the thesis that it·is this moment of continuity between the Jacobin and the Marxist political imaginary which has to be put in question by the project for a radical democracy. The rejection of privileged points of rupture and the confluence of struggles into a unified political space, and the acceptance, on the contrary, of the plurality and indeterminacy of the social, seem to us the two fundamental bases from which a new political imaginary can be constructed, radically libertarian and infinitely more ambitious in its objectives than that of the classic left. This demands, in the first place, a description of the historical terrain in which it emerged, which is the field of what we shall call the 'democratic revolution'.

The Democratic Revolution

The theoretical problematic which we have presented excludes not only the concentration of social conflict on a priori privileged agents, but also reference to any *general* principle or substratum of an anthropological nature which, at the same time that it unified the different subject positions, would assign a character of inevitability to resistance against the diverse forms of subordination. There is therefore nothing inevitable or natural in the different struggles against power, and it is necessary to explain in each case the reasons for their emergence and the different modulations they may adopt. The struggle against subordination cannot be the result of the situation of subordination itself. Although we can affirm, with Foucault, that wherever there is power there is resistance, it must also be recognized that the forms of resistance may be extremely varied. Only in certain cases do these forms of resistance take on a political character and become struggles directed towards putting an end to relations of subordination as such. If throughout the centuries there have been multiple forms of resistance by women against male domination, it is only under certain conditions and specific forms that a feminist movement which demands equality (equality before the law in the first place, and subsequently in other areas) has been able to emerge. Clearly, when we speak here of the 'political' character of these struggles, we do not do so in the restricted sense of demands which are situated at the level of parties and of the State. What we are referring to is a type of action whose objective is the transformation of a social relation which constructs a subject in a relationship of subordination. Certain contemporary feminist practices, for example, tend to transform the relationship between masculinity and femininity without passing in any way through parties or the State. Of course, we are not seeking to deny that certain practices require the intervention of the political in its restricted sense. What we wish to point out is that politics as a practice of creation, reproduction and transformation of social relations cannot be located at a determinate level of the social, as the problem of the political is the problem of the institution of the social, that is, of the definition and articulation of social relations in a field criss-crossed with antagonisms.

Our central problem is to identify the discursive conditions for the emergence of a collective action, directed towards struggling against inequalities and challenging relations of subordination. We might also say that our task is to identify the conditions in which a relation of subordination becomes a relation of oppression, and thereby constitutes itself into the site of an antagonism. We enter here onto a terrain constituted by numerous terminological shifts which have ended by establishing a synonymity between 'subordination', 'oppression', and 'domination'. The base which makes this synonymity possible is, as is evident, the anthropological assumption of a 'human nature' and of a unified subject: if we can determine *a priori* the essence of a subject, every relation of subordination which denies it automatically becomes a relation of oppression. But if we reject this essentialist perspective, we need to differentiate 'subordination' from 'oppression' and explain the precise conditions in which subordination becomes oppressive. We shall understand by a *relation of subordination* that in which an agent is subjected to the decisions of another — an employee with respect to an employer, for example, or in certain forms of family organization the woman with respect to the man, and so on. We shall call *relations of oppression,* in contrast, those relations of subordination which have transformed themselves into sites of antagonisms. Finally, we shall call *relations of domination* the set of those relations of subordination which are considered as illegitimate from the perspective, or in the judgement, of a social agent external to them, and which, as a consequence, may or may not coincide with the relations of oppression actually existing in a determinate social formation. The problem is, therefore, to explain how relations of oppression are constituted out of relations of subordination. It is clear why relations of subordination, considered in themselves, cannot be antagonistic relations: a relation of subordination establishes, simply, a set of differential positions between social agents, and we already know that a system of differences which constructs each social identity as *positivity* not only cannot be antagonistic, but would bring about the ideal conditions for the elimination of all antagonisms — we would be faced with a sutured social space, from which every equivalence would be excluded. It is only to the extent that the positive differential character of the subordinated subject position is subverted that the antagonism can emerge. 'Serf', 'slave', and so on, do not designate in themselves antagonistic positions; it is only in the terms of a different discursive formation, such as 'the rights inherent to every human being', that the differential positivity of these categories can be subverted and the subordination constructed as oppression. This means that there is no relation of oppression without the presence of a discursive 'exterior' from which the discourse of subordination can be interrupted.[4] The logic of equivalence in this sense displaces the effects of some discourses towards others. If, as was the case with women until the seventeenth century, the ensemble of discourses which constructed them as subjects fixed them purely and simply in a subordinated position, feminism as a movement of struggle against women's subordination could not emerge. Our thesis is that it is only from the moment when the democratic discourse becomes available to articulate the different forms of resistance to subordination that the conditions will exist to make possible the struggle against different types of inequality. In the case of women we may cite as an example the role played in England by Mary Wollstonecraft, whose book *Vindication of the Rights of Women,* published in 1792, determined the birth of feminism through the use made in it of the democratic discourse, which was thus displaced from the field of political equality between citizens to the field of equality between the sexes.

But in order to be mobilized in this way, the democratic principle of liberty and equality first had to impose itself as the new matrix of the social imaginary; or, in our terminology, to constitute a fundamental nodal point in the construction of the political. This decisive mutation in the political imaginary of Western societies took place two hundred years ago and can be defined in these terms: the logic of equivalence was transformed into the fundamental instrument of production of the social. It is to designate this mutation that, taking an expression from de Tocqueville, we shall speak of 'democratic revolution'. With this we shall designate the end of a society of a hierarchic and inegalitarian type, ruled by a theological–political logic in which the social order had its foundation in divine will. The social body was conceived of as a whole in which individuals appeared fixed in differential positions. For as long as such a holistic mode of institution of the social predominated, politics could not be more than the repetition of hierarchical relations which reproduced the same type of subordinated subject. The key moment in the beginnings of the democratic revolution can be found in the French Revolution since, as François Furet has indicated, its affirmation of the absolute power of its people introduced something truly new at the level of the social imaginary. It is there, according to Furet, that the true discontinuity is located: in the establishment of a new legitimacy, in the invention of democratic culture: 'The French Revolution is not a transition, it is an origin, and the phantom of an origin. What is unique about it is what constitutes its historical interest, and, what is more, it is this "unique" element that has become universal: the first experience of democracy.'[5] If, as Hannah Arendt has said, 'it was the French and not the American Revolution that set the world on fire',[6] it is because it was the first to found itself on no other legitimacy than the people. It thus initiated what Claude Lefort has shown to be a new mode of institution of the social. This break with the ancien régime, symbolized by the Declaration of the Rights of Man, would provide the discursive conditions which made it possible to propose the different forms of inequality as illegitimate and anti-natural, and thus make them equivalent as forms of oppression. Here lay the profound subversive power of the democratic discourse, which would allow the spread of equality and liberty into increasingly wider domains and therefore act as a fermenting agent upon the different forms of struggle against subordination. Many workers' struggles in the nineteenth century constructed their demands discursively on the basis of struggles for political liberty. In the case of English Chartism, for instance, the studies of Gareth Stedman Jones[7] have revealed the fundamental role of the ideas of

English radicalism, profoundly influenced by the French Revolution, in the constitution of the movement and the determining of its objectives.[7] (Hence the central role of the demand for universal suffrage, of which little account is taken by interpretations of Chartism as a phenomenon of a fundamentally social character, an expression of the class consciousness of the new industrial proletariat.)

From the critique of political inequality there is effected, through the different socialist discourses, a displacement towards the critique of economic inequality, which leads to the putting in question of other forms of subordination and the demanding of new rights. The socialist demands should therefore be seen as a moment internal to the democratic revolution, and only intelligible on the basis of the equivalential logic which the latter establishes. And the irradiation effects multiply in a growing variety of directions. In the case of feminism, it was a question of gaining access for women first to political rights; later to economic equality; and, with contemporary feminism, to equality in the domain of sexuality. As de Tocqueville pointed out: 'It is impossible to believe that equality will not finally penetrate as much into the political world as into other domains. It is not possible to conceive of men as eternally unequal among themselves on one point, and equal on others; at a certain moment, they will come to be equal on all points.'[8]

In every case it is the impossibility of constituting relations of subordination as a closed system of differences — an impossibility implying the *externality* of the subordinator and subordinated identities to each other, rather than their absorption into the system through their positions — which lies at the base of the relation of oppression. It is instructive, in this respect, to consider the transformations experienced by the antagonistic potential of workers' struggles. There were without a doubt *radically* anti-capitalist struggles in the nineteenth century, but they were not struggles of the proletariat — if by 'proletariat' we understand the type of worker produced by the development of capitalism, rather than the artisans whose qualifications and modes of life were threatened by the establishment of the capitalist system of production. The strongly antagonistic character of the struggles of these 'reactionary radicals' — in Craig Calhoun's phrase — their calling into question of the whole of the capitalist system, are explained by the fact that these struggles expressed resistance to the destruction of artisanal identities and the whole set of social, cultural and political forms which went with them. From that stemmed the total rejection of the new relations of production which capitalism was in the process of implanting; the complete externality existing between two systems of social organization generated the division of social space into two camps, which, as we know, is the condition for every antagonism. Calhoun, in his critique of E.P. Thompson's *The Making of the English Working Class,* has shown convincingly that a heterogeneous set of social groups are there grouped under the label 'working class', without sufficient recognition of the profound difference between 'old' and 'new' workers in their objectives and their forms of mobilization. According to Calhoun, 'the former fought on the basis of strong community foundations but against the preponderant forces of economic change. The latter fought on a weaker social basis but within the emergent industrial order. This distinction militates strongly against a notion of the continuous development and increasing radicalization of the working class.'[9]

It is towards the middle of the nineteenth century in Britain, and towards the end of the century in the rest of Europe, that there emerges a labour movement which can be strictly considered a product of capitalism; but this labour movement tends to call less and less into question capitalist relations of production as such — these having by then solidly implanted — and concentrates on the struggle for the transformation of relations *in* production. Those struggles which the Marxist tradition would term 'reformist', and consider as a backward step with respect to previous social struggles, correspond more in reality to the mode adopted by the mobilizations of the industrial proletariat than do the more radical earlier struggles. The relations of subordination between workers and capitalists are thus to a certain extent absorbed as legitimate differential positions in a unified discursive space.

If we turn our attention to another period of radical mobilizations by workers — that of the workers' council movements in Italy and Germany at the end of the First World War — we see that they too have at their base an overdetermined set of circumstances: the collapse of the social order following the war, the militarization of the factories, the beginnings of Taylorization, the transformation of the role of skilled workers in production. All of these conditions were linked either to an organic crisis which reduced the hegemonic capacity of the logics of difference, or to transformations which called into question traditional forms of worker identity. We should not forget, for example, the central role played in these struggles by skilled workers, a role which is generally recognized but explained in different ways.[10] For some it is a question of the defence of skills against the already present danger of Taylorization. For others it is the experience that these workers had acquired during the war which made them think of the possibilities of self-organization of the process of production and pressed them to a confrontation with their employees. In either case, however, it is the defence of a certain identity which the workers had acquired (their skills or their organizational functions in production) which leads them to rebel. We can therefore establish a parallel with the 'radical reactionaries' we mentioned above, as they too were defending a type of identity under threat.

It would be wrong, however, to understand this externality of power in a purely 'stagist' sense, as if the fact of belonging to a phase in the process of being transcended were the necessary condition for radicalism in a struggle; if this were the case, such radicalism would be characteristic only of defensive struggles. If the 'anachronistic' struggles which we mentioned above illustrate well the externality of power which is a condition of every antagonism, certain social transformations can, in contrast, constitute new forms of radical subjectivity on the basis of discursively constructing as an external imposition — and therefore as forms of oppression — relations of subordination which until that moment had not been questioned. This is the point at which the equivalential displacement peculiar to the democratic imaginary comes into play. The image of radical struggles as things from the past is perfectly unrealistic. It derives in good part from the neo-capitalist euphoria of the two decades after the Second World War, which appeared to offer an unlimited capacity for transformist absorption on the part of the system, and showed a linear tendency towards a homogeneous society in which every antagonistic potential would be dissolved, and each collective identity fixed in a system of differences. We shall try, on the contrary, to show that the complexity and the frequently contradictory aspects of this process of expansion, as the very act of satisfying a wide range of social demands during the apogée of the Welfare State, far from assuring the indefinite integration of the dominant hegemonic formations, frequently laid bare the arbitrary character of a whole set of relations of subordination. Thus the terrain has been created which makes possible a new extension of egalitarian equivalences, and thereby the expansion of the democratic revolution in new directions. It is in this terrain that there have arisen those new forms of political identity which, in recent debates, have frequently been grouped under the name of 'new social movements'. We should therefore study the democratic potential and the ambiguities of these movements, as well as the historical context in which they have emerged.

Democratic Revolution and New Antagonisms

The equivalential displacement between distinct subject positions — which is a condition for the emergence of an antagonism — may thus present itself in two fundamental variants. Firstly, it may be a question of relations of subordination already in existence which, thanks to a displacement of the democratic imaginary, are re-articulated as relations of oppression. To take the case of feminism once again, it is because women as women are denied a right which the democratic ideology recognizes in principle for all citizens that there appears a fissure in the construction of the subordinated feminine subject from which an antagonism *may* arise. It is also the case with the ethnic minorities who demand their civil rights. But the antagonism can also arise in other circumstances — for example, when acquired rights are being called into question, or when social relations which had not been constructed under the form of subordination begin to be so under the impact of certain social transformations. In this case it is because it is negated by practices and discourses bearing new forms of inequality that a subject position can become the site of an antagonism. But in every case what allows the forms of resistance to assume the character of collective struggles is the existence of an external discourse which impedes the stabilization of subordination as difference.

The unsatisfactory term 'new social movements' groups together a series of highly diverse struggles: urban, ecological, anti-authoritarian, anti-institutional, feminist, anti-racist, ethnic, regional or that of sexual minorities. The common denominator of all of them would be their differentiation from workers' struggles, considered as 'class' struggles. It is pointless to insist upon the problematic nature of this latter notion: it amalgamates a series of very different struggles at the level of the relations of production, which are set apart from the 'new antagonisms' for reasons that display all too clearly the persistence of a discourse founded upon the privileged status of 'classes'. What interests us about these new social movements, then, is not the idea of arbitrarily grouping them into a category opposed to that of class, but the *novel* role they play in articulating that rapid diffusion of social conflictuality to more and more numerous relations which is characteristic today of advanced industrial societies. This is what we shall seek to analyse through the theoretical problematic presented above, which leads us to conceive these movements as an extension of the democratic revolution to a whole new series of social relations. As for their novelty, that is conferred upon them by the fact that they call into question new forms of subordination. We should distinguish two aspects of this relation of continuity/discontinuity. The aspect of continuity basically involves the fact that the conversion of liberal-democratic ideology into the 'common sense' of Western societies laid the foundation for that progressive challenge to the hierarchical principle which Tocqueville called the 'equalization of conditions'. It is the permanence of this egalitarian imaginary which permits us to establish a continuity between the struggles of the nineteenth century against the inequalities bequeathed by the ancien régime and the social movements of the present. But from a second point of view we can speak of discontinuity, as a good proportion of the new political subjects have been constituted through their antagonistic relationship to recent forms of subordination, derived from the implanting and expansion of capitalist relations of production and the growing intervention of the state. It is to these new relations of subordination and to the antagonisms constituted within them that we shall now address ourselves.

It was in the context of the reorganization which took place after the Second World War that a series of changes occurred at the level of social relations and a new hegemonic formation was consolidated. The latter articulated modifications at the level of the labour process, the form of state and the dominant modes of cultural diffusion which were to bring about a profound transformation in the existing forms of social intercourse. If we examine the problem from an economic point of view, the decisive change is what Michel Aglietta has termed the transition from an extensive to an intensive regime of accumulation. The latter is characterized by the spread of capitalist relations of production to the whole set of social relations, and the subordination of the latter to the logic of production for profit. According to Aglietta the fundamental moment of this transition is the introduction of Fordism, which he describes as 'the principle of an articulation between process of production and mode of consumption'.[11] More specifically, it is the articulation between a labour process organized around the semi-automatic production line, and a mode of consumption characterized by the individual acquisition of commodities produced on a large scale for private consumption. This penetration of capitalist relations of production, initiated at the beginning of the century and stepped up from the 1940s on, was to transform society into a vast market in which new 'needs' were ceaselessly created, and in which more and more of the products of human labour were turned into commodities. This 'commodification' of social life destroyed previous social relations, replacing them with commodity relations through which the logic of capitalist accumulation penetrated into increasingly numerous spheres. Today it is not only as a seller of labour-power that the individual is subordinated to capital, but also through his or her incorporation into a multitude of other social relations: culture, free time, illness, education, sex and even death. There is practically no domain of individual or collective life which escapes capitalist relations.

But this 'consumer society' has not led to the end of ideology, as Daniel Bell announced, nor to the creation of a one-dimensional man, as Marcuse feared. On the contrary, numerous new struggles have expressed resistance against the new forms of subordination, and this from within the very heart of the new society. Thus it is that the waste of natural resources, the pollution and destruction of the environment, the consequences of productivism have given birth to the ecology movement. Other struggles, which Manuel Castells terms 'urban',[12] express diverse forms of resistance to the capitalist occupation of social space. The general urbanization which has accompanied economic growth, the transfer of the popular classes to the urban periphery or their relegation to the decaying inner cities, and the general lack of collective goods and services have caused a series of new problems which affect the organization of the whole of social life outside work. Hence the multiplicity of social relations from which antagonisms and struggles may originate: habitat, consumption, various services can all constitute terrains for the struggle against inequalities and the claiming of new rights.

These new demands must also be set within the context of the Keynesian Welfare State, the constitution of which has been another fundamental fact of the post-war period. It is without doubt an ambiguous and complex phenomenon, for if on the one hand this new type of state was necessary in order to perform a series of functions required by the new capitalist regime of accumulation, it is also the result of what Bowles and Gintis have called 'the post-World War accord between capital and labour',[13] and the result, therefore, of struggles against changes in the social relations generated by capitalism. It is, for example, the destruction of the networks of traditional solidarity of a community or family type (based, let us not forget, on the subordination of women) which has forced the state to intervene in diverse 'social services' for the sick, the unemployed, the old, and so on. Elsewhere, under pressure from workers' struggles, the state has intervened to assure a new labour policy (minimum wage, length of the working day, accident and unemployment insurance, and the social wage). If we can accept with Benjamin Coriat[14] that this state-plan intervenes in the reproduction of the labour force in order to subordinate it to the needs of capital, thanks to the practice of the collective contract and the negotiated agreements which link rises in wages to those in productivity, it is no less the case that these are gains which have brought real and important benefits to the workers.

But this intervention by the state at ever broader levels of social reproduction has been accompanied by a growing bureaucratization of its practices which has come to constitute, along with commodification, one of the fundamental sources of inequalities and conflicts. In all the domains in which the state has intervened, a politicization of social relations is at the base of numerous new antagonisms. This double transformation of social relations, resulting from the expansion of capitalist relations of production and of the new bureaucratic-state forms, is found in different combinations in all the advanced industrial countries. Their effects are generally mutually reinforcing, although this is not always so. Claus Offe has indicated, for example, how the provision by the state of services linked to the social wage can have effects which go in the direction of 'decommodification'.[15] This latter phenomenon may adversely affect the interests of capitalist accumulation, to the extent that a range of activities which could be sources of profit begin to be provided by the public sector. For Offe this phenomenon, linked to that of the 'deproletarianization' arising out of the various payments which allow workers to survive without being obliged to sell their labour-power at any price, is an important factor in the present crisis in the capitalist economies. But what crucially concerns us here is to trace the consequences of this bureaucratization underlying new antagonisms. The important fact is the imposition of multiple forms of vigilance and regulation in social relations which had previously been conceived as forming part of the private domain. This shifting of the line of demarcation between the 'public' and the 'private' has ambiguous effects. On the one hand, it serves to reveal the political character (in the broad sense) of social relations, and the fact that these are always the result of modes of institution that give them their form and meaning; on the other, given the bureaucratic character of state intervention, this creation of 'public spaces' is carried out not in the form of a true democratization, but through the imposition of new forms of subordination. It is here that we have to look for the terrain on which numerous struggles emerge against bureaucratic forms of state power. This should not blind us, however, to numerous other aspects which point in the opposite direction, and which give the Welfare State its characteristic ambiguity: the emergence of a new type of right designated as 'positive liberties' has also profoundly transformed the dominant common sense, lending legitimacy to a whole series of demands for economic equality and insistence upon new social rights. Movements such as the 'Welfare Rights Movement' in the United States, studied by Piven and Cloward,[16] are an example of this extension of the demands directed at the state, once its responsibility for the welfare of citizens is accepted. It is the notion of citizenship itself which has been transformed with the social state, as 'social rights' are now attributed to the citizen. As a consequence, the categories of 'justice', 'liberty', 'equity', and 'equality' have been redefined and liberal-democratic discourse has been profoundly modified by this broadening of the sphere of rights.

One cannot understand the present expansion of the field of social conflictuality and the consequent emergence of new political subjects without situating both in the context of the commodification and bureaucratization of social relations on the one hand, and the reformulation of the liberal-democratic ideology — resulting from the expansion of struggles for equality — on the other. For this reason we have proposed that this proliferation of antagonisms and calling into question of relations of subordination should be considered as a moment of deepening of the democratic revolution. This has also been stimulated by the third important aspect in the mutation of social relations which has characterized the hegemonic formation of the post-war period: namely, the new cultural forms linked to the expansion of the means of mass communication. These were to make possible a new mass culture which would profoundly shake traditional identities. Once again, the effects here are ambiguous, as along with the undeniable effects of massification and uniformization, this media-based culture also contains powerful elements for the subversion of inequalities: the dominant discourses in consumer society present it as social progress and the advance of democracy, to the extent that it allows the vast majority of the population access to an ever-increasing range of goods. Now, while Baudrillard is right to say that we are 'ever further away from an equality vis-à-vis the object',[17] the reigning appearance of equality and the cultural democratization which is the inevitable consequence of the action of the media permit the questioning of privileges based upon older forms of status. Interpellated as equals in their capacity as consumers, ever more numerous groups are impelled to reject the real inequalities which continue to exist. This 'democratic consumer culture' has undoubtedly stimulated the emergence of new struggles which have played an important part in the rejection of old forms of subordination, as was the case in the United States with the struggle of the black movement for civil rights. The phenomenon of the young is particularly interesting, and it is no cause for wonder that they should constitute a new axis for the emergence of antagonisms. In order to create new necessities, they are increasingly constructed as a specific category of consumer, which stimulates them to seek a financial autonomy that society is in no condition to give them. On the contrary, the economic crisis and unemployment make their situation difficult indeed. If we add to this the disintegration of the family cell and its growing reduction to pure functions of consumption, along with the absence of social forms of integration of these 'new subjects' who have received the impact of the general questioning of existing hierarchies, we easily understand the different forms which the rebellion of the young has adopted in industrial societies.

The fact that these 'new antagonisms' are the expression of forms of resistance to the commodification, bureaucratization and increasing homogenization of social life itself explains why they should frequently manifest themselves through a proliferation of particularisms, and crystallize into a demand for autonomy itself. It is also for this reason that there is an identifiable tendency towards the valorization of 'differences' and the creation of new identities which tend to privilege 'cultural' criteria (clothes, music, language, regional traditions, and so on). Insofar as of the two great themes of the democratic imaginary — equality and liberty — it was that of equality which was traditionally predominant, the demands for autonomy bestow an increasingly central role upon liberty. For this reason many of these forms of resistance are made manifest not in the form of collective struggles, but through an increasingly affirmed individualism. (The Left, of course, is ill prepared to take into account these struggles, which even today it tends to dismiss as 'liberal'. Hence the danger that they may be articulated by a discourse of the Right, of the defence of privileges.) But in any case, and whatever the political orientation through which the antagonism crystallizes (this will depend upon the chains of equivalence which construct it), *the form of the antagonism as such* is identical in all cases.

That is to say, it always consists in the construction of a social identity — of an overdetermined subject position — on the basis of the equivalence between a set of elements or values which expel or externalize those others to which they are opposed. Once again, we find ourselves confronting the *division* of social space.

The last in time of these 'new social movements', and without doubt one of the most active at the present moment, is the peace movement. It appears to us that it falls perfectly into the theoretical framework which we have put forward. With the expansion of what E.P. Thompson has called the 'logic of exterminism', a growing number of people feel that the most basic of all rights, that of life, has been called into question. In addition, the deployment in numerous countries of foreign nuclear weapons whose use is not under national control, generates new demands rooted in the extension to the field of national defence of the principles of democratic control which citizens have the right to exercise in the political field. Discourse concerning defence policy — traditionally the enclosed preserve of restricted military and political elites — is thus subverted as the democratic principle of control lodges itself at its heart.

The central idea which we have defended thus far is that the new struggles — and the radicalization of older struggles such as those of women or ethnic minorities — should be understood from the double perspective of the transformation of social relations characteristic of the new hegemonic formation of the post-war period, and of the effects of the displacement into new areas of social life of the egalitarian imaginary constituted around the liberal–democratic discourse. It is this which has provided the framework necessary for the questioning of the different relations of subordination and the demanding of new rights. That the democratic imaginary has played a fundamental role in the eruption of new demands since the 1960s, is perfectly well understood by the American neo–conservatives, who denounce the 'excess of democracy' and the wave of 'egalitarianism' which in their view caused an overload in the political systems of the West. Samuel Huntington, in his report to the Trilateral Commission in 1975, argued that the struggles in the United States in the 1960s for greater equality and participation had provoked a 'democratic surge' which had made society 'ungovernable'. He concluded that 'the strength of the democratic ideal poses a problem for the governability of democracy.'[18] The increasingly numerous demands for real equality have led society, according to the neo–conservatives, to the edge of the 'egalitarian precipice'. This is where they see the origins of the double transformation which, in their opinion, the idea of equality has undergone: it has passed from equality of opportunity to equality of results, and from equality between individuals to equality between groups. Daniel Bell considers that this 'new egalitarianism' puts in jeopardy the true ideal of equality, whose objective cannot be equality of results, but a 'just meritocracy'.[19] The present crisis is, then, seen as the result of a 'crisis of values', the consequence of the development of an 'adversary culture' and of the 'cultural contradictions of capitalism'.

Thus far we have presented the emergence of new antagonisms and political subjects as linked to the expansion and generalization of the democratic revolution. In reality, it can also be seen as a prolongation of various other areas of political effects which we have come across frequently throughout our analysis. In particular, the proliferation of these antagonisms makes us see in a new light the problem of the fragmentation of the 'unitary' subjects of the social struggles with which Marxism found itself confronted in the wake of its first crisis, at the end of the last century. All the discussion on strategies for recomposition of working-class unity, seen in perspective, is nothing other than the first act of a recognition — reluctant, it is true — of the plurality of the social, and the unsutured character of all political identity. If we read *sous rature* the texts of Rosa Luxemburg, Labriola, and of Kautsky himself, we shall see that this unassimilable moment of plurality is in one way or another present in their discourse, undermining the coherence of their categories. It is clear that this multiformity was not necessarily a negative moment of fragmentation or the reflection of an artificial division resulting from the logic of capitalism, as the theorists of the Second International thought, but the very terrain which made *possible* a deepening of the democratic revolution. As we shall see, this deepening is revealed even in the ambiguities and difficulties which every practice of articulation and recomposition has to face. Renunciation of the category of subject as a unitary, transparent and sutured entity opens the way to the recognition of the specificity of the antagonisms constituted on the basis of different subject positions, and, hence, the possibility of the deepening of a pluralist and democratic conception. The critique of the category of unified subject, and the recognition of the discursive dispersion within which every subject position is constituted, therefore involve something more than the enunciation of a general theoretical position: they are the *sine qua non* for thinking the multiplicity out of which antagonisms emerge in societies in which the democratic revolution has crossed a certain threshold. This gives us a theoretical terrain on the basis of which the notion of *radical and plural democracy* — which will be central to our argument from this point on — finds the first conditions under which it can be apprehended. Only if it is accepted that the subject positions cannot be led back to a positive and unitary founding principle — only then can pluralism be considered radical. Pluralism is *radical* only to the extent that each term of this plurality of identities finds within itself the principle of its own validity, without this having to be sought in a transcendent or underlying positive ground for the hierarchy of meaning of them all and the source and guarantee of their legitimacy. And this radical pluralism is *democratic* to the extent that the autoconstitutivity of each one of its terms is the result of displacements of the egalitarian imaginary. Hence, the project for a radical and plural democracy, *in a primary sense,* is nothing other than the struggle for a maximum auto-nomization of spheres on the basis of the generalization of the equivalential-egalitarian logic.

This approach permits us to redimension and do justice to workers' struggles themselves, whose character is distorted when they are contrasted *en bloc* to the struggles of the 'new political subjects'. Once the conception of the working class as a 'universal class' is rejected, it becomes possible to recognize the plurality of the antagonisms which take place in the field of what is arbitrarily grouped under the label of 'workers' struggles', and the inestimable importance of the great majority of them for the deepening of the democratic process. Workers' struggles have been numerous, and have assumed an extraordinary variety of forms as a function of transformations in the role of the state, the trade-union practices of different categories of workers, the antagonisms within and outside the factories, and the existing hegemonic equilibria. An excellent example is afforded us by the so-called 'new workers' struggles', which took place in France and in Italy at the end of the 1960s. They show well how the forms of struggles within the factory depend upon a discursive context much vaster than that of simple relations of production. The evident influence of the struggles and slogans of the student movement; the central role played by young workers, whose culture was radically different from that of their older col-leagues; the importance of immigrants in France and southerners in Italy — all this reveals to us that the other social relations in which workers are enrolled will determine the manner in which they react inside the factory, and that as a result the plurality of these relations cannot be magically erased to constitute a *single* working class. Nor, then, can workers' demands be reduced to a unique antagonism whose nature is ontologically different from that of other social and political subjects.

Thus far we have spoken of a multiplicity of antagonisms whose effects, converging and overdetermined, are registered within the framework of what we have called the 'democratic revolution'. At this point it is necessary, nevertheless, to make it clear that the democratic revolution is simply the terrain upon which there operates a logic of displacement supported by an egalitarian imaginary, but that it does not predetermine the *direction* in which this imaginary will operate. If this direction were predetermined we should simply have constructed a new teleology — we would be on a terrain similar to that of Bernstein's *Entwicklung*. But in that case there would be no room at all for a hegemonic practice. The reason why it is not thus, and why no teleology can account for social articulations, is that the discursive compass of the democratic revolution opens the way for political logics as diverse as right-wing populism and totalitarianism on the one hand, and a radical democracy on the other. Therefore, if we wish to construct the hegemonic articulations which allow us to set ourselves in the direction of the latter, we must understand in all their radical heterogeneity the range of possibilities which are opened in the terrain of democracy itself.

It cannot be doubted that the proliferation of new antagonisms and of 'new rights' is leading to a crisis of the hegemonic formation of the post-war period. But the form in which this crisis will be overcome is far from being predetermined, as the manner in which rights will be defined and the forms which struggle against subordination will adopt are not unequivocally established. We are faced here with a true polysemia. Feminism or ecology, for example, exist in multiple forms, which depend upon the manner in which the antagonism is discursively constituted. Thus we have a radical feminism which attacks men as such; a feminism of difference which seeks to revalorize 'femininity'; and a Marxist feminism for which the fundamental enemy is capitalism, considered as linked indissolubly to patriarchy. There are therefore a plurality of discursive forms of constructing an antagonism on the basis of the different modes of women's subordination. Ecology, in the same way, may be anti-capitalist, anti-industrialist, authoritarian, libertarian, socialist, reactionary, and so on. The forms of articulation of an antagonism, therefore, far from being predetermined, are the result of a hegemonic struggle. This affirmation has important consequences, as it implies that these new struggles do not necessarily have a progressive character, and that it is therefore an error to think, as many do, that they spontaneously take their place in the context of left-wing politics. Many have devoted themselves since the 1960s to the search for a new privileged revolutionary subject which might come to replace the working class, with the latter seen as having failed in its historical mission of emancipation. The ecological movements, the student movements, feminism and the marginal masses have been the most popular candidates for the carrying out of this new role. But it is clear that such an approach does not escape the traditional problematic, but simply displaces it. There is no *unique* privileged position from which a uniform continuity of effects will follow, concluding with the transformation of society as a whole. All struggles, whether those of workers or other political subjects, left to themsleves, have a partial character, and can be articulated to very different discourses. It is this articulation which gives them their character, not the place from which they come. There is therefore no subject — nor, further, any 'necessity' — which is absolutely radical and irrecuperable by the dominant order, and which constitutes an absolutely guaranteed point of departure for a total transformation. (Equally, there is nothing which permanently assures the stability of an established order.) It is in relation to this point that we consider that certain highly interesting analyses such as those of Alain Touraine and André Gorz, do not go far enough in their break with the traditional problematic.[20] Gorz, for example, given that he attributes to the 'non-class of non-workers' the privilege which he denies to the proletariat, really does no more than invert the Marxist position. It is still the location at the level of relations of production which is determining, even when, as in Gorz's case, the revolutionary subject is defined by the *absence* of that insertion. As for Touraine, his search for the social movement which can play in the 'programmed society' the role which was played by the working class in industrial society indicates clearly that he too does not question the idea of the uniqueness of the social force which can bring about a radical change in a determinate society.

That the forms of resistance to new forms of subordination are polysemic and can perfectly well be articulated into an anti-democratic discourse, is clearly demonstrated by the advances of the 'new right' in recent years. Its novelty lies in its successful articulation to neo-liberal discourse of a series of democratic resistances to the transformation of social relations. Popular support for the Reagan and Thatcher projects of dismantling the Welfare State is explained by the fact that they have succeeded in mobilizing against the latter a whole series of resistances to the bureaucratic character of the new forms of state organization. That the chains of equivalence which each hegemonic articulation constitutes can be of greatly differing natures is patently demonstrated by this neo-conservative discourse: the antagonisms constituted around bureaucratization are articulated in the defence of the traditional inequalities of sex and race. The defence of acquired rights founded on white, male supremacy which feeds the conservative reaction thereby broadens the area of its hegemonic effects. An antagonism is thus constructed between two poles: the 'people', which includes all those who defend the traditional values and freedom of enterprise; and their adversaries: the state and all the subversives (feminists, blacks, young people and 'permissives' of every type). An attempt is thus made to construct a new historic bloc in which a plurality of economic, social and cultural aspects are articulated. Stuart Hall has pointed out, for example, how Thatcherite populism 'combines the resonant themes of organic Toryism — nation, family, duty, authority, standards, traditionalism — with the aggressive themes of a revived neo-liberalism — self-interest, competitive individualism, anti-statism.'[21] In the case of the United States, Allen Hunter shows that the attack of the New Right on the Welfare State is the point at which the cultural and economic critiques come together. Both affirm that the state interferes 'with the economic and ethical features of the market in the name of a specious egalitarianism. They also attack welfare liberalism for creating state intervention in the private lives of the people and the moral structure of society in such areas as the socialization of children and the relation between the sexes.'[22]

It is precisely this polysemic character of every antagonism which makes its meaning dependent upon a hegemonic articulation to the extent that, as we have seen, the terrain of hegemonic practices is constituted out of the fundamental ambiguity of the social, the impossibility of establishing in a definitive manner the meaning of any struggle, whether considered in isolation or through its fixing in a relational system. As we have said, there are hegemonic practices because this radical unfixity makes it impossible to consider the political struggle as a game in which the identity of the opposing forces is constituted from the start. This means that any politics with hegemonic aspirations can never consider itself as *repetition*, as taking place in a space delimiting a pure internality, but must always mobilize itself on a plurality of planes. If the meaning of each struggle is not given from the start, this means that it is fixed — partially — only to the extent that the struggle moves outside itself and, through chains of equivalence, links itself structurally to other struggles. Every antagonism, left free to itself, is a floating signifier, a 'wild' antagonism which does not predetermine the form in which it can be articulated to other elements in a social formation. This permits us to establish the radical difference between the current social struggles and those which took place before the democratic revolution. The latter always took place in the context of the denial of *given* and relatively stable identities; as a result, the frontiers of the antagonism were plainly visible and did not require to be constructed — the hegemonic dimension of politics was consequently absent. But in the present industrial societies, the very proliferation of widely differing points of rupture, the precarious character of all social identity, lead also to a blurring of the frontiers. In consequence, the *constructed* character of the demarcating lines is made more evident by the greater instability of the latter, and the displacement of the frontiers and internal divisions of the social become more radical. It is in this field and from this perspective that the neo-conservative project acquires all its hegemonic dimensions.

The Anti-Democratic Offensive

What the neo-conservative or neo-liberal 'new right' calls into question is the type of articulation which has led democratic liberalism to justify the intervention of the state in the struggle against inequalities, and the installation of the Welfare State. The critique of this transformation is not a recent development. As long ago as 1944, in *The Road to Serfdom*, Hayek launched a violent attack on the interventionist state and the various forms of economic planning that were being implemented at the time. He announced that the Western societies were in the process of becoming collectivist, and thus taking off in the direction of totalitarianism. According to him, the threshold of collectivism is passed at the moment in which the law, instead of being a means of controlling the administration, is utilized by it in order to attribute new powers to itself, and to facilitate the expansion of the bureaucracy. From this point on it is inevitable that the power of the law will decline, while that of the bureaucracy increases. In reality, what is at issue through this neo-liberal critique is the very articulation between liberalism and democracy which was performed during the course of the nineteenth century.[23] This 'democratization' of liberalism, which was the result of multiple struggles, would eventually have a profound impact upon the form in which the very idea of liberty was conceived. From the traditional liberal definition of Locke — 'liberty is to be free from restraint and violence from others' — we had passed with John Stuart Mill to the acceptance of 'political' liberty and democratic participation as an important component of liberty. More recently, in social-democratic discourse, liberty has come to mean the 'capacity' to make certain choices and to keep open a series of real alternatives. It is thus that poverty, lack of education, and great disparities in the conditions of life are today considered offences against liberty.

It is this transformation which neo-liberalism wishes to question. Hayek is, without doubt, the one who has devoted himself most strenuously to reformulating the principles of liberalism in order to combat those shifts of meaning which have permitted the broadening and deepening of liberties. He proposes to reaffirm the 'true' nature of liberalism as the doctrine which seeks to reduce to the minimum the powers of the state, in order to maximize the central political objective: individual liberty. This comes once again to be defined negatively as 'that condition of men in which coercion of some by others is reduced as much as possible in society'.[24] Political liberty is ostensibly excluded from this definition. According to Hayek, 'democracy (is) essentially a means, a utilitarian device for safeguarding internal peace and individual freedom.'[25] This attempt to return to the traditional conception of liberty, which characterizes it as non-interference with the right of unlimited appropriation and with the mechanisms of the capitalist market economy, exerts itself to discredit every 'positive' conception of liberty as being potentially totalitarian. It affirms that a liberal political order can only exist in the framework of a capitalist free market economy. In *Capitalism and Freedom* Milton Friedman declares that this is the only type of social organization which respects the principle of individual liberty, as it constitutes the only economic system capable of coordinating the activities of a great number of people without recourse to coercion. All state intervention, except in connection with matters that cannot be regulated through the market, is considered as an attack on individual liberty. The notion of social or redistributive justice, insofar as it is invoked to justify intervention by the state, is one of the favourite targets of the neo-liberals. According to Hayek, it is a notion which is completely unintelligible in a liberal society, as 'in such a system in which each is allowed to use his knowledge for his own purposes the concept of "social justice" is necessarily empty and meaningless, because in it nobody's will can determine the relative incomes of the different people, or prevent that they be partly dependent on accident.'[26]

From a 'libertarian' perspective Robert Nozick has equally questioned the idea that there can exist such a thing as a distributive justice which the state should provide.[27] In his view, the sole function of the state compatible with liberty is that of protecting what legitimately belongs to us, while it does not have the right to establish taxes which go beyond what is required for the development of policing activities. In contrast to the American ultralibertarians, who reject all state intervention,[28] Nozick justifies the existence of the minimal state — that is to say, law and order. But a state which went beyond that would be unjustifiable, as in that case it would violate the rights of individuals. In any case, Nozick claims, there would not be anything available which could be legally distributed by the state, as everything that existed would be possessed by individuals or be under their legitimate control.

Another way of attacking the subversive effects of the articulation between liberalism and democracy is, in the manner of the neoconservatives, to redefine the notion of democracy itself in such a way as to restrict its field of application and limit political participation to an ever narrower area. Thus Brzezinski proposes to 'increasingly separate the political system from society and to begin to conceive the two as separate entities.'[29] The objective is to remove public decisions more and more from political control, and to make them the exclusive responsibility of experts. In such a case the effect would be a depoliticization of fundamental decisions, at the economic level as well as at social and political levels. Such a society, in his view, would be democratic 'in a libertarian sense; democratic not in terms of exercising fundamental choices concerning policy-making but in the sense of maintaining certain areas of autonomy for individual self-expression'.[30] Although the democratic ideal is not openly attacked, an attempt is made to empty it of all substance and to propose a new definition of democracy which in fact would serve to legitimize a regime in which political participation might be virtually non-existent.

In France, among the theoreticians of the new right, there has been a far more audacious and frontal critique of democracy. Thus its principal spokesman, Alain de Benoist, declares openly that the French Revolution marked one of the fundamental stages of degeneration of Western civilization — a degeneration which began with Christianity, the 'Bolshevism of Antiquity'. He further argues that it is the spirit itself of the 1789 Declaration of the Rights of Man which has to be rejected. Skilfully recapturing a series of libertarian themes from the movement of 1968, Alain de Benoist considers that in attributing a fundamental role to universal suffrage, democracy places all individuals on the same level and fails to recognize the important differences among them. Thence derives a uniformization and massification of the citizenry, upon whom is imposed a single norm which shows the necessarily totalitarian character of democracy. In the face of the chain of equivalences equality= identity=totalitarianism, the new right proclaims the 'right to difference', and affirms the sequence difference=inequality=liberty. De Benoist writes: 'I call "right-wing" the attitude which considers the *diversity* of the world, and hence inequalities, as a good, and the progressive homogenization of the world, favoured and brought about by the bimillennarian discourse of the totalitarian ideology, as an evil.'[31]

It would be an error to underestimate the importance of these attempts to redefine notions such as 'liberty', 'equality', 'justice' and 'democracy'. The traditional dogmatism of the Left, which attributed secondary importance to problems at the centre of political philosophy, based itself upon the 'superstructural' character of such problems. In the end, the Left interested itself only in a limited range of issues linked to the infrastructure and the subjects constituted within it, while the whole of the vast field of culture and the definition of reality built upon the basis of it, the whole effort of hegemonic rearticulation of the diverse discursive formations, was left free for the initiative of the right. And, in effect, if the whole of the liberal-democratic conception of the state, as associated with the Right, was simply seen as the superstructural form of bourgeois domination, it was difficult — without falling into crass opportunism — to consider a different attitude possible. However, once we have abandoned the base/superstructure distinction, and rejected the view that there are privileged points from which an emancipatory political practice can be launched, it is clear that the constitution of a hegemonic left alternative can only come from a complex process of convergence and political construction, to which none of the hegemonic articulations constructed in any area of social reality can be of indifference. The form in which liberty, equality, democracy and justice are defined at the level of political philosophy may have important consequences at a variety of other levels of discourse, and contribute decisively to shaping the common sense of the masses. Naturally, these irradiation effects cannot be considered as the simple adoption of a philosophical point of view at the level of 'ideas', but should rather be seen as a more complex set of discursive-hegemonic operations embracing a variety of aspects, both institutional and ideological, through which certain 'themes' are transformed into nodal points of a discursive formation (i.e. of a historic bloc). If neo-liberal ideas have acquired an unquestionable political resonance, it is because they have permitted the articulation of resistances to the growing bureaucratization of social relations to which we referred earlier. Thus the new conservatism has succeeded in presenting its programme of dismantling the Welfare State as a defence of individual liberty against the oppressor state. But in order for a philosophy to become 'organic ideology', certain analogies must exist between the type of subject which it constructs and the subject positions which are constituted at the level of other social relations. If the theme of individual liberty can be mobilized so effectively, it is also because, despite its articulation with the democratic imaginary, liberalism has continued to retain as a matrix of production of the individual what Macpherson called 'possessive individualism'. This latter constructs the rights of individuals as existing before society, and often in opposition to it. To the extent that more and more numerous subjects demanded these rights in the framework of the democratic revolution, it was inevitable that the matrix of possessive individualism would be broken, as the rights of some came into collision with the rights of others. It is in this context of crisis of democratic liberalism that it is necessary to locate the offensive which seeks to dissolve the subversive potential of the articulations between liberalism and democracy, reaffirming the centrality of liberalism as the defence of individual liberty against all interference from the state and in opposition to the democratic component, which is founded upon equal rights and popular sovereignty. But this effort to restrict the terrain of democratic struggle, and to preserve the inequalities existing in a number of social relations, demands the defence of a hierarchical and anti-egalitarian principle which had been endangered by liberalism itself. This is why the liberals increasingly resort to a set of themes from conservative philosophy, in which they find the necessary ingredients to justify inequality. We are thus witnessing the emergence of a new hegemonic project, that of liberal-conservative discourse, which seeks to articulate the neo-liberal defence of the free market economy with the profoundly anti-egalitarian cultural and social traditionalism of conservatism.

Radical Democracy: Alternative for a New Left

The conservative reaction thus has a clearly hegemonic character. It seeks a profound transformation of the terms of political discourse and the creation of a new 'definition of reality', which under the cover of the defence of 'individual liberty' would legitimize inequalities and restore the hierarchical relations which the struggles of previous decades had destroyed. What is at stake here is in fact the creation of a new historic bloc. Converted into organic ideology, liberal–conservatism would construct a new hegemonic articulation through a system of equivalences which would unify multiple subject positions around an individualist definition of rights and a negative conception of liberty. We are once again faced, then, with the displacement of the frontier of the social. A series of subject positions which were accepted as *legitimate differences* in the hegemonic formation corresponding to the Welfare State are expelled from the field of social positivity and construed as negativity — the parasites on social security (Mrs Thatcher's 'scroungers'), the inefficiency associated with union privileges, and state subsidies, and so on.

It is clear, therefore, that a left alternative can *only* consist of the construction of a different system of equivalents, which establishes social division on a new basis. In the face of the project for the reconstruction of a hierarchic society, the alternative of the Left should consist of locating itself fully in the field of the democratic revolution and expanding the chains of equivalents between the different struggles against oppression. *The task of the Left therefore cannot be to renounce liberal-democratic ideology, but on the contrary, to deepen and expand it in the direction of a radical and plural democracy.* We shall explain the dimensions of this task in the following pages, but the very fact that it is possible arises out of the fact that the *meaning* of liberal discourse on individual rights is not definitively fixed; and just as this unfixity permits their articulation with elements of conservative discourse, it also permits different forms of articulation and redefinition which accentuate the democratic moment. That is to say, as with any other social element, the elements making up the liberal discourse never appear as crystallized, and may be the field of hegemonic struggle. It is not in the abandonment of the democratic terrain but, on the contrary, in the extension of the field of democratic struggles to the whole of civil society and the state, that the possibility resides for a hegemonic strategy of the Left. It is nevertheless important to understand the radical extent of the changes which are necessary in the political imaginary of the Left, if it wishes to succeed in founding a political practice fully located in the field of the democratic revolution and conscious of the depth and variety of the hegemonic articulations which the present conjuncture requires. The fundamental obstacle in this task is the one to which we have been drawing attention from the beginning of this book: essentialist apriorism, the conviction that the social is sutured at some point, from which it is possible to fix the meaning of any event independently of any articulatory practice. This has led to a failure to understand the constant displacement of the nodal points structuring a social formation, and to an organization of discourse in terms of a logic of 'a priori privileged points' which seriously limits the Left's capacity for action and political analysis. This logic of privileged points has operated in a variety of directions. From the point of view of the determining of the fundamental antagonisms, the basic obstacle, as we have seen, has been *classism*: that is to say, the idea that the working class represents the privileged agent in which the fundamental impulse of social change resides — without perceiving that the very orientation of the working class depends upon a political balance of forces and the radicalization of a plurality of democratic struggles which are decided in good part *outside* the class itself. From the point of view of the *social levels* at which the possibility of implementing changes is concentrated, the fundamental obstacles have been *statism* — the idea that the expansion of the role of the state is the panacea for all problems; and *economism* (particularly in its technocratic version) — the idea that from a successful economic strategy there necessarily follows a continuity of political effects which can be clearly specified.

But if we look for the ultimate core of this essentialist fixity, we shall find it in the fundamental nodal point which has galvanized the political imagination of the Left: the classic concept of 'revolution', cast in the Jacobin mould. Of course, there would be nothing in the concept of 'revolution' to which objection could be made if we understood by it the overdetermination of a set of struggles in a point of political rupture, from which there follow a variety of effects spread across the whole of the fabric of society. If this were all that was involved, there is no doubt that in many cases the violent overthrow of a repressive regime is the condition of every democratic advance. But the classic concept of revolution implied much more than this: it implied the *foundational* character of the revolutionary act, the institution of a point of concentration of power from which society could be 'rationally' reorganized. This is the perspective which is incompatible with the plurality and the opening which a radical democracy requires. Once again radicalizing certain of Gramsci's concepts, we find the theoretical instruments which allow us to redimension the revolutionary act itself. The concept of a 'war of position' implies precisely the *process* character of every radical transformation — the revolutionary act is, simply, an internal moment of this process. The multiplication of political spaces and the preventing of the concentration of power in one point are, then, preconditions of every truly democratic transformation of society. The classic conception of socialism supposed that the disappearance of private ownership of the means of production would set up a chain of effects which, over a whole historical epoch, would lead to the extinction of all forms of subordination. Today we know that this is not so. *There are not,* for example, necessary links between anti-sexism and anti-capitalism, and a unity between the two can only be the result of a hegemonic articulation. It follows that it is only possible to construct this articulation on the basis of separate struggles, which only exercise their equivalential and overdetermining effects in *certain* spheres of the social. This requires the autonomization of the spheres of struggle and the multiplication of political spaces, which is incompatible with the concentration of power and knowledge that classic Jacobinism and its different socialist variants imply. Of course, every project for radical democracy implies a socialist dimension, as it is necessary to put an end to capitalist relations of production, which are at the root of numerous relations of subordination; but socialism is *one* of the components of a project for radical democracy, not vice versa. For this very reason, when one speaks of the socialization of the means of production as one element in the strategy for a radical and plural democracy, one must insist that this cannot mean only workers' self-management, as what is at stake is true participation by all subjects in decisions about what is to be produced, how it is to be produced, and the forms in which the product is to be distributed. Only in such conditions can there be *social appropriation* of production. To reduce the issue to a problem of workers' self-management is to ignore the fact that the workers' 'interests' can be constructed in such a way that they do not take account of ecological demands or demands of other groups which, without being producers, are affected by decisions taken in the field of production.[32]

From the point of view of a hegemonic politics, then, the crucial limitation of the traditional left perspective is that it attempts to determine *a priori* agents of change, levels of effectiveness in the field of the social, and privileged points and moments of rupture. All these obstacles come together into a common core, which is the refusal to abandon the assumption of a sutured society. Once this is discarded, however, there arises a whole set of new problems which we should now tackle. These may be summarized in three questions which we shall address in turn: 1) How do we determine the *surfaces of emergence* and the *forms of articulation* of the antagonisms which a project for radical democracy should embrace? 2) To what extent is the pluralism proper to a radical democracy compatible with the effects of equivalence which, as we have seen, are characteristic of every hegemonic articulation? 3) To what extent is the logic implicit in the displacements of the democratic imaginary sufficient to define an *hegemonic project?*

On the first point it is evident that, just as the apriorism implicit in a topography of the social has proved untenable, so it is impossible to define *a priori* the surfaces on which antagonisms will be constituted. Thus, although several left politics may be conceived and specified in certain contexts, there is not *one* politics of the Left whose *contents* can be determined in isolation from all contextual reference. It is for this reason that all attempts to proceed to such determination *a priori* have necessarily been unilateral and arbitrary, with no validity in a great number of circumstances. The exploding of the uniqueness of meaning of the political — which is linked to the phenomena of combined and uneven development — dissolves every possibility of fixing the signified in terms of a division between left and right. Say we try to define an ultimate content of the left which underlies all the contexts in which the word has been used: we shall never find one which does not present exceptions. We are exactly in the field of Wittgenstein's language games: the closest we can get is to find 'family resemblances'. Let us examine a few examples. In recent years much has been talked about the need to deepen the line of separation between state and civil society. It is not difficult to realize, however, that this proposal does not furnish the Left with any theory of the surface of emergence of antagonisms which can be generalized beyond a limited number of situations. It would appear to imply that every form of domination is incarnated in the state. But it is clear that civil society is also the seat of numerous relations of oppression, and, in consequence, of antagonisms and democratic struggles. With a greater or lesser clarity in their results, theories such as Althusser's analysis of 'ideological state apparatuses' sought to create a conceptual framework with which to think these phenomena of displacement in the field of domination. In the case of the feminist struggle, the state is an important means for effecting an advance, frequently *against* civil society, in legislation which combats sexism. In numerous underdeveloped countries the expansion of the functions of the central state is a means of establishing a frontier in the struggle against extreme forms of exploitation by landowning oligarchies. Furthermore, the state is not a homogeneous medium, separated from civil society by a ditch, but an uneven set of branches and functions, only relatively integrated by the hegemonic practices which take place within it. Above all, it should not be forgotten that the state can be the seat of numerous democratic antagonisms, to the extent that a set of functions within it — professional or technical, for example — can enter into relations of antagonism with centres of power, within the state itself, which seek to restrict and deform them. None of this means to say, of course, that in certain cases the division between state and civil society *cannot* constitute the fundamental political line of demarcation: this is what happens when the state has been transformed into a bureaucratic excrescence imposed by force upon the rest of society, as in Eastern Europe, or in the Nicaragua of the Somozas, which was a dictatorship sustained by a military apparatus. At any event, it is clearly impossible to identify either the state or civil society *a priori* as *the* surface of emergence of democratic antagonisms. The same can be said when it is a question of determining the positive or negative character, from the point of view of the politics of the Left, of certain organizational forms. Let us consider, for example, the 'party' form. The party as a political institution can, in certain circumstances, be an instance of bureaucratic crystallization which acts as a brake upon mass movements; but in others it can be the organizer of dispersed and politically virgin masses, and can thus serve as an instrument for the expansion and deepening of democratic struggles. The important point is that inasmuch as the field of 'society in general' has disappeared as a valid framework of political analysis, there has also disappeared the possibility of establishing a *general* theory of politics on the basis of topographic categories — that is to say, of categories which fix in a permanent manner the meaning of certain contents as differences which can be located within a relational complex.

The conclusion to be drawn from this analysis is that it is impossible to specify *a priori* surfaces of emergence of antagonisms, as there is no surface which is not constantly subverted by the overdetermining effects of others, and because there is, in consequence, a constant displacement of the social logics characteristic of certain spheres towards other spheres. This is, among other things, the 'demonstration effect' that we have seen in operation in the case of the democratic revolution. A democratic struggle can autonomize a certain space within which it develops, and produce effects of equivalence with other struggles in a different political space. It is to this plurality of the social that the project for a radical democracy is linked, and the possibility of it emanates directly from the decentred character of the social agents, from the discursive plurality which constitutes them as subjects, and from the displacements which take place within that plurality. The original forms of democratic thought were linked to a *positive* and *unified* conception of human nature, and, to that extent, they tended to constitute a single space within which that nature would have to manifest the effects of its radical liberty and equality: it was thus that there was constituted a public space linked to the idea of citizenship. The public/private distinction constituted the separation between a space in which differences were erased through the universal equivalence of citizens, and a plurality of private spaces in which the full force of those differences was maintained. It is at this point that the overdetermination of effects linked to the democratic revolution begins to displace the line of demarcation between the public and the private and to *politicize* social relations; that is, to multiply the spaces in which the new logics of equivalence dissolve the differential positivity of the social: this is the long process which stretches from the workers' struggles of the nineteenth century to the struggle of women, diverse racial and sexual minorities, and diverse marginal groups, and the new anti-institutional struggles in the present century. Thus what has been exploded is the idea and the reality itself of a unique space of constitution of the political. What we are witnessing is a politicization far more radical than any we have known in the past, because it tends to dissolve the distinction between the public and the private, not in terms of the encroachment on the private by a unified public space, but in terms of a proliferation of radically new and different political spaces. We are confronted with the emergence of a *plurality of subjects,* whose forms of constitution and diversity it is only possible to think if we relinquish the category of 'subject' as a unified and unifying essence.

Is this plurality of the political not in contradiction, however, with the unification resulting from the equivalential effects which, as we know, are the condition of antagonisms? Or, in other words, is there not an incompatibility between the proliferation of political spaces proper to a radical democracy and the construction of collective identities on the basis of the logic of equivalence? Once again, we are faced here with the apparent dichotomy autonomy/hegemony, to which we have already referred in the previous chapter, and whose political implications and effects we should now consider. Let us consider the question from two perspectives: a) from the point of view of the *terrain* on which the dichotomy can present itself as exclusive; and b) from the point of view of the possibility and the historical conditions of the emergence of that terrain of exclusion.

Let us begin, then, by considering the terrain of the incompatibility between equivalential effects and autonomy. First, the logic of equivalence. We have already indicated that, inasmuch as antagonism arises not only in the dichotomized space which constitutes it but also in the field of a plurality of the social which always overflows that space, it is only by coming out of itself and hegemonizing external elements that the identity of the two poles of the antagonism is consolidated. The strengthening of specific democratic struggles requires, therefore, the expansion of chains of equivalence which extend to other struggles. The equivalential articulation between anti-racism, anti-sexism and anti-capitalism, for example, requires a hegemonic construction which, in certain circumstances, may be the condition for the consolidation of each one of these struggles. The logic of equivalence, then, taken to its ultimate consequences, would imply the dissolution of the autonomy of the spaces in which each one of these struggles is constituted; not necessarily because any of them become subordinated to others, but because they have all become, strictly speaking, equivalent symbols of a unique and indivisible struggle. The antagonism would thus have achieved the conditions of total transparency, to the extent that all unevenness had been eliminated, and the differential specificity of the spaces in which each of the democratic struggles was constituted had been dissolved. Second, the logic of autonomy. Each of these struggles retains its differential specificity with respect to the others. The political spaces in which each of them is constituted are different and unable to communicate with each other. But it is easily seen that this *apparently* libertarian logic is only sustained on the basis of a new closure. For if each struggle transforms the moment of its specificity into an absolute principle of identity, the set of these struggles can only be conceived of as an *absolute system of differences,* and this system can only be thought as a closed totality. That is to say, the transparency of the social has simply been transferred from the uniqueness and intelligibility of a system of equivalences to the uniqueness and intelligibility of a system of differences. But in both cases we are dealing with discourses which seek, through their categories, to dominate the social as a *totality*. In both cases, therefore, the moment of totality ceases to be a *horizon* and becomes a *foundation*. It is only in this rational and homogeneous space that the logic of equivalence and the logic of autonomy are contradictory, because it is only there that social identities are presented as *already* acquired and fixed, and it is only there, therefore, that two *ultimately* contradictory social logics find a terrain in which these *ultimate* effects can develop fully. But as, by definition, this ultimate moment never arrives, the incompatibility between equivalence and autonomy disappears. The status of each changes: it is no longer a case of *foundations* of the social order, but of *social logics,* which intervene to different degrees in the constitution of every social identity, and which partially limit their mutual effects. From this we can deduce a basic precondition for a radically libertarian conception of politics: the refusal to dominate — intellectually or politically — every presumed 'ultimate foundation' of the social. Every conception which seeks to base itself on a knowledge of this foundation finds itself faced, sooner or later, with the Rousseauian paradox according to which men should be obliged to be free.

This change in the status of certain concepts, which transforms into social logics what were previously foundations, allows us to understand the variety of dimensions on which a democratic politics is based. It allows us, first of all, to identify with precision the meaning and the limits of what we may call the 'principle of democratic equivalence'. We are able to specify the meaning because it becomes clear that the mere displacement of the egalitarian imaginary is not sufficient to produce a transformation in the identity of the groups upon which this displacement operates. On the basis of the principle of equality, a corporatively constituted group can demand its rights to equality with other groups, but to the extent that the demands of various groups are different and in many cases incompatible among themselves, this does not lead to any real equivalence between the various democratic demands. In all those cases in which the problematic of possessive individualism is maintained as the matrix of production of the identity of the different groups, this result is inevitable. For there to be a 'democratic equivalence' something else is necessary: the construction of a new 'common sense' which changes the identity of the different groups, in such a way that the demands of each group are articulated equivalentially with those of the others — in Marx's words, 'that the free development of each should be the condition for the free development of all'. That is, equivalence is always hegemonic insofar as it does not simply establish an 'alliance' between given interests, but modifies the very identity of the forces engaging in that alliance. For the defence of the interests of the workers not to be made at the expense of the rights of women, immigrants or consumers, it is necessary to establish an equivalence between these different struggles. It is only on this condition that struggles against power become truly democratic, and that the demanding of rights is not carried out on the basis of an individualistic problematic, but in the context of respect for the rights to equality of other subordinated groups. But if this is the meaning of the principle of democratic equivalence, its limits are also clear. This total equivalence never exists; every equivalence is penetrated by a constitutive precariousness, derived from the unevenness of the social. To this extent, the precariousness of every equivalence demands that it be complemented/limited by the logic of autonomy. It is for this reason that the demand for *equality* is not sufficient, but needs to be balanced by the demand for *liberty,* which leads us to speak of a radical and *plural* democracy. A radical and non-plural democracy would be one which constituted *one* single space of equality on the basis of the unlimited operation of the logic of equivalence, and did not recognize the irreducible moment of the plurality of spaces. This principle of the separation of spaces is the basis of the demand for liberty. It is within it that the principle of pluralism resides and that the project for a plural democracy can link up with the logic of liberalism. It is not liberalism as such which should be called into question, for as an ethical principle which defends the liberty of the individual to fulfil his or her human capacities, it is more valid today than ever. But if this dimension of liberty is constitutive of every democratic and emancipatory project, it should not lead us, in reaction to certain 'holistic' excesses, to return purely and simply to the defence of 'bourgeois' individualism. What is involved is the production of *another* individual, an individual who is no longer constructed out of the matrix of possessive individualism. The idea of 'natural' rights prior to society — and, indeed, the whole of the false dichotomy individual/society — should be abandoned, and replaced by another manner of posing the problem of rights. It is never possible for individual rights to be defined in isolation, but only in the context of social relations which define determinate subject positions. As a consequence, it will always be a question of rights which involve other subjects who participate in the same social relation. It is in this sense that the notion of 'democratic rights' must be understood, as these are rights which can only be exercised collectively, and which suppose the existence of equal rights for others. The spaces constitutive of the different social relations may vary enormously, according to whether the relations involved are those of production, of citizenship, of neighbourhood, of couples, and so on. The forms of democracy should therefore also be plural, inasmuch as they have to be adapted to the social spaces in question — direct democracy cannot be the only organizational form, as it is only applicable to reduced social spaces.

It is necessary, therefore, to broaden the domain of the exercise of democratic rights beyond the limited traditional field of 'citizenship'. As regards the extension of democratic rights from the classic 'political' domain to that of the economy, this is the terrain of the specifically anti-capitalist struggle. Against those champions of economic liberalism who affirm that the economy is the domain of the 'private', the seat of natural rights, and that the criteria of democracy have no reason to be applied within it, socialist theory defends the right of the social agent to equality and to participation as a producer and not only as a citizen. Some advances have been made in this direction by theorists of the pluralist school such as Dahl and Lindblom,[33] who today recognize that to speak of the economy as the domain of the private in the era of multinational corporations is senseless, and that it is therefore necessary to accept certain forms of worker participation in the running of enterprises. Our perspective is certainly very different, as it is the very idea that there can be a natural domain of the 'private' which we wish to question. The distinctions public/private, civil society/political society are only the result of a certain type of hegemonic articulation, and their limits vary in accordance with the existing relations of forces at a given moment. For example, it is clear that neo-conservative discourse today is exerting itself to restrict the domain of the political and to reaffirm the field of the private in the face of the reduction to which this has been submitted in recent decades under the impact of the different democratic struggles.

Let us take up again at this point our argument regarding the mutual and necessary limitations between equivalence and autonomy. The conception of a plurality of political spaces is incompatible with the logic of equivalence only on the assumption of a closed system. But once this assumption is abandoned, it is not possible to derive from the proliferation of spaces and the ultimate indeterminacy of the social the impossibility of a society signifying itself — and thus thinking itself — as a totality, or the incompatibility of this totalizing moment with the project for a radical democracy. The construction of a political space with equivalential effects is not only not incompatible with democratic struggle, but is in many cases a requirement for it. The construction of a chain of democratic equivalences in the face of the neo-conservative offensive, for example, is one of the conditions of the struggle of the Left for hegemony in the present circumstances. The incompatibility therefore does not lie in equivalence as a social logic. It arises only from the moment at which this space of equivalences ceases to be considered as *one* political space among others and comes to be seen as the centre, which subordinates and organizes all other spaces. It arises, that is, in the case where there takes place not only the construction of equivalents at a certain level of the social, but also the transformation of this level into a unifying principle, which reduces the others to differential moments internal to itself. We see then, paradoxically, that it is the very logic of openness and of the democratic subversion of differences which creates, in the societies of today, the possibility of a closure far more radical than in the past: to the extent that the resistance of traditional systems of differences is broken, and indeterminacy and ambiguity turn more elements of society into 'floating signifiers', the possibility arises of attempting to institute a centre which radically eliminates the logic of autonomy and reconstitutes around itself the totality of the social body. If in the nineteenth century the limits of every attempt at radical democracy were found in the survival of old forms of subordination across broad areas of social relations, at the present those limits are given by a new possibility which arises in the very terrain of democracy: the logic of totalitarianism.

Claude Lefort has shown how the 'democratic revolution', as a new terrain which supposes a profound mutation at the symbolic level, implies a new form of institution of the social. In earlier societies, organized in accordance with a theological-political logic, power was incorporated in the person of the prince, who was the representative of God — that is to say, of sovereign justice and sovereign reason. Society was thought as a body, the hierarchy of whose members rested upon the principle of unconditional order. According to Lefort, the radical difference which democratic society introduces is that the site of power becomes an empty space; the reference to a transcendent guarantor disappears, and with it the representation of the substantial unity of society. As a consequence a split occurs between the instances of power, knowledge, and the law, and their foundations are no longer assured. The possibility is thus opened up of an unending process of questioning: 'no law which can be fixed, whose dictates are not subject to contest, or whose foundations cannot be called into question; in sum, no representation of a centre of society: unity is no longer able to erase social division. Democracy inaugurates the experience of a society which cannot be apprehended or controlled, in which the people will be proclaimed sovereign, but in which its identity will never be definitively given, but will remain latent.'[34] It is in this context, according to Lefort, that the possibility must be understood of the emergence of totalitarianism, which consists of an attempt to re-establish the unity which democracy has shattered between the loci of power, law and knowledge. Once all references to extra-social powers have been abolished through the democratic revolution, a purely social power can emerge, presenting itself as total and extracting from itself alone the principle of law and the principle of knowledge. With totalitarianism, rather than designating a vacant site, power seeks to make itself material in an organ which assumes itself to be the representative of a *unitary* people. Under the pretext of achieving the unity of the people, the social division made visible by the logic of democracy is thereupon denied. This denial constitutes the centre of the logic of totalitarianism, and it is effected in a double movement: 'the annulment of the signs of the division of the state and society, and of those of the internal division of society. These imply the annulment of the differentiation of instances which govern the constitution of political society. There are no longer ultimate criteria of the law, nor ultimate criteria of knowledge, which are separate from power.'[35]

If we examine them in the light of our problematic, it is possible to link these analyses to what we have characterized as the field of hegemonic practices. It is because there are no more assured foundations arising out of a transcendent order, because there is no longer a centre which binds together power, law and knowledge, that it becomes possible and necessary to unify certain political spaces through hegemonic articulations. But these articulations will always be partial and subject to being contested, as there is no longer a supreme guarantor. Every attempt to establish a definitive suture and to deny the radically open character of the social which the logic of democracy institutes, leads to what Lefort designates as 'totalitarianism'; that is to say, to a logic of construction of the political which consists of establishing a point of departure from which society can be perfectly mastered and known. That this is a *political logic* and not a type of social organization is proved by the fact that it cannot be ascribed to a particular political orientation: it may be the result of a politics of the 'left', according to which every antagonism may be eliminated and society rendered completely transparent, or the result of an authoritarian fixing of the social order in hierarchies established by the state, as in the case of fascism. But in both cases the state raises itself to the status of the sole possessor of the truth of the social order, whether in the name of the proletariat or of the nation, and seeks to control all the networks of sociability. In the face of the radical indeterminacy which democracy opens up, this involves an attempt to reimpose an absolute centre, and to re-establish the closure which will thus restore unity.

But if there is no doubt that one of the dangers which threatens democracy is the totalitarian attempt to pass beyond the constitutive character of antagonism and deny plurality in order to restore unity, there is also a symmetrically opposite danger of a lack of all reference to this unity. For, even though impossible, this remains a horizon which, given the absence of articulation between social relations, is necessary in order to prevent an implosion of the social and an absence of any common point of reference. This unravelling of the social fabric caused by the destruction of the symbolic framework is another form of the disappearance of the political. In contrast to the danger of totalitarianism, which imposes immutable articulations in an authoritarian manner, the problem here is the absence of those articulations which allow the establishment of meanings common to the different social subjects. Between the logic of complete identity and that of pure difference, the experience of democracy should consist of the recognition of the multiplicity of social logics along with the necessity of their articulation. But this articulation should be constantly re-created and renegotiated, and there is no final point at which a balance will be definitively achieved.

This leads us to our third question, that of the relationship between democratic logic and hegemonic project. It is evident from everything we have said so far that the logic of democracy cannot be sufficient for the formulation of any hegemonic project. This is because the logic of democracy is simply the equivalential displacement of the egalitarian imaginary to ever more extensive social relations, and, as such, it is only a logic of the elimination of relations of subordination and of inequalities. The logic of democracy is not a logic of the positivity of the social, and it is therefore incapable of founding a nodal point of any kind around which the social fabric can be reconstituted. But if the subversive moment of the logic of democracy and the positive moment of the institution of the social are no longer unified by any anthropological foundation which transforms them into the fronts and reverse sides of a single process, it follows clearly that every possible form of unity between the two is contingent, and is therefore itself the result of a process of articulation. This being the case, no hegemonic project can be based exclusively on a democratic logic, but must also consist of a set of proposals for the positive organization of the social. If the demands of a subordinated group are presented purely as negative demands subversive of a certain order, without being linked to any viable project for the reconstruction of specific areas of society, their capacity to act hegemonically will be excluded from the outset. This is the difference between what might be called a 'strategy of opposition' and a 'strategy of construction of a new order'. In the case of the first, the element of negation of a certain social or political order predominates, but this element of negativity is not accompanied by any real attempt to establish different nodal points from which a process of different and positive reconstruction of the social fabric could be instituted — and as a result the strategy is condemned to marginality. This is the case with the different versions of 'enclave politics', whether ideological or corporative. In the case of the strategy of construction of a new order, in contrast, the element of social positivity predominates, but this very fact creates an unstable balance and a constant tension with the subversive logic of democracy. A situation of hegemony would be one in which the management of the positivity of the social and the articulation of the diverse democratic demands had achieved a maximum of integration — the opposite situation, in which social negativity brings about the disintegration of every stable system of differences, would correspond to an organic crisis. This allows us to see the sense in which we can speak of the project for a radical democracy as an alternative for the Left. This cannot consist of the affirmation, from positions of marginality, of a set of anti-system demands; on the contrary, it must base itself upon the search for a point of equilibrium between a maximum advance for the democratic revolution in a broad range of spheres, and the capacity for the hegemonic direction and positive reconstruction of these spheres on the part of subordinated groups.

Every hegemonic position is based, therefore, on an unstable equilibrium: construction starts from negativity, but is only consolidated to the extent that it succeeds in constituting the positivity of the social. These two moments are not theoretically articulated: they outline the space of a contradictory tension which constitutes the specificity of the different political conjunctures. (As we have seen, the contradictory character of these two moments does not imply a contradiction in our argument, as, from a logical point of view, the coexistence of two different and contradictory social logics, existing in the form of a mutual limitation of their effects, is perfectly possible). But if this plurality of social logics is characteristic of a tension, it also requires a plurality of spaces in which they are to be constituted. In the case of the strategy of construction of a new order, the changes which it is possible to introduce in social positivity will depend not only on the more or less democratic character of the forces which pursue that strategy, but also upon a set of structural limits established by other logics — at the level of state apparatuses, the economy, and so on. Here it is important not to fall into the different forms of utopianism which seek to ignore the variety of spaces which constitute those structural limits, or of apoliticism, which reject the traditional field of the political in view of the limited character of the changes which it is possible to implement from within it. But it is also of the greatest importance not to seek to limit the field of the political to the management of social positivity, and to accept only those changes which it is possible to implement at present, rejecting every charge of negativity which goes beyond them. In recent years there has been much talk, for example, of the need for a 'laicization of politics'. If by this one understands a critique of the essentialism of the traditional Left, which proceeded with absolute categories of the type *'the* Party', *'the* Class', or *'the* Revolution', one would not dissent. But frequently such 'laicization' has meant something very different: the total expulsion of utopia from the field of the political. Now, without 'utopia', without the possibility of negating an order beyond the point that we are able to threaten it, there is no possibility at all of the constitution of a radical imaginary — whether democratic or of any other type. The presence of this imaginary as a set of symbolic meanings which totalize as negativity a certain social order is absolutely essential for the constitution of all left-wing thought. We have already indicated that the hegemonic forms of politics always suppose an unstable equilibrium between this imaginary and the management of social positivity; but this tension, which is one of the forms in which the impossibility of a transparent society is manifested, should be affirmed and defended. Every radical democratic politics should avoid the two extremes represented by the totalitarian myth of the Ideal City, and the positivist pragmatism of reformists without a project.

This moment of tension, of openness, which gives the social its essentially incomplete and precarious character, is what every project for radical democracy should set out to institutionalize. The institutional diversity and complexity which characterizes a democratic society should be conceived of in a very different manner from the diversification of functions proper to a complex bureaucratic system. In the latter it is always exclusively a question of the management of the social as positivity, and every diversification takes place, in consequence, within a rationality which dominates the whole set of spheres and functions. The Hegelian conception of the bureaucracy as a universal class is the perfect theoretical crystallization of this perspective. It has been transferred to the sociological plane in so far as the diversification of levels within the social — following a functionalist, structuralist or any other similar perspective — is linked to a conception of each of these levels as constituting moments of an intelligible totality which dominates them and gives them their meaning. But in the case of the pluralism proper to a radical democracy, *diversification* has been transformed into a *diversity*, as each of these diverse elements and levels is no longer the expression of a totality which transcends it. The multiplication of spaces and the institutional diversification which accompanies it no longer consist of a rational unfolding of functions, nor do they obey a subterranean logic which constitutes the rational principle of all change, but they express exactly the opposite: through the irreducible character of this diversity and plurality, society constructs the image and the management of its own impossibility. The compromise, the precarious character of every arrangement, the antagonism, are the primary facts, and it is only within this instability that the moment of positivity and its management take place. The advancing of a project for radical democracy means, therefore, forcing the myth of a rational and transparent society to recede progressively to the horizon of the social. This becomes a 'nonplace', the symbol of its own impossibility.

But, for this very reason, the possibility of a *unified discourse* of the Left is also erased. If the various subject positions and the diverse antagonisms and points of rupture constitute a *diversity* and not a *diversification,* it is clear that they cannot be led back to a point from which they could all be embraced and explained by a single discourse. Discursive *discontinuity* becomes primary and constitutive. The discourse of radical democracy is no longer the discourse of the universal; the epistemological niche from which 'universal' classes and subjects spoke has been eradicated, and it has been replaced by a polyphony of voices, each of which constructs its own irreducible discursive identity. This point is decisive: there is no radical and plural democracy without renouncing the discourse of the universal and its implicit assumption of a privileged point of access to 'the truth', which can be reached only by a limited number of subjects. In political terms this means that just as there are no surfaces which are privileged *a priori* for the emergence of antagonisms, nor are there discursive regions which the programme of a radical democracy should exclude *a priori* as possible spheres of struggle. Juridical institutions, the educational system, labour relations, the discourses of the resistance of marginal populations construct original and irreducible forms of social protest, and thereby contribute all the discursive complexity and richness on which the programme of a radical democracy should be founded. The classic discourse of socialism was of a very different type: it was a discourse of the universal, which transformed certain social categories into depositories of political and epistemological privileges; it was an a priori discourse concerning differential levels of effectiveness within the social — and as such it reduced the field of the discursive surfaces on which it considered that it was possible and legitimate to operate; it was, finally, a discourse concerning the privileged points from which historical changes were set in motion — the Revolution, the General Strike, or 'evolution' as a unifying category of the cumulative and irreversible character of partial advances. Every project for radical democracy necessarily includes, as we have said, the socialist dimension — that is to say, the abolition of capitalist relations of production; but it rejects the idea that from this abolition there necessarily follows the elimination of the other inequalities. In consequence, the de-centring and autonomy of the different discourses and struggles, the multiplication of antagonisms and the construction of a plurality of spaces within which they can affirm themselves and develop, are the conditions *sine qua non* of the possibility that the different components of the classic ideal of socialism — which should, no doubt, be extended and reformulated — can be achieved. And as we have argued abundantly in these pages, this plurality of spaces does not deny, but rather requires, the overdetermination of its effects at certain levels and the consequent hegemonic articulation between them.

Let us come to a conclusion. This book has been constructed around the vicissitudes of the concept of hegemony, of the new logic of the social implicit within it, and of the 'epistemological obstacles' which, from Lenin to Gramsci, prevented a comprehension of its radical political and theoretical potential. It is only when the open, unsutured character of the social is fully accepted, when the essentialism of the totality and of the elements is rejected, that this potential becomes clearly visible and 'hegemony' can come to constitute a fundamental tool for political analysis on the left. These conditions arise originally in the field of what we have termed the 'democratic revolution', but they are only maximized in all their deconstructive effects in the project for a radical democracy, or, in other words, in a form of politics which is founded not upon dogmatic postulation of any 'essence of the social', but, on the contrary, on affirmation of the contingency and ambiguity of every 'essence', and on the constitutive character of social division and antagonism. Affirmation of a 'ground' which lives only by negating its fundamental character; of an 'order' which exists only as a partial limiting of disorder; of a 'meaning' which is constructed only as excess and paradox in the face of meaninglessness — in other words, the field of the political as the space for a game which is never 'zero-sum', because the rules and the players are never fully explicit. This game, which eludes the concept, does at least have a name: hegemony.

Notes to Chapter 4

1. A. Rosenberg, *Democrazia e socialismo. Storia politica degli ultimi centocinquanti anni* (1789-1937), Bari 1971.
2. Ibid., p. 119.
3. Strictly considered, this affirmation is of course exaggerated. The realignment of forces during the French Revolution also required hegemonic operations, and implied certain changes of alliances: think of episodes such as the Vendée. It is only from a historical perspective, and in comparison with the complexity of the hegemonic articulations which characterize subsequent phases of European history, that one can argue for the relative stability of the framework of basic divisions and oppositions in the course of the French Revolution.
4. On the concept of 'interruption' see D. Siverman and B. Torode, *The Material Word*, London 1980, chapter one.
5. F. Furet, *Penser la Révolution Française*, Paris 1978, p. 109.
6. H. Arendt, *On Revolution*, London 1973, p. 55.
7. G. Stedman Jones, 'Rethinking Chartism', in *idem, Languages of Class*, Cambridge, England, 1983.
8. A. de Tocqueville, *De la Démocratie en Amérique*, Paris 1981, vol. 1, p. 115.
9. C. Calhoun, *The Question of Class Struggle*, Chicago 1982, p. 140. For a related argument see L. Paramio, 'Por una interpretación revisionista de la historia del movimiento obrero europeo,' *En Teoria* 8/9, Madrid, 1982.
10. On this theme see C. Siriani, 'Workers Control in the Era of World War I', *Theory and Society*, 9:1 (1980), and C. Sabel, *Work and Politics*, Cambridge, England, 1982, Chapter 4.
11. M. Aglietta, *A Theory of Capitalist Regulation*, London 1979, p. 117.
12. Cf. M. Castells, *La question urbaine*, Paris 1972.

194

13. S. Bowles and H. Gintis, 'The crisis of Liberal Democratic Capitalism', *Politics and Society*, vol. 2, no. 1 (1982).

14. B. Coriat, *L'atelier et le chronomètre*, Paris 1979, p. 155.

15. C. Offe, *Contradictions of the Welfare State*, edited by J. Keane, London 1984, p. 263.

16. Cf. F. Piven and R. Cloward, *Poor People's Movements*, New York 1979.

17. J. Baudrillard, *Le système des objets*, Paris 1968, p. 183.

18. S. Huntington, 'The Democratic Distemper', in N. Glazer and I. Kristol(eds.), *The American Commonwealth*, New York 1976, p. 37.

19. D. Bell, 'On Meritocracy and Equality', *The Public Interest*, Fall 1972.

20. Cf. A. Touraine, *L'après-socialisme*, Paris 1980; A. Gorz, *Adieux au prolétariat*, Paris 1980. For an interesting discussion of Touraine see J.L. Cohen, *Class and Civil Society: The Limits of Marxian Critical Theory*, Amherst 1982.

21. S. Hall and M. Jacques (eds.), *The Politics of Thatcherism*, London 1983, p. 29. The way in which sexism has been mobilized to create a popular base for Thatcherism is indicated in B. Campbell, *Wigan Pier Revisited: Poverty and Politics in the '80s*, London 1984.

22. A. Hunter, 'The Ideology of the New Right' in *Crisis in the Public Sector. A Reader*, New York 1981, p. 324. For a thoughtful analysis of the present political conjuncture in American politics see D. Plotke 'The United States in Transition: Towards a New Order', *Socialist Review*, No 54, 1980 and 'The Politics of Transition: The United States in Transition' *Socialist Review*, no. 55, 1981.

23. This articulation has been analysed by C.B. Macpherson in *The Life and Times of Liberal Democracy*, Oxford 1977.

24. F. Hayek, *The Constitution of Liberty*, Chicago 1960, p. 11.

25. F. Hayek, *The Road to Serfdom*, London 1944, p. 52.

26. F. Hayek, *Law, Legislation and Liberty*, vol. 2, Chicago 1976, p. 69.

27. Cf. R. Nozick, *Anarchy, State and Utopia*, New York 1974.

28. For a presentation of their position consult M.N. Rothbard, *For a New Liberty. The Libertarian Manifesto*, New York 1973.

29. Z. Brzezinski, cited by P. Steinfelds, *The Neo-Conservatives*, New York 1979, p. 269.

30. Ibid., p. 270.

31. A. de Benoist, *Les idées à l'endroit*, Paris 1979, p. 81.

32. Apart from the fact that our reflexion is located in a very different theoretical problematic, our emphasis on the need to articulate a plurality of forms of democracy corresponding to a multiplicity of subject positions distinguishes our approach from that of the theorists of 'participatory democracy' with whom we nevertheless share many important concerns. On 'participatory democracy', see C.B. Macpherson, op. cit. chapter 5 and C. Pateman, *Participation and Democratic Theory*, Cambridge, England, 1970.

33. Cf. R. Dahl, *Dilemmas of Pluralist Democracy*, New Haven and London 1982, and C. Lindblom, *Politics and Markets*, New York 1977.

34. C. Lefort, *L'invention démocratique*, Paris 1981, p. 173.

35. Ibid., p. 100.

Index